DESERT
RECKONING

DESERT
RECKONING

A Town Sheriff, a Mojave Hermit,
and the Biggest Manhunt in
Modern California History

WITHDRAWN

DEANNE STILLMAN

NATION
BOOKS
New York

Designed by Linda Mark

Library of Congress Cataloging-in-Publication Data
Stillman, Deanne.
   Desert reckoning : a town sheriff, a Mojave hermit, and the biggest
manhunt in modern California history / Deanne Stillman.
      p. cm.
   Includes bibliographical references and index.
   ISBN 978-1-56858-608-3 (hardcover : alk. paper)
   ISBN 978-1-56858-691-5 (e-book)
   1. Criminal investigation—California—Mojave Desert—Case studies.
I. Title.
   HV8073.S7332 2012
   363.2'32--dc23

                                                      2012004961

10 9 8 7 6 5 4 3 2 1

To my father, Edward Stillman, 1927–1996,
coyote, shapeshifter, writer at heart

A FEW WORDS ON NAMES

Many people let me into their lives so I could write this book. Some requested anonymity, and that request has been honored, either by a name change or not using a name at all. Other names were changed to accommodate the privacy of family members who were not interviewed for this book. Pseudonyms are generally indicated in the text.

CONTENTS

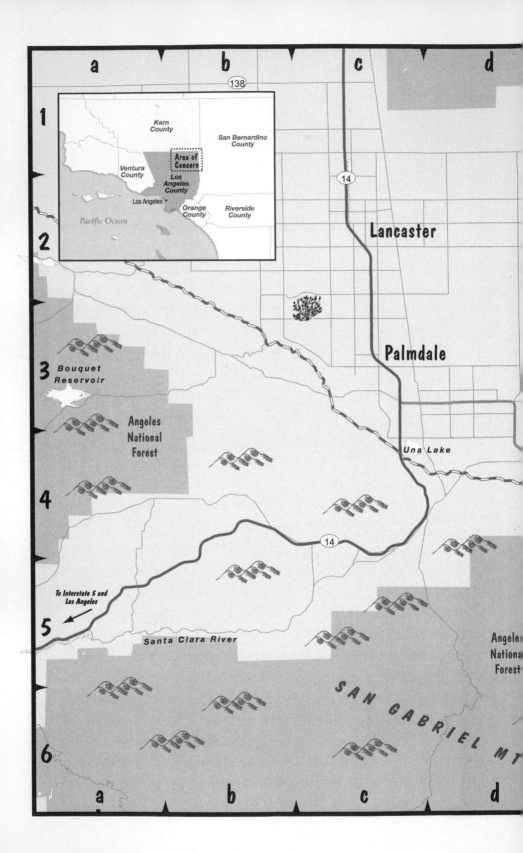

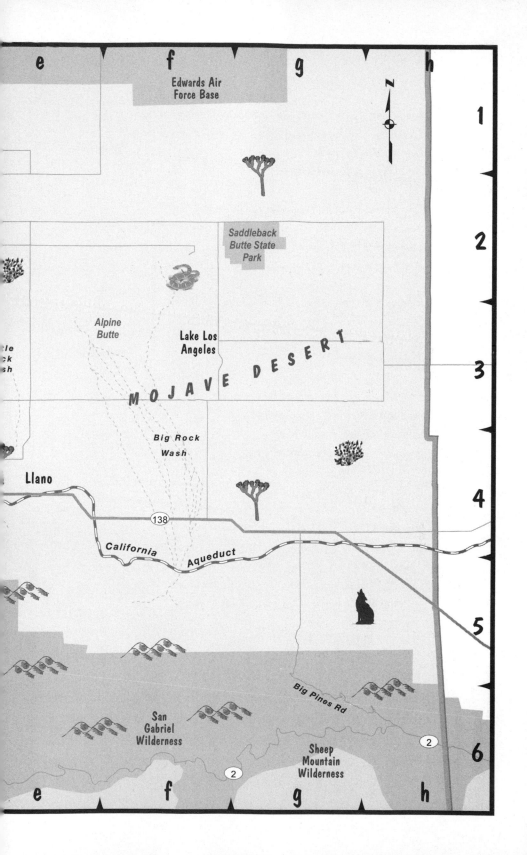

e   f   g   h

Edwards Air
Force Base

1

N

Saddleback
Butte State
Park

2

Alpine
Butte

Lake Los
Angeles

MOJAVE DESERT

3

Big Rock
Wash

Llano

4

138

California Aqueduct

5

Big Pines Rd

San
Gabriel
Wilderness

2

Sheep
Mountain
Wilderness

2

6

e   f   g   h

Oh Mama, I'm in fear for my life from the long arm of the law
Oh Mama, I'm in fear for my life from the long arm of the law
Lawman has put an end to my runnin'
And I'm so far from my home

Oh, Mama, I can hear you a cryin'
You're so scared and all alone
Hangman is comin' down from the gallows
And I don't have very long

The jig is up, the news is out, they finally found me
A renegade who had it made, retrieved for a bounty
Nevermore to go astray, this will be the end today
I'm a wanted man

Oh, Mama, I've been here on the lam
And had a high price on my head
Lawman said get dead or alive
I was for sure he'd shoot me dead.

Dear Mama, I can hear you a cryin'
You're so scared and all alone
Hangman is comin' down from the gallows
And I don't have very long

The jig is up, the news is out, they finally found me
A renegade who had it made, retrieved for a bounty
Nevermore to go astray
This will be the end today
I'm a wanted man

I'm a wanted man
And I don't wanna go, No, No
          —Styx, "Renegade"

"What's the use of holding down a job like this? Look at you. What'd you ever get out of it? Enough to keep you eating. And what for? "... That's right.... They don't even hang the right ones. You risk your life catching somebody, and the damned juries let them go so they can come back and shoot at you. You're poor all your life, you got to do everything twice, and in the end they pay you off in lead. So you can wear a tin star. It's a job for a dog, son."

—John M. Cunningham, "The Tin Star," short story that became *High Noon*

Old Rattler, it is part of Nature's plan
That I should grind you underneath my heel—
The age-old feud between the snake and man—
As Adam felt in Eden, I should feel.

And yet, Old Rattlesnake, I honor you;
You are a partner of the pioneer;
You claim your own, as you've a right to do—
This was your Eden—I intruded here.

—Vaida Stewart Montgomery, "To a Rattlesnake"

DAY
ONE

A Strange Request

Alone in his small trailer, Donald Charles Kueck had been singing a song. It wasn't a pretty song, nor was it a song that the casual passerby would hear on the off chance that he or she was in the vicinity of the remote little abode. No, the weird and discordant tune emanating from the trailer, always calling, calling, calling for someone to come and put him out of his misery, was broadcast on a frequency few could monitor, its sound waves fading in and out of the radio dead zones that pockmarked the vast desert expanse. But the singer was persistent and unwavering, and his song encircled the sage and drifted across the nest of the last desert tortoise; it traveled down washes cut by ancient floods and caressed the tough backs of scorpions, and one day it crossed a bajada, and the singer, yearning for his days to end, sang more furiously, sending the dirge into the higher elevations, up a butte studded with Joshua trees and granite slabs and bobcats and up higher until it was swept away by a Santa Ana wind—that high-voltage swirl of hot air that is born in the Mojave and is said to carry messages of evil—and

it wafted across the high-desert scrub, over mountains and sea, and was heard by sensitive souls in other lands, far-flung sisters of the man who sang his own death song, and they called each other from Okinawa and Pensacola and Arizona and knew something was wrong. In another desert community outside of Los Angeles there was a daughter who also sensed impending doom, and she wrung her hands as she knew the end was near. Animals with their keener hearing responded to the softer notes of the singer's grim melody (for all living things respond to music) and would come in from points south, east, north, and west of the trailer to be fed and nourished by the man who loved them but hated cops. In the mornings, the jackrabbits were the first to arrive, arranging themselves around a special outdoor breakfast table with portions of food placed at individual settings. Other critters would stop by throughout the day on their rounds. There was a raven that would alight on the man's arm. Kangaroo rats—amazing for their ability to go for days without water and often seen skittering across the sands—would slow themselves, finding a rare moment of rest in their perpetual state of panic, oblivious to the Daewoo automatic rifle inside the trailer, the magazines loaded with high-velocity rounds, and the handwritten will, perhaps calmed by the repeating reverberations of the death song (for all living things love an echo). But the company of animals was not enough to stop the man's desire to die. It is certainly within reason to figure that some of the animals, a coyote licking his chops possibly, or a tangle of rattlesnakes, may have even watched or slithered by as one night, perhaps under a full moon, while he was tweaked on a desert cocktail of meth, Darvon, and Soma, with the sound of his own blood thundering through his body, the Devil threw him a spade. "Oh, it's you," the man said. "Now what?" The Devil did not answer and the man said, "I see." He approached the spade and walked around it, knowing that when he picked it up, the deal was done. At the call of the raven, he picked it up and said, "Where do I dig?" "Between a rock and a hard place," the Devil replied, laughing at his own absurd joke. The man did not resist. He began to pace his property, looking for the right spot to bury himself, taking to the task with a kind of grim purpose, for he liked projects, and in fact eked out a meager living by assembling desert flotsam and jetsam into items that other desert dwellers found necessary, which is why his property was cluttered with junk. On this, the first night, he gazed at the skies, which were ablaze with constellations and shooting stars, and he stopped at various sites but they did not feel right and the same thing happened on the second. The Devil returned and said, "What's so great about the stars? Did they ever grant you a wish?" and the man said, "I can't remember," and then walked to the edge of his property. "Looks good to me," the Devil said, and so the man commenced to dig, with great fervor, sinking spade into hardpack and heaving the first shovelful to the side.

There might have come the quick flight of rattlesnakes deranged by the shifting grains of sand above their nest, but this would not have deterred the man, for these were his neighbors and he liked them. As his spade reached deeper and perhaps hit a layer of granite, there might have come the howling of jackals on the plain, and this may have given the man pause, for even a man used to living with the screaming voice of Mephistopheles would have been surprised by the hellish sound such digging might have unleashed. When the digging became difficult, the Devil laughed and threw him a pickaxe, which he wielded to break through to the lower regions. Sometimes, when even the pickaxe didn't do the job, the Devil shrieked wildly and ordered the man to hurry as he pried the massive boulders of pyrite and quartz from the dirt with his bare hands. On some nights, when the sky would grow black and there were no starlit shadows and it got so still that all you could hear was the thunder of blood rushing away from and back to your heart, perhaps the man with the Fu Manchu carried a lantern to his grave and watched the progress of his painstaking work, saw the shovelfuls of sand piling up as he heaved the dirt from his desert bed, until the last flickers of false light were pierced by another wrenching Mojave sunrise.

One night there was a full moon, which illuminated the silhouettes of night hunters across the desert—you could see the hair on the ground-hugging tarantulas and likewise on the fleet-footed bobcats up in the buttes—and the man who was both gravedigger and corpse admired his work and said, "I'm finished." But the Devil told him to lie down in his grave to be sure. The man balked at first, but of course the Devil prevailed. So the man laid down and gazed at the heavens and then closed his eyes. His breathing came easy and he was surprised at how good it felt. As he rested, he thought of his work and within his grim accomplishment he found a certain kind of pride, because now there would be no remaining tasks or fetters, no more rebukes from the world he had failed, no remorse over the lives he had ruined, only the hole awaiting him at the end of his song.

In the morning, his eyes opened, and it was not the frothing heads of Cerberus he beheld but another infinite and wrenching Mojave sunrise. He cursed the Devil for giving him more time and climbed out of his grave. "Motherfucker," he called across the empty bajada. "I'll fucking kill you." Then he retreated into his wretched little trailer where the temperature sometimes reached 110 degrees. Like all living things in the desert heat, he remained still—but unlike many of them, his mind did not. (Later, when it was all over, his sister, a nurse in the navy, would suggest that perhaps he was suffering from a brain tumor—how else to explain his peculiar degeneration in the desert? Why else would a man literally dig his own grave?) As the blazing sun crackled the shell of his home, he was filled with a kind of exquisite torment that could not be shut down, the chattering of voices that he recognized. *Daddy, why did you leave us? . . . Mr. Kueck, put your hands where I can see 'em. . . . Okay, shit for brains, it's thirty days in the hole. . . . Don, do you need some help? We're your sisters. . . . Dad, everything's okay now*—and it was this last voice that always got him because it was his son, lying in the gutter with a dirty needle jammed into his arm and father would tell son that he was sorry but the voices would not be quelled, instead nourished and then subdued and then raging again, depending on the nature and strength of his desert cocktail. . . . Sometimes when the voices screamed, or when they left him and there was nothing, he prepared for the arrival of the sheriff, who occasionally drove by while patrolling the desert. He would pick up his rifle and wait. *You never know with cops*, he would tell himself. *I am not going back to jail. I don't do incarceration.* But the moment would pass and soon his friends would return—raven and jackrabbit and desert quail and lizard, pausing on scrub and rocky perches, charmed by the softer notes of the man's weird and discordant song, longing, as did he, for a moment of grace. One day a pair of sheriff's boots crunched across the white Mojave gravel, its occupant drawn to the strange and urgent song emanating from the man's trailer. In the blink of the raven's eye, the creatures of the desert vanished, and the man became the final incarnation of himself. "The time has come," he said to a snake. "Adios, my friend."

FRONTIER LOS ANGELES

When Jesus heard of it, he departed thence by ship into a desert place apart: and when the people had heard thereof, they followed him on foot out of the cities.

—Matthew 14:13 (King James version)

NORTH OF LOS ANGELES—THE STUDIOS, THE BEACHES, RODEO Drive—lies a sparsely populated region that comprises fully one-half of Los Angeles County. Sprawling across 2,200 square miles, this shadow side of Los Angeles is called the Antelope Valley. It's in the high Mojave Desert, surrounded on all sides by mountain ranges, literally walled off from the city. It is a terrain of savage dignity, a vast amphitheater of startling wonders that puts on a show as the megalopolis burrows through the San Gabriel Mountains in its northward march. Packs of coyotes range the sands, their eyes refracting the new four-way stoplight at dusk, green snakes with

triangle heads slither past Trader Joe's, vast armies of ravens patrol the latest eruption of tract mansions that, until a few years ago, were selling for NOTHING DOWN! Now foreclosed and empty, they are once again available for a small down payment, as the region waits for the endless boom-and-bust cycle to head north as it always does.

Over the years, many have taken the Mojave's dare, fleeing the quagmire of LA and starting over in desert towns like Lake Los Angeles, population 14,000. Nestled against giant rocky buttes studded with Joshua trees and chollas and sage, Lake Los Angeles is a frontier paradise where horses graze in front yards and the neighbors say howdy. "It looks just like the Wild West here," many remark upon driving through the town for the first time, and in fact it sounds like the Wild West: on the outskirts of nearby Lancaster, drivers can cruise down a remote stretch of road and hear "The William Tell Overture"—the theme from *The Lone Ranger*—as their tires traverse a specially engineered patch of singing pavement. The Wild West atmosphere brings occasional income to the region, with various westerns shot on the sets that dot the area, sometimes featuring manhunts of yesteryear. Yet re-creating the past was not the original plan for Lake Los Angeles; like other planned communities across Southern California, it was supposed to be about the present—a history-free place where people would do something fun in the sun, like water skiing, even though there was no place to do so.

Oddly, this sort of dreaming was a tradition itself, dating back to the nineteenth century, when land featuring Joshua trees impaled with oranges was sold to eager buyers back east, expecting to find citrus groves on their property when they arrived. Decades later, amid the Antelope Valley's land speculation fever of the 1960s, developers purchased 4,000 acres near the northeastern edge, subdivided them into 4,465 lots, filled a dry lakebed, and named the place Lake Los Angeles. Ads depicted a happy resort town where water skiers jetted across the desert lake with stunning showcase homes on a nearby hill. But that portrait never materialized; much of the land was sold to buyers who never visited the area, and many of the homes were never built. Speculators lost interest and the lake dried up, never to be refilled, although every now and then, there are calls to turn on some spigot, somewhere, and make one more dryland playground.

Over the years, Lake Los Angeles filled up anyway, with people looking for work and solace, and sometimes finding both. Today, those who live here would not, and in some cases, cannot live anywhere else. Many are Mojave diehards. For the most part, the town's longtime residents—a mix of fighter pilots, ranchers, real estate developers, winemakers, Hispanics who work the region's onion fields, and blue-collar crews who grease the engine of the Hollywood studio system "down below"—get along just fine. But Lake Los Angeles is also a siphon for fuckups, violent felons, meth chefs, and paroled gangbangers who live in government-subsidized housing. For years, law-abiding locals felt they were under siege, as the city and its problems climbed Highway 14 into the desert, an underpatrolled area where if you called a cop, it might take two hours for a black-and-white to arrive. In 2000, the beleaguered town finally got its own resident deputy—Stephen Sorensen, a ten-year veteran of the sheriff's department. "Resident deputy" meant that you lived where you worked, a gig that was undesirable to some because it involved solitary travel to remote locations on calls involving violent people. "Out there, you're a loner," Sgt. Vince Burton of the area's Palmdale station told me awhile ago. "Whatever happens you have to deal with it yourself."

WHEN THE LAW CAME

Say, what was your name in the states?
Was it Brown or Jackson or Bates
Did you murder your wife and flee for your life?
Say, what was your name in the states?
   —Popular frontier ditty

IN THE BEGINNING, IT WAS NOT TOMBSTONE, DEADWOOD, OR Dodge City that laid claim to being the most violent of American outposts. It was Los Angeles County, although LA is not thought of as being part of the West, or even the Wild West for that matter. LA is the place that manufactures the West, or at least America's idea of the West—and itself. But there was a time that LA itself was the Wild West of mythology—and nearly as sprawling as half of California. While today LA County is as big as Rhode Island—2,200 square miles—in 1850, when the boundaries were first drafted, it was over twice the size, with a sparse population of a

little over 7,000 people spread out across a vast area that was bigger than many eastern states. West to east, the county line ran from the Pacific Ocean to the Colorado River, and north to south from Santa Barbara to the far edge of San Juan Capistrano. About half of the population lived in the pueblo of Los Angeles—the hive that flourished and festered around a plaza downtown, encircled by adobe houses and, beyond that, private farms and community grazing areas as the city radiated outward. During a one-year period from 1850 to 1851, the murder rate was one per day—the highest rate reported in any city at any time in American history. In fact, the figure was probably higher; it does not include homicides in which the victims were Indians (in 1852, the majority of LA County's population), blacks, Asians, and Mexicans, which were not considered crimes. And it does not include murders that nobody ever knew about in the vast California wilderness.

Much of the reported violence took place in what is now downtown Los Angeles, originally known as El Pueblo de la Reina de Los Angeles—"the town of the queen of the angels." The place with the beautiful name was a squalid enclave of brawls, knifings, and human trafficking, where blood ran in the arroyos and dead dogs often floated by. "Los Angeles was a town of dust and mud and flies," writes Nat B. Read in *Don Benito Wilson: From Mountain Man to Mayor, Los Angeles, 1841 to 1878*. "There were so many flies that Frenchman John La Rue would simply dip his fingers in to fish out a fly before serving the cup of coffee to a guest in his eating joint. . . . There were more wild dogs than humans. . . . Roving in large packs, they hounded carts, killed humans with their rabies, and created an awful din." Locals would toss poison into the streets to get rid of the marauding dogs, and their corpses floated down the *zanjas*—the canals that provided the city's drinking water. The affliction of the day was gold fever, which drove countless newcomers to California—a region with no government except Miner's Law, the gnarly code that prevailed at the many camps that sprouted across the mountains and deserts of the West. The pilgrims came by land and by sea, on foot and horseback, quickly displacing Mexican ranchers who had settled on land granted to their ancestors by the king of Spain, along with Native Americans whose populations had already been decimated by the early Spanish incursions into the New World. Joining these emigrants were prostitutes and outlaws, themselves heading for LA. Their community came to be known as Sonora Town, after the most violent of the High Sierra mining camps. If LA didn't work out for the misfits of gold country, they quickly headed for Mexico, as local attorney and writer Horace Bell noted at the time. Mexican outlaws had the same idea in reverse, often heading for California. On the dusty streets of the pueblo, the pirates would meet, fight, and frequently kill each other, in disputes that were resolved immediately.

From out of the city of angels flowed endless vectors of conflict, creating violence across all pockets of the far-flung region. Highwaymen preyed on wayfarers riding the Butterfield stagecoach across the Old Spanish Trail and its desert tributaries as they headed to Southern California. Other outposts up and down El Camino Real along the coast were magnets for raids. East of the old pueblo, the mission at San Gabriel—today a quaint and often bypassed historic site off the Santa Ana freeway—was the site of the biggest horse theft in frontier history, with the mountain man Peg-Leg Smith and the Ute Indian Wakara making off with thousands of mustangs, driving them through the Cajon Pass and into the Mojave, kicking up a trail of dust that could be seen from downtown Los Angeles. There were shoot-outs in the passes and draws where nowadays traffic is stalled for hours, and bloody standoffs in seaside outposts today known for good surf. Hastily formed posses drawn from dirty dozens in bars, the streets, and inmates in LA County lockup would pursue the outlaws. All too often the vigilantes would hang the fugitives, on the spot or right in the center of the City of the Queen of the Angels, as citizens cheered them on. Between

1850 and 1865, there were thirty-five unlawful executions, in addition to the many legal executions of record. "A person could be tried and condemned at six in the evening," wrote one local, "and hanged at sunrise the following morning, if not sooner. It all depended on the mood of the moment. As one publication noted, 'Life was cheaper than printer's ink and white space.'"

It was amid this little-known creation myth of Los Angeles that the Los Angeles County Sheriff's Department was born, decades before lawmen such as Wyatt Earp, Bat Masterson, and Pat Garrett galloped across the mesas into the American dreamtime. The early sheriffs of LA County were involved in deadly episodes that are hard to picture in a place that is the national epicenter of the here and now, where the tides and the light and the winds are engaged in a constant sweeping of what just happened, where no one cares where you came from and little for where you are going. The first sheriff in these parts was George Thompson Burrill, a classic prototype for a long line of colorful sheriffs who have presided over this troubled, far western frontier. Elected in 1851, Burrill was a handsome dark-haired man with a handlebar mustache who generally sported an infantry dress sword, a flourish he acquired while living in Mexico. As sheriff, he found himself in charge of a burgeoning county whose residents harbored a deep distrust of rules and those who enforced them, which is why he was paid the unusually high salary of $10,000 per year. At the time, officials didn't really know exactly how they were supposed to run things. Several, including Burrill, penned a letter to Peter Burnett, the state's first governor, asking for guidelines. "In the absence of laws," they wrote, "it has been found impractical to organize the courts, or otherwise enter upon the discharge of their duties. . . . We would respectfully ask Your Excellency for some suitable instructions."

Among the sheriff's first tasks was tax collection for a new local government from recent settlers who had no desire to hand over official revenue, and from Native Americans, who had no reason—a desert version of "taxation without representation." The Indians themselves were engaged in a battle with arriviste marauders. A band of Cupenos had been fending off the Jim Irving gang, outlaws who had been raiding ranches across LA and San Diego counties, preying on remote homesteads and settlements where Indians had lived for centuries. In a battle near latter-day Palm Springs, the Cupenos killed a number of outlaws, and residents on the coast became nervous. Enter Sheriff Burrill, accompanied by a posse from Los Angeles—the first official sheriff's mounted posse in the region, armed with government-issued lances and any weapons the men provided on their own. In an operation that foreshadowed modern SWAT teams, this small tactical unit mustered fast and joined other lawmen in a desert pursuit, soon capturing the Indians. Within weeks, the leaders of the revolt were tried and executed by firing squad. Pockets of Native American resistance continued across Southern California, culminating in the early-twentieth-century hunt for Willie Boy, the notorious Chemehuevi Indian who killed a tribal chief and then ran away with his daughter, pursued by three armed posses for over two weeks across the Mojave. "He was a bad Indian," a wire service reporter wrote of the man who became known as "the last Indian hold-out." "The white man said so," the reporter explained. "So the white man hunted him down, just as though he had been a wild beast, until a 30–30 bullet made him a good Indian."

Sheriff Burrill was engaged in other violent episodes, including one in which the Irving gang resurfaced, riding into downtown LA in an attempt to kidnap men in jail and hold them for ransom. But the sheriff had been tipped off, and the vigilantes were confronted by a team of federal troops and told to head for Mexico. They did, raiding a ranch outside of town, only to be ambushed in a mountain pass by a band of Cahuilla Indians. Burrill went on to serve one more term and was succeeded on January 1, 1852, by Sheriff James R. Barton, a carpenter who had served with Capt. Steven Kearny's Army of the West. The army had helped wrest New Mexico and

California from Spanish rule in fierce battles at Santa Fe and San Diego. Like Burrill, Barton soon found himself in confrontations with vigilantes, embroiled in the daily violence of maelstrom Los Angeles. He would be killed in action on January 23, 1857—the first LA County lawman to lose his life in the line of duty. But before that final first, Barton would oversee the first legal use of the death penalty since the county was formed. It was applied to Ygnacio Herrera, a young Mexican who was accused of killing a man who had reportedly flirted with his girlfriend. According to local papers, Herrera was "freed from his worldly existence" by Sheriff Barton, as thousands of Angelenos gathered to watch the public hanging.

In that hyperviolent era, there was yet one more first for the second sheriff of LA County; this was the lynching of a prisoner by vigilantes (such things had happened before, but not under the watch of the newly formed department). The hanged man was one Dave Brown, who had murdered someone in Los Angeles. Although he had been condemned, his execution was stayed, angering local citizens, including Mayor Stephen C. Foster, who immediately resigned and led a party of vigilantes to the jail. Barton and his small band of deputies were unable to fend off the mob, which battered down the jail doors, dragged Brown across the street, and hanged him from a crossbeam above the gates to a corral. So popular was the act that Foster was reelected as mayor. Sheriff Barton stepped down in repudiation, returning a year later for two more terms.

By then, Los Angeles County was diminishing in size. San Bernardino had become its own jurisdiction, but fewer square miles did not reduce the county's violence. It was during Barton's final term that he led one of the great manhunts of the nineteenth century, the one that took his life.

In January 1857, a band of Mexican outlaws escaped from San Quentin State Prison and headed south for the border—joining a pantheon of future renegades such as Joaquin Murrietta and Tiburcio

Vazquez, Jesse James–like figures whose desert flights were later recalled during the fevered hunt for Donald Kueck. Among the fugitives from San Quentin was Juan Flores, who had been sent to jail for horse theft two years earlier. Like Murrietta and Vazquez, Flores would be immortalized in a cottage industry of pulp literature and ripped-from-the-headlines drama, portrayed as a martyr or demon. But after his capture, he never had a proper trial, and to this day his story is retold and debated. However, of one thing we can be sure: kill a sheriff, and all bets are off, especially if you mutilate the body and flee.

After breaking out of San Quentin, it didn't take long for Juan Flores to get into trouble again. Arriving in San Juan Capistrano after a day or two on the road, las Manillas—or "the hands," as his gang was known—killed a storekeeper while he was preparing dinner, then placed his body on the table and ate his meal. Meanwhile other banditos ran amok through town, plundering stores and terrorizing merchants. Receiving word of the murder, Sheriff Barton called for volunteers to ride with him to San Juan Capistrano. On the night of January 22, he and six men left Los Angeles and headed south, stopping for breakfast at Refugio, the main house owned by Jose Sepulveda, one of California's wealthiest dons. Among the vaqueros and servants at the don's house was Juan Flores's Indian sweetheart. Leaving their guns in an outbuilding, Sheriff Barton and his men sat down for their morning meal, during which they were warned that Flores was well armed and mounted, with a force of fifty or sixty men, greatly outnumbering the members of county law enforcement. But Barton would not wait for reinforcements, and rode on for twelve miles until he and his men were ambushed by las Manillas in Santiago Canyon. Grabbing their guns to return fire, they realized that someone— Flores's girlfriend?—had removed the ammunition from their weapons. Sheriff Barton and three deputies were killed, while the others fled to Los Angeles.

As word of the murders spread, LA erupted in frenzy. Committees of Safety and Vigilance were quickly assembled, the latter to "avenge the foul deed and bring the culprits," wrote an eyewitness. "The El Monte boys, as usual, took an active part. The city was placed under martial law. . . . Suspicious houses were searched, and forty or fifty persons were arrested." Within hours, eleven of these men were lynched, and the state legislature released funds for the pursuit.

Four posses totaling over one hundred men formed immediately, joined by federal troops from Ft. Tejon and Indian crews from the Mojave. As they headed south into the high chaparral, troops from San Diego poured in, mounted rangers began to scour the countryside, and "American, German, and French citizens vied with one another for the honor of risking their lives," reported an eyewitness, "along with two detachments of Californios." The outlaws were chased into the mountains, and the horses of the lead posse gave out as others galloped into the higher elevations, trailed by horse-drawn wagons carrying coffins for the slain sheriffs. Soon, the mangled and defaced bodies of Sheriff Barton and his three deputies were discovered. Placed in the coffins, they were escorted back to Los Angeles. At noon on the following Sunday, the city closed down and went into mourning. On the following day the funerals were held, attended by thousands.

Meanwhile the fugitives pushed deeper into the Santa Ana Range. Most were soon captured. Two were hanged on the spot. Fifty-two were arrested and taken to the LA County jail. Eleven were lynched or legally hanged. Flores was caught on top of a peak in what is today the Tucker Wildlife Sanctuary in Orange County. It's a scenic remove where many animals and plants perished in the Santiago fire in 2007, one of the worst cases of arson in California's history, touched off by someone who remains at large—the kind of person who is the most bizarre sort of killer, enraged at the land. Two days later, Juan Flores escaped again, this time from Don Sepulveda's ranch, where he was being held pending return to Los

Angeles. It happened eleven days later. "All those in favor of hanging Juan Flores will signify by saying, 'Aye!'" the judge said at the
courthouse in the City of the Queen of the Angels, where people
sat in judgment after he was taken in for the last time.

"Aye!" said the citizens.

Then they marched to the jail, secured Flores, and escorted
him to Fort Hill—a rise behind the jail with a temporary gallows.
He was promptly dispatched in front of a crowd that seemed to
include "practically every man, woman, and child in the pueblo,"
according to an eyewitness, "not to mention many people from
various parts of the State who had flocked into town."

No one knows what happened to the body of Juan Flores. And
the place where he died is not marked. Where he was caught, however, is another matter: the mountain in the Cleveland National
Forest is called Flores Peak; although its notoriety is not advertised
and means little to most people, the tribute places him on par with
John Dillinger, the Clanton Brothers, and other American outlaws
whose last taste of freedom has been memorialized and marketed at
the point of capture.

The sheriff too is commemorated, where he drew his last
breath. This is the site known as California Historical Landmark
number 218, aka Barton Mound, on the southeast corner of Inter-
state 405 and State Highway 133, two miles south of East Irvine. It
says: "Juan Flores, who had escaped from San Quentin, was being
sought by James Barton with a posse of five men. Near this mound,
Flores surprised Barton and three of his men; all four were killed.
When Los Angeles learned of the slaughter, posses were formed,
and Flores and his men were captured." But you'll never be able to
read the plaque in person; it's buried under landscaping for a housing development.

The first decade of the Los Angeles County Sheriff's Department would see one more sheriff gunned down. This was twenty-
three-year-old Sheriff Billy Getman, a member of the posse that

had captured Juan Flores. He was killed on January 7, 1858, one year after Sheriff Barton lost his life. The episode involved someone whom local papers referred to as "a maniac," and it may be the region's first recorded suicide by cop. A heavily armed man had barricaded himself inside a pawn shop in downtown Los Angeles. With his two revolvers, pair of derringers, and Bowie knife, he was trying to provoke the store proprietor into killing him—or possibly contacting law enforcement for aid, which would then trigger a shoot-out. When Getman arrived and tried to force the door open, the man burst through, firing point blank at Getman and killing him instantly. Then he fled. A running gun battle in the streets of Los Angeles ensued, with armed locals joining in and killing the fugitive after firing at least thirty rounds. In El Pueblo de la Reina de Los Angeles, Sheriff Getman had been in office for seven days. At his funeral two days later, citizens poured out en masse to mourn another sheriff. Some began to wonder if Los Angeles County was too unruly for law enforcement. With its bloated dog carcasses floating through town, gangsters plying the outlying trails, public lynchings and daily homicides, was it a God-forsaken region at the mercy of forces in play since Cain and Abel? Or would higher angels prevail in the land whose name invoked them? Sheriff Lee Baca—the thirtieth sheriff of the county and a spiritual man—often finds himself wrestling with such questions. In 2003, shortly after he received word that a deputy had been killed in a remote pocket of the Antelope Valley, he choppered out to the crime scene, stood before cameras, and issued an answer. "We're down to what's known in this business as dead or alive," he said, and soon flyers bearing the ancient message were plastered across the Mojave.

BREACHING A
HERMIT KINGDOM

You talkin' to me?
—Travis Bickle, *Taxi Driver*

Nobody knows why Deputy Sheriff Steve Sorensen decided to drive onto Donald Kueck's property on Saturday, August 2, 2003. It was Sorensen's day off, but when a neighbor of Kueck's called him that morning, the deputy said no problem, he'd come right over, as he always did if someone on his remote desert beat had a need. The neighbor—let's call him Frank Baker —was a master carpenter in the studio system "down below," then working on the set of the new Jodie Foster movie. He was concerned about a man we shall refer to as Mr. X, a particularly tenacious squatter whose trail of raw sewage was approaching Baker's well-traveled

airfield, where members of the local ultralight community gathered and kept their planes.

A hardworking guy with a wife and kids, Frank had lived in Llano for twenty years, accumulating forty acres of desert land on a breathtaking plain just to the east of a series of buttes where westerns are shot and Predator drones—the kind used in the war in Iraq—take off from a secret test site and cruise the glittering night skies. The only person who had lived in this area longer than Frank Baker was Donald Kueck. For years, Kueck's home had been a tent a few miles away and then, more recently, a trailer on property his sisters had bought for him after he was kicked off his old site because of trouble with a landlord. But unlike Baker, Kueck had checked out of society a long time ago. In fact, both he and Mr. X, who was squatting on land adjacent to both men, were really living in Frank's world. According to Baker, Sorensen had visited Mr. X at least twenty times, trying to monitor the situation until the eviction papers had moved through the system. To make sure Mr. X got the point, two weeks before the vacate date of August 2, Sorensen visited the property along with a couple of tow trucks and had Mr. X's cars removed, leaving one of the squatter's vehicles so he could take his belongings when he left. Concerned for his family, Frank wanted Sorensen to make sure that Mr. X had vacated the premises that day.

The Mojave is known for its legions of squatters—people who have moved into the many abandoned sheds that mark the desert, some of which date from the homesteading era and were photographed by Dorothea Lange. Although ramshackle, they retain a certain rustic quality; of course, others are barely standing, but they still serve as dwellings for all manner of pilgrims, outcasts, ne'er-do-wells, eccentrics, ex-felons, fugitives, lost and tweaked-out kids, stray animals—a large off-the-grid population that either is stranded or wants to be left alone. Years ago, I met a Vietnam vet who had found refuge at the edge of Randsburg, a California town once the site of a gold strike; treasure hunters still find the precious metal while combing through its hills. The soldier I met had been living in a mine shaft pretty much since his return from the war, emerging occasionally for provisions or to visit with a few compadres, other vets who were living in a little community of tents nearby. They were never coming in, they told me; unwelcomed when the war was over, they had found a home in the womb of the desert. Although the squatter who lived in the mine shaft had known some of these men for a long time, his best friend was a rattlesnake who lived in the shaft with him. She had been there since he moved in, he told me, and there the pair had formed some sort of arrangement or alliance whereby he anticipated her moves and understood her ways and she left him alone. He liked that she was always there, although he did not say why; it was understood that he had found comfort with a companion who was a silent presence, a creature who was misunderstood if not reviled by most people, an emissary from another world that no one wished to see.

Deep inside this world of squatters is another one, comprised of solitary people who have chosen to participate in nothing other than their own lives and a deep communion with the desert; they are not unlike the Christian hermits of 2,000 years ago, who would wander into the wastes seeking enlightenment or something other than what was found among more concentrated populations. Across American deserts, they form a kind of hermit kingdom, some living in sheds or shacks, others in makeshift lean-tos, others in abandoned vehicles or storage units or caves. Many a notorious latter-day hermit has gone out in a blaze of glory, whacked those who crossed the borders of their world, or been found in all manner of states of preservation or decay. They have names like Cougar Dave and Buckskin Bill, Wheelbarrow Annie and Beaver Dick. In his book *Wild Game*, the writer Frank Bergon tells the story of a notorious hermit named Bristlewolf, who lived for many years in a dugout at Pinto Hot Springs in the Virginia Range of Nevada.

An old Basque shepherd would attend to his needs from time to time; as the years passed, he would stop by and bathe the hermit's arthritic legs in the healing waters of the springs. One day, two college hikers stumbled into Bristlewolf's camp. Fearing eviction, he shot them. Several days later, his old friend showed up. Unhinged, he shot and killed him too.

Some squatters are fastidious, arranging their possessions just so and obsessively wiping away the dirt that accumulates in their lean-tos and tunnels. The squatter who had drawn the attention of Antelope Valley locals was not a tidy one; he had been leaving piles of trash everywhere, taking dumps all over the desert, turning the view from Frank's forty-acre spread into one big toilet. Nor was he popular with other squatters and hermits who were his neighbors. Every scene has its own class system and in general hermits don't like squatters because hermits are often living legally—in their own place, someone else's who doesn't mind their occupancy, or somewhere no one cares about or ever visits. Squatters are pretty much doing what the term says—squatting—wherever they can, sometimes inside a hermit's domain, until forced to move on. The area of concern—a far-flung outpost called Llano—wasn't in Sorensen's immediate jurisdiction, but he lived two miles away, and that meant it was in his backyard, and he regularly patrolled its maze of dirt roads. The unassuming berg was once home to a utopian community Aldous Huxley wrote about when he lived in nearby Pearblossom years later, fleeing there after World War II, convinced that man's only sanctuary was the desert. The commune was a spawning ground for ideas considered subversive at the time, such as feminism and the minimum wage. Like most utopian communities, Llano vanished, and today all that's left are the stark crumbling stone walls of its visionaries and the remnants of a hearth. Often, packs of desert dogs gather at the fire that burns no more, playful but quick to expose fangs to a stranger who approaches too quickly, sentinels of the new kind of utopia that now flourishes at Llano—a strange brew of loners, outlaws, ultralight pilots, people hunkered in compounds behind KKK signs, meth cookers and asthmatics, those who crave quiet, and serious desert freaks who work hard at blue-collar jobs and out here where land is cheap live like kings.

Yet even for longtime residents who love this region and know its nooks and crannies, it demands certain precautions. For instance, you don't often see people walking alone in the middle of the Antelope Valley—and if you do, they are probably homeless or tweaked. The experience causes extreme discomfort and is dangerous—or at least feels that way. The valley is flat, surrounded on all sides by mountains and buttes; across its floor, vegetation is sparse, dotted with creosote and the occasional Joshua tree. In the relentless white daylight of the summer sun, there is no place to hide, except tunnels and mine shafts, or under or behind a rock. From any direction, you are completely exposed and vulnerable. If you are wearing a uniform, you are broadcasting a message that is generally not welcome in this part of the desert—and as you traverse the sands, someone may be watching you through a rifle scope from hundreds of yards away. Or someone may simply be firing rounds—a not uncommon act in American deserts, especially the Mojave, which is, apart from law enforcement and military, the most heavily armed region in the country.

The August morning heated up, heading past 100 degrees. It was even too hot for rattlesnakes, and to escape the furnace they retreated to pockets of shade—under the greasewood or into the sand. Attuned to human and animal sounds, Deputy Sorensen walked the site where he had recently served eviction papers to the squatter, saw no sign of him, and told the Bakers. Then he got back in his Ford Expedition and started for home. But something changed his mind. To this day, what that was is not known. When he arrived, Mr. X was gone. He drove to Frank's place to tell the family and then headed north, toward home. But something—

what? Some ancient siren call? A strange dirge being broadcast on a frequency only the most attuned could hear?—made Sorensen turn left, back toward the squatter's site, east on Avenue T-8 (many streets of the Antelope Valley are named for the alphabet, and their remote tributaries are numbered), for about fifty yards and then he paused, just past the old tires that marked Kueck's driveway.

The ex-surfer from the South Bay knew his desert and knew who lived on his beat. So it is safe to say that on his many previous trips to Mr. X's, he had stopped at the same juncture for a quick recon; it is safe to say he knew that the man who lived down this driveway was once a friend of Mr. X; it is safe to say he had heard the man was named Don (no last names in the desert; the desert doesn't care who you are and generally neither does anyone else); it is safe to say that as Sorensen looked down this driveway, perhaps with binoculars, he saw things that looked suspicious: the trashed cars common to many a desert pack rat, giant drums of what could have contained chemicals for manufacturing meth, stacks of pipes that could have been used to make bombs, classic desert junk piles that suggested everything from scavenging to chop shop. Clearly and at the very least, whoever lived here was in violation of various codes, and perhaps the place was even a hazmat site. But until August 2, as far as anyone knows, he had not approached the occupant of the property. On that blazing day on the edge of fall, something must have looked slightly different; there must have been a shift—more junk, more cars—or maybe one of the area's ultralight pilots had flown over the site and told local officials that he had spotted a meth lab—"I'm sick and tired of all the trash—human and otherwise—and I want it out of this desert *now*."

So Sorensen turned down the driveway and headed south in his SUV, perhaps looking to his right and down toward the ground where the grave awaited the land's occupant. Perhaps he saw the planks that covered it, and their six-foot-by-three-foot configuration fueled his suspicion, or perhaps he even stopped, got out of his car, lifted the planks, saw the grave, and then continued, unholstering his 9 mm Beretta and wondering what he was getting himself into.

But the death song had trapped him, and on he went, for another twenty feet or so, at which point he saw the wretched little trailer from which only silence emanated. In a few minutes, his brains would be in a bucket.

Kueck, a longtime heavy user of Darvon and Soma, may have been basking, semi-asleep, like the rattlesnake in the bucket at his front door, the living embodiment of the great American battle cry, "Don't tread on me!" As Sorensen sat in his car, there were subtle atmospheric changes, and Kueck—like the snake—may have tasted the movement on the inhale, and Sorensen, the seasoned desert cop, perhaps suspected but did not know for a fact that he was now being watched by a pair of bloodshot eyes that squinted from a sill, suspected but did not know for a fact that a paranoid man who had eked out a life in the Mojave and was now permanently baked had reached for his automatic rifle with the high-velocity rounds, suspected but did not know for a fact that he was a dead man walking into the land of no return.

He spotted an old Dodge Dart and ran the plates. It is not known if Sorensen received the information from the DMV database, and if he did, if it meant anything to him, because the dispatcher garbled the name of the man who owned the car, and therefore Sorensen may not have known that the owner was Donald Charles Kueck, a man who had spent months trying to get him fired, writing letters to everyone from the FBI to then LA County sheriff Sherman Block, after Sorensen had pulled him over on a remote desert road next to an alfalfa field for reckless driving on a hot summer day in 1994 at about noon. "I live alone in a rural location," Kueck wrote in a lengthy and detailed statement that accompanied his complaint against Sorensen at that time, "and now I fear for my safety."

Seven years later the sun beat down and once again, it was al-most high noon. The two men were about to finish the dance. "Excuse me, anybody home?" Sorensen might have called out as he approached the lonesome pad. "What's up?" came the reply. Although Kueck was living on land bought for him by one of his sisters, he knew he was in violation of a myriad of codes, living in a ramshackle trailer without the proper permits. Worst of all, he feared going back to jail—"a concentration camp," as he later told police. "Sir, I'm checking on a call about some squatters. Can I see some ID?" "Hold it right there," a voice came from the trailer. "I know my rights." It was the 24/7 refrain of the Mojave—indeed, the Mojave was one big rights fest, where every pack rat, every meth freak, every hermit in every desert bunker knew the Bill of Rights as well as his Buddy Weiser, quoting the Second Amend-ment and search-and-seizure law like scripture, but in the end always destroyed by that American urge to go out like Custer. "Dude, did you see my sign? It says no trespassing. Do you have a warrant?"

By now Sorensen was halfway between his car and the trailer with no cover in sight, approaching a troubled ex-con who had moved out here to get away from society's relentless demands for smog checks and housing permits. And now that system was clos-ing in on his front door, in the form of a deputy with a gun. "Sir, come out with your hands up," Sorensen might have said, hearing the rattle of the snake in the bucket.

What happened next, according to police, is that Kueck kicked open his front door, aimed his Daewoo at Sorensen and blasted him with .223s. The high-velocity bullets screamed into the deputy's body below his vest, shattering and buckling him like a piece of glass as he spun around and managed to get off three shots before Kueck blasted into Sorensen's right side and arm, tear-ing the 9 mm from his grasp as rivulets of blood quenched the Mojave's hot sand.

But Kueck wasn't finished. We know from witnesses who heard the shots that a second volley of bullets was fired, two more to the side of Sorensen's chest, and then as he lay mortally wounded, Kueck pumped him with eight more rounds, including one that blasted through an eye and blew his brains out. When it was over, Kueck had raked the deputy's body with fourteen shells.

Unbeknownst to Kueck, he was being watched. After hearing the shots from their home a mile away, Frank Baker's wife and kids had climbed their lookout tower and now, through a scope, observed Kueck ransacking Sorensen's Ford. They immediately dialed 911. Kueck disappeared from their view; he was on his knees, hidden by the SUV, tying a rope around Sorensen's legs, trussing him like a bagged deer, right ankle over left. He dragged the body toward the back of his yellow Dodge Dart and tied it to the bumper. Then he picked up the deputy's brains and threw them in a bucket. As sirens wailed across the Mojave, Donald Charles Kueck vanished. A few minutes later the phone rang at his daughter's house. "I'm sorry," he said, in tears. "I know I've been a terrible father. I won't be coming over on Monday."

In a land infamous for its outlaws, Kueck was about to become the target of one of the largest manhunts the desert had ever known.

THE FEVER DREAM OF LLANO:
A CASTLE FOR EVERY MAN

Can You Build?
After Every Whirlwind of Revolution
Comes the Task of the Builders!
Today: Ahead of the Revolution,
Integral Co-operation is
Building, NOW, the Impregnable
Breastwork, the Llano co-operative
Colonies!
Before Your Very Eyes, Individualism
Disintegrates! The Palaces of the
Profiteers Crumble and Fall Apart!
Be one of the Master Builders!
Spread the Cement of
Co-operation!

    —Billboard for Llano, 1913

We've partnered with lifestyle expert Martha Stewart to create high-quality homes inspired by her very own homes in New York, Connecticut, and Maine.

—Press release for KB homes, 2003

ON MARCH 11, 2006, ABOUT THIRTY MEMBERS OF THE SAN Fernando Band of Mission Indians gathered near the site of a new development in Palmdale, one of the two cities in the Antelope Valley. Representing the Tataviam and Fernandeno tribes in the Antelope, Santa Clarita, and Victor valleys, they had come to rebury six of their Vanyume ancestors who had been unearthed two years earlier as land was being bulldozed to make way for the 5,000-home Anaverde community just off the Avenue S exit ramp. The six individuals—men, women, and a baby—were about 800 to 1,000 years old. They were found in separate graves, with a crumbling stone hearth nearby—perhaps a remnant of a burial ritual. One of the ancients, most likely a shaman, was buried with 1,500 shell beads. As late-winter snowflakes fell to the earth, some members of the gaily bedecked group placed offerings of tobacco, sage, and knives in the graves, gifts for the eternal journey, and there was traditional singing and drumming and the shaking of rattles. A backhoe covered the graves, and within a few weeks, a steamroller had finished the job. There was a new paved road over the old burial site, and the latest wave of suitors began to arrive in the Antelope Valley.

* * *

Everything was going according to plan. In June 2003, just a few months before the deadly encounter between Deputy Steve Sorensen and Donald Kueck in Llano, there was a ribbon-cutting ceremony in which leaders of the four federal agencies that oversee

the banking industry posed for a picture brandishing a pair of gar-
dening shears. Then they scissored a giant sheaf of regulations
wrapped up in red tape. The photograph was widely circulated,
symbolizing the efficiency with which regulators could cut through
unnecessary rules. It seemed innocuous on its face—what's wrong
with cutting red tape?—but it also meant that the era of banking
oversight was finished.

That summer became a frenzy of subprime mortgage loans,
and the mantra was NOTHING DOWN! Nowhere was it chanted
more loudly than in the Antelope Valley, which was already entering a periodic boom cycle. Now McMansion developments
erupted everywhere. As Mike Davis had written in *City of Quartz*,
"The Antelope Valley is a virgin bride, engridded to accept the future hordes."

They had been coming for decades, and to accommodate each
wave of arrivals, the grid of alphabet avenues bisected with numbered streets was perpetually spinning off bewildering subsets of
letters and numbers. In the 1970s, several developments flowered
along Avenue K, becoming home to Vietnam vets who were returning and getting jobs in the aerospace industry at the valley's
various plants or at Edwards Air Force Base. In the desert, they
could buy into the American dream of affordable housing quite
easily, enticed by low-interest, long-term mortgages on comfortable ranch houses where—in the ad parlance of the time—you
could "live better electrically." In 1986 the Antelope Valley's
county-sponsored area-wide general plan outlined ways to further
facilitate home sales. "Review government procedures," it said, "to
determine ways in which they can be altered to reduce development permit processing time and reduce the cost of housing." As
the twentieth century closed out and the new one was ushered in
by a moment of punctuation known forever as 9/11, Americans
were urged by President George Bush to "go shopping"—and we
did, buying up McMansions like houses on the Monopoly board as

the banks unleashed an endless river of cash. Some of the new home buyers would be moving into Martha Stewart homes, replicas of her various East Coast mansions built by KB Homes, one of the primary developers in the West and progenitor of instant "neighborhoods" across Southern California. Stewart's partnership with KB Homes was announced in 2005, just after the lifestyle queen had been released from prison, where she had done time for making false statements to federal authorities. But the idea had been in the works for some time.

The first development of Martha Stewart homes was in the California desert town of Perris; the model called Katonah was based on the New York mansion where Stewart spent five months on supervised release after her time in jail, an inadvertent nod to the many ex-felons who live in lesser abodes across the Mojave. "Martha's influence is seen in the many options available to home-buyers," said the publicity material, "such as specialized flooring, bathroom and kitchen fixtures, lighting, paint colors, cabinetry selections, and other special touches such as distinctive mantels, shelving, molding and wainscoting. To provide additional design inspiration, model homes will contain furniture and decorative accents from Martha Stewart Living." In the Antelope Valley city of Lancaster, the development offering designer shelter was called Terrane Vista. Consisting of ninety-two homes, it was erected on a sprawling parcel of sand at Thirty-Fifth Street East and Avenue A-8. The instant community would feature "the best of California living," Stewart said, along with "distinctive designs that include stone-decorated fronts and kitchen islands."

The desert is a land of grand dreams and colossal failure. You may say that this is not unlike other regions, and to a degree you would be right. But things last forever in the desert; the sand and wind and heat may take their toll, but sooner or later what people dreamed up and loved and killed each other over presents itself or is uncovered, even if it diminishes slowly as it sinks into nature's hourglass, losing its initial pride or grandeur. Just a few miles—or nineteen letters and 125 numbers—away from Terrane Vista are the crumbling ruins of Llano, in whose shadows Donald Kueck toiled away on his desert empire. He had eked out a living on the land, just like a group of communitarians who had fled the adobe jungle decades earlier and sunk roots in the sands of the Antelope Valley. In the end they could not get away from the tentacles of civilization. Strangely, it was that torqued-out version of their legacy that was putting the squeeze play on the latter-day pilgrims of the Mojave Desert, as tract housing marched across the region's open spaces.

Their kingdom was called Llano del Rio, and it was founded in 1914 by Job Harriman, attorney and one-time Socialist candidate for governor of California, vice president of the United States, and mayor of Los Angeles. A slender man born in rural Indiana in 1861, Harriman attended law school in Colorado Springs, a town that was originally one of hundreds of utopian colonies that had sprung up across the land, based on all manner of ideals and practices, from polygamy to making furniture. He came to California in 1886, well-versed in the popular ideas of utopian novelists such as Edward Bellamy (who posited a city in the year 2000 where material goods are delivered to every home via pneumatic tubes) and William Dean Howells, who coined a place called Altruria, whose colonists raised their own produce and sold it to surrounding city dwellers. For a time, Harriman managed a utopian colony in Santa Rosa and then moved to San Francisco, where he set up shop as a lawyer, basing his practice on the radical idea that workers were entitled to a fair wage and a safe workplace. By 1900, he was running for vice president on the Socialist Party ticket, with labor organizer Eugene Debs as the candidate for president. They won 6 percent of the vote.

Today, it's hard to imagine a self-proclaimed socialist gaining traction in any sphere; the word is stripped of history and devoid of all meaning except slander, used to demonize everybody from Barack Obama to fry cooks who would like a sprinkler system in the workplace. But in the early 1900s, the Socialist Party was a major political force; "it was a time when many people in the area [Los Angeles County] were poor and jobless," a communard wrote of Harriman's utopia. "Soup kitchens fed hundreds of penniless and starving people. Others were dissatisfied. Any effort that would lead to a more satisfying life would fill a need and have a strong appeal."

In 1910, nearly every trade worker in Los Angeles went on strike, from butchers and trolley car operators to brewers and printers who worked at the *Los Angeles Times*. By then, the well-known Harriman had moved to Los Angeles, was defending people involved in worker protests, and was running for mayor—losing the election after a volatile season during which a bomb went off in the *LA Times* building and twenty workers were killed. Harriman decided to hit the road; the desert was calling, and there he went, sounding this rousing charge: "We will build a city and make homes for many a homeless family. We will show the world a trick they do not know, which is how to live without war or interest on money or rent on land or profiteering in any manner."

He began to explore the city's sere and empty backyard, and put together a team of partners to bring his Mojave venture to fruition. One day, a farmer from the Antelope Valley came to Harriman in his downtown Los Angeles office. He knew of the perfect place for a utopian community—a 10,000 square-mile parcel ninety miles northeast of Los Angeles, between Mescal and Big Rock Creek, yards away from the parcel of land where Donald Kueck would eke out his own dream in the twenty-first century. It was isolated and remote, yet still relatively close to the city. More importantly, it had water—or so it seemed at the time. It was owned by the nearly bankrupt Mescal Water and Land Company and probably could be had for a song.

After surveying the property, Harriman and his partners bought 2,000 acres for $80,000. One of his partners was from the Texas town of Llano (which means "plain"), and thus the flatlands were named, with the appendage "del Rio" for the creek running through it.

There was something about these desert flats that attracted visionaries. It had first been settled in the early 1890s and was called Almondale. After three years Almondale ran into water problems, and the colonists dispersed. The record does not tell us if the organizers of Llano knew about the site's water problems, and even if they did, would they have gone elsewhere? The longing for a desert paradise is primal, perhaps imprinted on our DNA, and the existence of places that the late writer Marc Reisner called "hydraulic civilizations"—Las Vegas, Phoenix, Cairo—would certainly suggest that Harriman had dreamed with the best of them—Bugsy Siegel, the ancient Pharaohs—and in the scheme of time, can an empire truly be judged as lesser if it endures for years and not longer?

In 1913, ads for Llano began to appear in socialist publications; soon, they proclaimed, the Mojave would be as "green as the map of Ireland." Organizers were building a "unique and beautiful" agricultural and industrial community of 6,000 residents, "far removed from the hurly-burly of the artificial cities, in God's open country, right on the land." Billboards along the road to Llano trolled for residents, pitching life in utopia with hyperactive rhetoric that in an odd way foreshadowed the latter-day wave of breathless pitches for homes that could be acquired for less than a song.

In the case of Llano, anyone could become a master builder for hardly anything down—$500, a good deal even at that time, or so it seemed on paper. The remainder of the fee, $1,500, could be worked off at the colony at the rate of $4 per day. In the beginning, people flocked to Llano, eager to build a new society, plowing, digging, planting, laying pipe, hauling timber, making bricks, constructing barns and stables, milking cows, publishing a magazine, building a fish hatchery, chicken coops, a machine shop, a steam laundry, and finally, establishing a school, all the while living in tents as they awaited materials for housing that could not be constructed quickly enough to accommodate the influx of residents. The new housing—sixteen-by-twenty-four two-room adobes—would itself be temporary, pending the design of the new city, which would be cooked up by the community after consultation with a master architect.

For this position, Harriman once again rattled the status quo, hiring the feminist and self-trained architect Alice Constance Austin, a contemporary of Frank Lloyd Wright and Rudolf Schindler, and a visionary whose lesser-known creations were in some ways more influential than those of her male peers. To this day they are hallmarks of the American style of modern living, incorporated into countless tract homes across the land—and fueling their very existence. At Llano, she would be able to meld her ideas and create the dream home, and also plan the new city. "The Socialist City should be beautiful," she wrote after meeting with colonists. "It should be constructed on a definite plan, each feature having a vital relation to and complementing each other feature, thus illustrating in a concrete way the solidarity of the community; it should emphasize the fundamental principle of equal opportunity for all; and it should be the last word in the application of scientific discovery to the problems of everyday life, putting every labor-saving device at the service of every citizen." Several decades later, corporations such as General Electric said the same thing in a Madison Avenue kind of way: "Live better electrically, with GE"—a selling point of the tract homes that later erupted across the Antelope Valley and the rest of America.

In the beginning, colonists were plagued with problems. Because of a lumber shortage, there were families living in tents with bedsprings, "on the cold damp ground and the wind blowing a gale of rain and snow," as one resident recounted. "My wife had a sick child on each arm." Another family reported that a child was down with typhoid because of the brutal conditions.

But not all was troubling in paradise. Colonists persevered through that first Mojave winter, and there was great promise for its future. Pilgrims continued to arrive, along with a variety of eccentrics, including a water witch who dowsed the sands for springs, a turnip-obsessed farmer who was convinced that the future lay in mass production of the unsung root, and Wesley and Oliver Zornes, brothers who constructed a "flivver aeroplane" with a Model T motor and tried to fly it from Crystallaire, a then-unnamed spot that later became an ultralight airport, down the road a piece from the airstrip with the tower from which residents later witnessed Donald Kueck ransacking Deputy Sorensen's vehicle. At old Llano, Harriman continued to stoke interest, sounding the trumpet again in The Gateway to Freedom. As always, his tune was filled with socialist rhetoric, but he also called for a return to the primal: "In the turmoil of life the modern city is a battlefield where the fierceness of competition crushes, maims, and kills. . . . For the masses failure is inevitable. In the heart of nearly every man is the instinctive desire to get on the land."

Articles suggested that Llano was "a spot of destiny" that would soon be the "metropolis of the Antelope Valley." The community's own publications, *Western Comrade* and *Llano Colonist*, echoed the call in almost biblical terms. "Once this rich plain is touched by water and the plow," one of them proclaimed, "a veritable gold mine of virgin strength is tapped." These recruiting ads sometimes featured a litany of demographics and stats, covering everything from people to bees: according to the December 1915 issue of the *Comrade*, there were seven hundred colonists, two hundred pupils, over two hundred hogs, seventy-five work horses, two large tractors, three trucks, a number of cars, 2,000 egg-making birds, several hundred hares, 11,000 grape cuttings, thousands of fruit and shade trees, and several hundred colonies of bees with "several tons of honey on hand." Among those who joined the parade was a man from the Imperial Valley who drove his herd of cattle hundreds of miles to Llano and dozens of farmers from Texas, who were later surprised to learn they had bought shares in a commune.

With so many people showing up, it was time to enact a few laws—to the dismay of some colonists. Like many a desert dweller, they harbored a healthy dislike of the man and his attendant restrictions on freedom. Early that year, there were complaints that horses were trampling the alfalfa fields because someone kept leaving the gates open, kids were throwing stones through hotel windows, dogs and chickens were polluting the water supply, and people were drinking and swearing. Fines were levied for the various infractions, thus adding more people to the never-ending desert parade of those who cannot abide fetters.

Yet Llano was booming, and on May Day 1915, the community celebrated its first birthday. The day was chosen for its connection to the labor movement. Ever since the eight-hour work day became law on May 1, 1884, and the deadly Haymarket riots at a workers' rally in Chicago followed on the same day two years later, the first day of May had been considered a labor holiday. Socialist circles across the land held celebrations, and Llano was no exception: a Maypole was raised and festooned with ribbon, and visitors and residents danced around it, as the new gardens and orchards and grain and alfalfa fields were sprouting under the turquoise sky.

Soon after the celebration, things were going well enough that it was time for an official "Declaration of Principles," lest anarchy reign in the utopia where it was fostered. Colonists came up with eleven principles, covering everything from collective ownership to responses for greed and selfishness. All in all, it was a provocative desert blend of anarchism, the Ten Commandments, the Sermon on the Mount, and Edward Bellamy.

With the declaration in place, it was time for the next phase: the dream house and the dream city. What would these things look like? What kind of dwelling would best nurture the individual as well as the community? How would residents and visitors travel through Llano? Would there be trains? Parks? Stand under the sky ceiling in the ruins at Llano, and imagine this: A handsome woman is meeting with commune residents in a crowded room. Perhaps it is still under construction and not impervious to the desert winds. Some of the residents have been living in tents for quite some time, others in temporary adobes. Alice Constance Austin listens to the desires and concerns of the communitarians and shows them drawings and models. One day, after meeting like this every week for two years, she unveils the master plan, along with architect Leonard A. Cooke, who had designed the temporary adobes.

There would be 10,000 people on 640 acres—"the square mile area common to many ideal communities planned for the United States," noted Dolores Hayden in *Seven American Utopias*. There would be a green belt around the town, a civic center with "eight rectangular halls, like factories," as Austin had described them, "with sides almost wholly of glass," leading to a glass-domed assembly hall. Each family in the colony would have one car, housed in communal garages, and the road around the city would double "as a drag strip with stands for spectators on both sides." With NASCAR around the corner, and a car racing oval soon to be constructed at nearby Willow Springs, this was far-sighted indeed.

The housing itself, Austin wrote, would be "equal, with more or less equal access to community facilities (no house is more than half a mile from the community center)." For instance, there would be single-family houses that were part of a continuous street facade. But there were also choices for individuals, including alternative facade treatments for the homes—prefiguring Martha Stewart homes by decades. In addition, there was a variety of selections for the interiors.

Each home would have two bedrooms and a bath, living room, closet, patio, and pergola or sun parlor. It would feature built-in furniture, crafted by the colony's workshops, along with window frames "delicately carved in low relief on wood or stone," in Austin's words, "or painted in subdued designs"—all of which would serve as a new art industry at Llano. There would be sleeping porches in each house, to take advantage of the climate and stunning mountain views, awnings in case of rain, roll-away beds, plants on the roof parapets, "wide, easy stairs" with window seats at each landing, heated tile floors, and French windows designed to eliminate the need for high-maintenance drapes. On May 1, 1916, the second anniversary of Llano, Austin presented her model house and renderings of the civic center and school to colonists, and a great esprit de corps pervaded the community.

Across the region, Sundays at Llano were becoming legendary; there were theatre productions, literary readings and talks, and mandolin and guitar concerts. As anyone who has ever heard an impromptu desert symphony can attest, such an experience is transporting and mysterious and necessary; many a cowboy on the old cattle drives noted that when they broke out the fiddle under the starlight, people and animals alike wandered in and were calmed for a spell, especially the cows, whose days were numbered. Years later, Aldous Huxley moved to the region and regained his sight, attributing the miracle to the purifying and harsh glare of the sun in the Antelope Valley as it refracted off the endless white sands. From his house across the bajada, he gazed at the faltering and empty city of Llano and chronicled the story in his essay "Ozymandias," after the old poem about a pharaoh who laments the march of time. "What pleasure," he wrote, "to sit under one's privately owned cottonwood tree and listen, across a mile of intervening sagebrush, to the music of the Socialists. . . . The moon is full, and to the accompaniment of the steady croaks of frogs along the irrigation ditch and the occasional shrieks of coyotes, the strains of Sousa and Sweet Adeline transcribed for mandolins and saxophone come stealing with extraordinary distinctness upon the ear."

Alas, by 1917, the ship of Llano was sinking as the band played on, riven by internal quarrels and factions, outside enemies who had burrowed in, and forces beyond everyone's control, such as constant water shortages and disputes with neighbors over the limited supply. There was also a shortage of money and housing. The small down payments did not cover the costs of building material, and new houses could not be built quickly enough to accommodate everyone. Many of the colony's eight hundred residents were still living in tents or temporary adobes. Moreover, not all of the able-bodied people were working; there were deadbeats who were either angry at colony officials or just wanted to hang out in the desert. Lawsuits were filed, people vied for control of Llano, some colonists could not live on $4 a day and left to find work elsewhere, and others were taken by the draft to serve in World War I.

Meanwhile, certain powerful outsiders hoped for Llano's collapse. As early as 1915, the *LA Times* had proclaimed the end, with headlines such as "Red Utopians Are Disgusted" and "New Wail from Reds' Utopia." Over the months, the paper continued the drumbeat, soon running a doomsday photo of dilapidated rowboats stacked up in the colony's sand.

In 1917, some colonists decided to start over elsewhere and made their way to the site of New Llano in Louisiana. The record does not tell us exactly how many made the exodus out of the desert—perhaps there were as few as sixty-five or as many as six hundred. About seventy-five stayed in the Mojave and pressed on. But by 1924, the last communitarians of Llano were gone, and desert scavengers descended on the site. Job Harriman died of tuberculosis in 1925, in the end described by a colonist as "a broken-hearted man, bowed down with the tragedy of the human race, and knowing that there would be a long, weary struggle with the

changing of habits before mankind would ever find happiness."
Over time, Llano began to appear on certain maps as a Mojave
ghost town, and to this day, desert rats describe it as "the socialist
Stonehenge," knowing little of the true story of the vanished empire just north of Tweaker Highway.

Today the desert's many feral dogs seem to find comfort near
the old hearth at Llano, one of the few remaining features. Perhaps they are drawn by the way the wind whistles through the
failing stone walls or the dreams only they can see in the ghost
smoke of the chimney. But lest you think the legacy of our devoted communards is simply a nice story involving well-meaning
though perhaps naïve people, think again, for it is that and more:
you see, tract housing—the great scourge often pegged to the evil
empire of Levittown—was actually a desert dream, and it came
right out of Llano, cooked up by a student of Austin's who grew up
at the commune.

His name was Gregory Ain, and he lived with his family in the
futuristic community. Under Austin's tutelage, Ain grew up to become an architect, believing that architecture could forge a just
and egalitarian world through well-designed homes for the masses,
a dream whose building blocks were his early years at Llano. To
that end, with the help of other architects, he designed the famous
Mar Vista tract in Los Angeles called Modernique Homes. It was a
grand plan for ordinary people. The average size of the house was
1,060 feet, costing $12,000. Each resident could have from one to
three bedrooms, with folding and sliding panels. The houses were
painted in different color combinations, invoking the famous har-
monic color concepts introduced by LeCorbusier, the Old World
master whose New World ideas had influenced all the LA mod-
ernists. Thinking of mothers as Austin had taught him at Llano, Ain
designed an open kitchen so they could keep an eye on children.
As for children themselves, Ain planned for them too, incorporat-
ing the parenting philosophy of Dr. Spock into his designs for the

kitchen and living room cabinets. The community's landscape was designed by noted modernist Garrett Eckbo, who created a park-like atmosphere along the streets with plantings of magnolia, melaleuca, and ficus. Full-page ads for the tract were splashed across the pages of the *LA Times*. "Only Modernique Homes Have These Convertible Features," the ads said, going on to itemize such things as living, dining, and sleeping areas, indirect lighting, unique bath, closet space, and, most importantly, the great California promise of flexible financing.

Today, the dream homes cooked up in the sands of Llano are available to all—or were until the market collapsed. Thousands of them were marching toward its ruins in the summer of 2003, when Donald Kueck and Steve Sorensen had their deadly encounter. In the days preceding it, both men had expressed misgivings about the way things were going in the Mojave, perhaps sensing that they were in the wrong place, or that something bad was about to happen, and they lamented to various associates that it was getting too crowded, filling up with people fleeing the city or something or some place else, and they complained about too much riffraff in the desert, and really, they both said in their own ways, the lowlifes had to go.

What was it that they longed for? Like plants to the sun, they were drawn to a simpler time, a time without trouble, a time, really, that none of us have experienced except that we all have in our bones, the time when the valley was a valley and not a grid, before the numbers and letters came, before KB Homes and Martha Stewart interiors, before the last herds of antelope that gave the valley its name were mowed down in a canyon—yes, long before that, the time when the Indians of the valley, perhaps even the very shaman whose remains were unearthed as ground was broken for the development on Avenue S, walked the sands on which both men now tried to make their respective ways, living on porridge that they made from acorns in the eastern Mojave which they visited on trade journeys as they crossed the mountains and deserts that were home. Mountain man Jedidiah Smith described the Indians of the region as poor but friendly. They would be gone soon and so would the Spanish, who were saved by the Indians' gruel and then killed them, replaced by the white man, his laws, and those who enforced and broke them—the never-ending cycle of winner and loser in a play that has run for a very long time.

Bad Day at Big Creek Wash

It doesn't matter—man or woman, white, black, brown, or yellow. We all bleed blue.

     —Law and Order

At the report of gunfire, a Code 3—"Deputy down. . . . Deputy needs assistance"—went out across the region. Within minutes, dozens of patrol cars from nearby towns and counties were screaming across Highway 138 toward Kueck's trailer. In Long Beach, a Sikorsky H-3 helicopter took off carrying five LA County deputies for its regular run up the mountains to Barley Flats in the San Gabriel Mountains, but diverted to Llano as the repeated Code 3s were broadcast across the Mojave and up and down the PCH. Every cop on the West Coast from Tijuana to Port Washington knew that a brother was in trouble, clinging to life or, quite possibly, had just been whacked, and many of them grabbed their vehicles and headed for the desert as the chopper's crew of

sergeant, two deputy pilots, and a pair of EMS deputy paramedics prepared to debark and fan across Kueck's property. Ten minutes later, a SWAT team of three from LASD headquarters in East Los Angeles boarded another chopper and was on its way. Homicide detectives Joe Purcell and Phil Guzman, investigating another murder in the town of El Monte, dropped everything when they got the call and hitched a ride out on an LAPD chopper, as by now LASD helicopters had already deployed to Llano or were busy with other crimes—after all, it was Saturday, the night when someone in LA County always gets killed.

The first to arrive was Sgt. Larry Johnston, followed by Officer Victor Ruiz of the California Highway Patrol. Johnston spotted spent shell casings and human tissue all over the blood-soaked sand in front of the trailer. There was Sorensen's SUV, its passenger door flung open, his two-way radio gone. But the Dodge Dart was missing, and Sorensen himself was not in sight. Was he being held hostage? Was he bleeding to death in a nearby desert wash? Did the assailant have them in his sights just waiting to ambush two more cops? Other deputies arrived and helped Johnston set up the first perimeter. Ruiz got in his Crown Victoria on the 138 and headed east, siren shrieking, turning north at Two Hundredth Street and then east again on Avenue T, where pavement turns to sand, staying with the chopper as both vehicles headed toward the trailer, and listening to his radio, which was crackling with updates from the nearby glider airport. Within seconds, he made a turn, following a set of deep and freshly made tire grooves leading away from the bloody site, north toward Palmdale Boulevard, a major thoroughfare in the valley, where a fugitive could jack someone and get a ride out of town.

As the SWAT team landed in the brush, Officer Ruiz saw the body. At that point, his radio lost its signal, one more reminder that he had entered a dead zone. With the suspect possibly lurking, Ruiz stopped his vehicle and jumped out, hoping to save his brother and employing his training as an EMT. In a quick scan, he noticed that the deputy's eye was pushed in, right where he had taken a round. And his head was flat. Few could survive injuries like this. Still alert to a possible ambush, Ruiz listened for his carotid. There was no sign of life. He spotted two or three pink stains in Sorensen's abdomen, around his bullet-proof vest. If he were alive, there would have been excessive bleeding. There was not. Then he looked inside the skull. "I saw that the brain was missing," Ruiz later told me. "That stops the heart."

Trying again to reach someone on his hand-held, Officer Ruiz could not get a signal. A highway patrolman for over a decade, he had been called to scenes in which other cops had been shot at or seriously wounded a number of times, but this was the worst he had ever witnessed. Within minutes, the shaken officer was joined by fifteen other sheriff's units and five CHIPS vehicles converging at the scene, as SWAT swarmed the trailer.

Arriving around the same time as Ruiz was Deputy Melissa Sullivan, who had been in her patrol car when she heard dispatch calling, "114 Boy," and getting no answer. Knowing that was Sorensen's code, she was concerned and headed right to headquarters at the Lancaster station. En route, she learned that Sorensen had been killed; she diverted and drove to the scene, racing toward her colleague's body and shocked to see that he was wearing the same uniform she was wearing—a Class B LASD rig with a cloth star. Gazing at the mangled corpse, the veteran cop was overtaken with thoughts ranging from disbelief to the personal. "Why would someone shoot you for wanting to protect them and their family?" she thought. Then she recalled the lonely beat that deputies traversed in the Antelope Valley. "This could have been me." For example, there was the time she had to wait thirty minutes for backup on a domestic violence call in Lake Los Angeles. The situation hadn't been safe, and months after the incident, the thought of it still nagged her.

With cops fanning out across the desert, Deputy Sullivan and several others remained with Sorensen's body to protect it—and the crime scene, now one of at least two, including the site of the murder. Among those surrounding Sorensen were members of SWAT. Some teared up at the sight of a fellow lawman reduced to a pile of mangled flesh. A commander told them to suck it up, and someone said a prayer, and then they put a blanket over Sorensen lest the news media, now swarming the skies like vultures, broadcast the scene on the evening news. Amid the creosote and fresh tire tracks and footprints in the Mojave furnace, with Steve's body stiffening on the path behind her, Melissa Sullivan phoned her family to let them know that she was all right. Then she and the others surrounded the scene with yellow tape, attaching it to bushes and scrub as they marked off a strange new grid in the wilderness. As Sullivan performed the task, she wondered if she really was all right. When she had first seen Sorensen's body, she cried briefly but made herself stop; "suck it up" was the law enforcement mantra and this was not a time to ignore it. Soon there would be more grisly news, a discovery that would crank a manhunt that was gathering steam into a fever pitch. For now, Deputy Sullivan left to get drinks and crackers from an RV that was the command post at the corner of Palmdale Boulevard and Two Hundredth Street, and then returned with replenishment for the crew.

At the same time, another SWAT team was racing across the desert in the Peacekeeper, following the tire tracks that had led Ruiz to Sorensen's body and then continuing on into the wastes. The armored jeep carried a team of six, as well as two Emergency Services Division paramedics and a K-9 handler. The vehicle was packed with gear; except for the driver, the men were not inside it. Instead they were standing on foot rails that ran along the back and sides of the vehicle and holding onto a handlebar as the Peacekeeper coursed over the sands. SWAT teams are color-coded; among the men on the rails was Deputy Bruce Chase, an eleven-year SWAT veteran and number four on Team Gold, which was assigned to that day's task. In that position, he was in charge of intel for the day's plan. The plan was to keep following the tracks and try to avoid an ambush or being shot at; outside the vehicle, the men were totally exposed—a vulnerability that Chase and the other men on the hunt would feel for the next seven days, in every minute that they were trekking through the wide open expanse of the desert. Essentially they were moving targets.

Another part of the plan was to deploy the lone passenger inside the Peacekeeper. This was Rik, a Belgian Malinois, a sturdy and stouthearted breed that has become the preferred dog in law enforcement, the canine that is said to have accompanied Navy SEALS in their takedown of bin Laden, trained to engage in combat as well as detect human scent. His handler was Sgt. Joe Williams, an ex–Air Force MP; together, he and Rik looked like a GQ ad—a rippling and handsome man in uniform and a beautiful four-legged sentry by his side—and in fact they were a couple, of sorts: at LASD, dogs live with their partners, and together they are on call at a moment's notice. At the time of the incident, Joe and Rik had been a team for three years, deployed many times but never to anything like this. It wasn't just the gruesome nature of the crime that made this call different, or even the bizarre pursuit that would go on for seven days in the high summer heat of the Mojave. Early on, Joe realized that the man they were up against was a remarkable character; in his view, Donald Kueck was calculating, not afraid, and willing to die.

Less than two hours after Kueck shot Sorensen, the SWAT team found his yellow Dodge Dart two and a half miles from the deputy's body. Rik picked up a scent, then led deputies to an abandoned shed about fifty yards away. "Zuken," Joe said, issuing the Dutch command for "search," and Rik headed through a dilapidated doorway and began coming back with items belonging to Steve. First, it was his gun belt, empty and covered in blood. "Revere," Joe said, giving the command for "continue searching," and Rik ran back and returned with Steve's hat. It, too, was covered in blood. *"Revere,"* Joe said again, and Rik headed back through the doorway, coming back with Steve's bloody notebook. Although Joe knew that Sorensen had been shot and killed, the sight of his personal belongings surfacing sequentially and covered in blood was troubling; the hunters had already seen what happened to their brother, but now they came face-to-face with his remnants—the very totems of the job that had called him.

Still on the scent, Rik led the SWAT team away from the shed and east on a rutted dirt road until the road intersected and ended at 170th Street East, a paved road with occasional traffic. But there the scent vanished, and the search began to unravel. It was 6:14 PM. Had Kueck flagged someone down and hitched a ride out of town? Was there a carjacking? Could he have gotten to the nearby airstrip and literally vanished into thin air? A half hour later, SWAT received some disturbing information—Kueck's car was dumped a few hundred yards from Sorensen's home. Now they were gripped by other questions. Sorensen was married, and he had a two-year-old son. Was his wife, Christine, being held hostage? Where was the child? They raced to the house and kicked down the door, mounting a room-to-room search in the carefully wired compound, but no one was there. A few minutes later they got a tip that Kueck was hiding out next to his property, on the site of the recently evicted squatter. The SWAT team tore back across the desert in off-road vehicles, converging on the squatter's trailer and turning it upside down. An elaborate tunnel system splayed out before them, a demented leprechaun's world of canned food, a piss-stained mattress, *Hustler* centerfolds taped to the crumbling walls, and a cockatoo at the end of a hallway. The labyrinth was one that they would continue to hear about as the manhunt unfolded, as tip after tip poured in, alluding to ancient subterranean causeways, unmarked and classified underground missile silos, and a myriad of other strange Mojave hideouts.

Word of the incident had swept through the region, and cops from other desert precincts were converging in the Antelope Valley. News choppers were buzzing in from Los Angeles. Locals monitored the situation on their police band radios; learning that a fugitive was at large, they retrieved their weapons from wherever they kept them and placed them at the ready, lest a desperate stranger—or maybe even someone they knew—showed up, looking for aid and comfort.

Yet amid the chaos, nature took over. The sun began to sink, and the desert cooled, and another magnificent display of color swept the skies; the valley was now a red and orange tabernacle, and it encircled one and all, and everyone was silent and humbled, wiped of all memory of bad news, unless you're standing next to it or near it or you can smell it or sense it, and then the paradox of the beauty and the terrible event of a moment ago stops your clock and makes clear that two opposing aspects at any given time is the way of all things and that's really all there is to it. In a few days, there would be a full moon, but as red and orange faded to ink and then as dusk faded to black, there was an unusual occurrence in the region known for its sparkling night skies: no waxing moon was visible, nor were there stars. Yet a strange white light illumined the site where Deputy Sorensen's body was lying, and it cast harsh shadows and was accompanied by an ungodly hum. The false sun was coming from a large generator, which had been set up so the coroner could examine Steve's body. As he worked, cataloguing the elements of the scene, various members of law enforcement surrounded the felled deputy, and in the distance, on the paved two-lanes south and north of the remote enclave, sirens screamed and red lights flashed and danced in the strange modern constellation that spells trouble.

There was still no sign of Kueck. At the nearby Lancaster station, Captain Carl Deeley, Sorensen's commander, ran through some options. He knew his beat, and he knew that if Kueck were still in it, he'd be trying to flee the area, traveling at night, when the temperature had cooled and under the cover of darkness. It was time to call in the FLIRs—forward-looking infrared thermal imaging—used by the military to target the enemy in another desert war, the one raging at the same time in Iraq. In fact, the technology was borne of wide-open, flat space, having first been deployed in Operation Desert Storm during the Gulf War. Deeley contacted Edwards Air Force base and asked for support. A thermal imaging plane was dispatched, flying over the Mojave at 30,000 feet, scanning every inch of the desert floor, looking for the telltale blip of heat that would indicate a human form. A special SWAT team backed up the FLIRs, ripping across the sands on ATVs, now joined by deputies on foot and horseback, and by K-9 units from three jurisdictions.

By midnight, the FLIRs had picked up nothing but coyotes and kit foxes and all manner of desert predators on the move. The cops were right back where they started—at Kueck's abandoned car in the middle of the desert. "People are creatures of habit," Detective Paul Delhauer, a profiler with the sheriff's department, told me on the phone months later. "Their personality is their fingerprint." There was only one place Donald Kueck would hide—right in his own backyard, the Mojave. They were right. As the FLIRS were sweeping the area, he walked through an unlocked back door into the home of an associate and neighbor. This was C. T. Smith, a forty-year-old ex-con with an extensive arrest record. He had done time for two felonies, possession of controlled substances, and lewd and lascivious acts, and the last thing he wanted was further contact with law enforcement. C.T. lived about a mile away from Kueck in a dilapidated compound of sheds and had not seen his friend in months. He was surprised, not so much by the unannounced entry—these things happen in the desert—but by the whole picture: Kueck was tired, sunburned, and upset—and armed with an assault rifle and a short barrel revolver. "What's up, buddy?"

he said. "Got any water, man?" Kueck said. "I've been living in the desert." Did C.T. know that the local deputy had been killed? Had he heard the sirens and choppers in the area? It would have been hard not to, yet we do not know what condition he was in, nor do we know if there was talk of anything that happened that day among his immediate circle. "Sure, man," he said, and then filled a jug that his friend was carrying. After a while Kueck headed out the door and into the night. A solitary FLIR continued to sweep the valley floor, but Kueck eluded it for a while and then dug a hole that was wide enough to crouch in. He got in and covered himself up with a piece of cardboard. To many, the makeshift hideout sounds like a joke, but Kueck, a self-taught scientist among many other skills, knew that by then, the ground had cooled down enough to match human body temperature, and there would be no heat for the infrared to detect.

Time passed and the choppers peeled off. The coroner was finishing his gruesome inventory as Deputy Sullivan continued to stand guard near her fallen brother. When a few last measurements and tallies were completed, Deputy Sorensen was placed in the refrigerated van and taken out of the desert he had loved and patrolled, down the hill and back to the city, and into the county morgue. The generator had been turned off, and the desert went dark again, and the night became the worst version of itself. Sometimes, often in fact, you can hear the coyotes howl in the blackness, and those who are attuned hear all sorts of other things—all the sounds and whispers and quivers of the night hunters that assume different shapes from ours—the snakes and the bobcats and the smaller, less noted creatures. But on that night, Deputy Melissa Sullivan heard nothing. The dead zone was everywhere, she later remembered: the animals knew what happened.

DAY TWO

Crossing the Reptile Door

*May your trails be crooked, winding,
lonesome, and dangerous, leading to the most amazing view.*
        —Edward Abbey, *Desert Solitaire*

THE ANCIENTS SAID THAT LIZARDS DWELL IN THE DREAMTIME, and when they appear it's to tell us to break from the past, lose a tail, and hit the road. Of course, at the time the lizard appears, we may not recognize that any sort of portal or window has opened, any sign suggesting a geographic or inward journey, and certainly a child would not take the appearance of a reptile or any other creature as an invitation to change location. But then again perhaps only a child would recognize such a thing, even though the information may not resonate until some time later, might be buried under years of being told to do the right thing, adhere to the rules, get a job, get married, follow the middle-class way . . . until one day the future desert dweller finds him or herself on a different path, stepping through an entrance, forcing open a crack in the window, leaving things behind and why? The explanation never does satisfy those in his or her immediate circle, some of whom are obliterated by the break, but no matter . . . the call is answered and the man vanishes, and it only starts to make sense later, when the narrative is over.

Donald Charles Kueck was born on August 21, 1950, into a Southern family that prided itself on military service and law enforcement. His father's father served in Kaiser Wilhelm's navy, fleeing Germany after World War I as Hitler began to seize power. His father was a pilot at Eglin Air Force base in Mobile, Alabama, and that's where Don was raised—3,000 miles from the Mojave Desert. His mother's brother was head of the Louisiana State troopers, the top cop in the state. Two of his older sisters would later join the army and the navy.

Exactly when Don succumbed to the gravitational pull of the desert we do not know. But as a little boy, he would play in the woods, and it was there that lizards entered his life. They were blue ones—called runners or racers—and one day he picked one up and took it home. He named it Thing 1. Soon there were more—Thing 2 and Thing 3—and one day Thing 2 escaped and Don grabbed it and squished it by mistake. "He was heartbroken," an older sister Peggy recalls. But it was not just a momentary loss, she says; he had an affinity for the lizards and they for him, and it went beyond playing with reptiles, the thing that lots of boys did. Somehow you could just tell—there was some sort of harmonizing of energy, a cross-species understanding perhaps, the kind of thing found in the character of Dr. Doolittle or others who have a way with creatures.

Another thing that was noteworthy about Don was the fact that he had an IQ of 140. He was always thinking, making and rigging contraptions, wondering about how things worked. A friend would later say that he was "too smart for his own good," one step ahead of everybody and everything, rolling out theories of physics and mechanics and the ways of the universe to the degree that he had trouble shutting down all of the chatter. But he received one message loud and clear: he was not cut out for the family tradition of service in the military or law enforcement. In 1970 or so, at the age of twenty, he hit the hippie trail, heading to Southern California and beginning to orbit the desert. He was not alone: at the time many were walking away from family or national expectations, fleeing the military draft, heading north to Canada, west to San Francisco or Venice, or underground. Often such acts were fraught with difficulty and danger. Don's number was never called in the draft lottery, so on that front, he considered himself lucky. But a friend of his was drafted and the two made a pact: Don, already a longhair, would not cut his hair until his friend came home from Vietnam. His long hair had already made him an outcast in his native Mobile, Alabama, with people making jokes about his pony tail and cops giving him the evil eye even if he were just sitting in his car at a traffic light. Still, when he left, it was the fact that he had forsaken so much—Southern tradition and on top of that the Air Force, progenitor of the right stuff and US air supremacy—that really puzzled many in his community and family. What else was there? they wondered. What kind of a man would not want to claim his heritage in this world?

Arriving on the West Coast, Don found himself in the port city of Long Beach by way of a sojourn in San Francisco, where—as he later told friends—he had taken a lot of acid, so much that his vision was destroyed and he had gone blind for a while. When his sight returned, it was difficult to focus; there were floaters and patterns and stars, and it was only when he was away from cities that the chaos seemed to vanish, sucked into a world without clutter and diversion. Certainly Long Beach was filled with distractions; it bustled and screamed with the traffic of three So Cal freeways whizzing by, and every day the world's biggest cargo ships entered the harbor, offloading massive shipping containers that were hauled away by parades of big rigs that puffed particulates as they headed inland. But perhaps the fact that there was a navy base nearby provided some comfort, though it is not likely that Don would have thought that at the time, or even acknowledged it; he had wanted to get as far away from his family as possible. There were numerous jobs for able-bodied men at the shipping docks or in the aerospace factories that were then fueling the state's economy; thousands of men and women were making airplanes and machines and munitions for California's military compounds, including Edwards Air Force Base, another military base near which Don would soon be living.

It did not take long to find employment, and he was hired at a place that specialized in restaurant upholstery, where he met and fell in love with the owner's daughter. Soon the pair eloped and moved into a small, one-bedroom apartment in Bell Gardens, a working-class suburb that was home to many who toiled at the plants or the numerous mom-and-pop shops that serviced them. Don's wife, nineteen or twenty, had a daughter named Rebecca from an earlier marriage. She was two or three years old. Some people take to being parents, welcoming toddlers into their arms and delighting in the routine of bringing them into the tribe— teaching them song, how to hold a spoon, the names of things. We do not know how Don played this role, whether he took to it with joy or a sense of duty, resignation or even resentment perhaps, but we do know that the first thing he did when he woke up in the morning was smoke a joint. "He was Mr. Mellow, Mr. Cool," recalls his former brother-in-law, James Finch, not pegging the mellowness to pot smoking necessarily but to his general demeanor.

But there were few like-minded spirits in Don's orbit, and sometimes he would organize trips to Hollywood, a short hop up the 405 and then east across the 101 and into another world. "Let's go look at the freaks," Don would say to his wife and brother-in-law, and then they'd pile into the car and flee Long Beach. Don always brought his favorite drink, a can of Dr. Pepper mixed with cherry brandy, and he'd pass it around for all to share.

In 1974, his wife gave birth to her second child, a son by way of Don; he was named Charles Donald Kueck, a reversal of his father's first and middle names. Over time, the son became like his father in more ways than simply sharing a reversed name; they looked almost exactly alike, had the same temperament, the same exuberance and charm, the same brilliance and lack of follow-through, the same likes and dislikes, and one day the son would follow the father into the desert and there he, too, would bake.

Shortly after the birth of Charles, or Chuck as they started to call him, Don adopted Rebecca, and it seemed as if he wanted to have this family. But several years into the marriage, it was clear to Don that he was not cut out for the conventional life. What exactly triggered the dramatic separation is not clear. He had lost his job because of a back injury, and a lifelong descent into pain-killing drugs began. Perhaps the drugs numbed him against the difficulty of being a parent and husband; perhaps his trips to Hollywood where he could "see the freaks"—all the runaways, drifters, and street punks who had cut society's cord or had it severed—reminded him that he actually was one, and try as he might to fit in, such a thing was just not possible. "I don't love you," he said to his wife at dinner one night. "I'm going out for milk and cigarettes." He never came back, at least to this particular configuration of his family, and years later, the story of his departure would attain a weird sort of status among friends and associates of his children, especially his son, adding to Don's charisma with its drama and chill, inciting a certain kind of awe and wonder, even as the consequences of the exit were exacting a dire toll.

His first move was into an apartment in North Hollywood—ever closer to the Mojave, a world of salvation that lay just beyond the San Gabriel Mountains to the north. For the next thirteen years, he had no contact with his immediate family, his ex-wife, and his two kids. From his base in this LA suburb just outside the studio gates, he wandered and worked a series of jobs that led nowhere. Even for the most stalwart, the hermit in the making, even for those with no desire for fame or recognition or even a hearty pat on the back for a job well done, living in proximity to the studios would not have been without travail. We do not know if he ever queued up outside Warner Brothers or Universal, along with the hundreds who routinely came in response to calls for extras, hoping to get discovered, meet someone who knew someone, hobnob with the Hollywood proletariat—after all, as the scripture went, that's how Marilyn did it—her mother was a studio seamstress!—but with his Fu Manchu, long hair, and chiseled face, he was almost a stand-in for Clint Eastwood. And what's more, he had the gift of gab—all of the men and women who knew him will tell you that he told a great story around life's campfire, could keep you there all night, talking all silvery about philosophy and adventures and things of a spiritual nature, and later if you picked it apart, it didn't really make sense or perhaps it required too much thinking and hurt your brain, but you didn't really care at the time because it sure sounded good and you believed every word of his rap. But there are many pretty people at the studio gates, and some charming ones too, and in the end Donald Kueck would head out of North Hollywood and become a star of his own design—in his own drama, with a set that went on forever.

One day our hermit in the making could no longer pay his rent. He moved into his van and parked it next door in a friend's driveway. Every couple of days, he would take a shower inside his friend's house, becoming a brother to the woman who lived there, Barb Oberman. In Don she found a brother who did not fit well in the conventional world. He did not need or want money, she recalls, and was not embarrassed about living in his van. He was on a spiritual path, one that did not involve material things, and Barb understood how that had made it impossible for him to function as a family man—at least in the way he was expected to in Long Beach. To earn a few bucks every now and then, the two of them would deliver phone books to the homes that lined the residential streets near the studio backlots. For the daily needs of life, they improvised. For instance, if something was broken or needed repair, or if they needed something that they didn't have, Don could either make the repair or build the new thing. Unable to afford a proper back brace to treat his old injury, he made one out of rubber bands. A student of the night skies, he made a telescope from a cardboard tube and added some lenses, although with the bright lights of the city illuminating Los Angeles on a round-the-clock basis, it was not always possible to view the constellations or even the phases of the moon. Minus such things in life, some of us are disoriented, even bereft; others who do not consciously notice their absence are adrift, although they may not be aware of that either, except in the vaguest sense, and they would probably live out their lives with that inchoate longing for something that they could not name or describe. Donald Kueck longed to live in the desert and talked about finding a place there; the lizards were calling and it was time to go.

It wasn't just the stars he longed for, it was the whole thing and everything it was and represented. Once the pair went into the Mojave to go shooting, and Don brought his 50 mm muzzle-loading gun. Now, a 50 mm is not a minor gun, even though it's old-fashioned and from another time. It's a serious weapon and can do a lot of damage. But lots of people have them—they're their own scene, like pistols are for others—and on any given day, you can go out in the desert and discern their blasts coming from just over yonder. "He liked old guns," Barb tells me on the phone months after his death. "But he was not a gun freak." During their trip, she noticed that he seemed completely at home, at rest, in the hot, dry, wide-open space, and she understood that sooner or later he would be leaving North Hollywood. As it happened, she and her brother owned some land in the Colorado Desert between the Salton Sea and Colorado River. She told Don that he could go live there, but he declined; it was the wrong desert, she says, and some time later, he found a place just beyond the mountains, in the desert with the siren name, the Mojave, or the Mo-jave as some said in appreciation, pronouncing the *j* and drawing out the second syllable, savoring the name as if tasting the place as they named it. This was where he could park his van forever, and he went there.

Oddly, or perhaps not so, for how far do we really range from our home turf, the renegade boy from Alabama, brother to sisters in the navy and law enforcement, son of father in the Air Force, grandson of man who served with Kaiser Wilhelm, ended up on the perimeter of Edwards Air Force Base, launching pad for the space shuttle, testing grounds for the Stealth bomber, one of the most heavily armed regions in the world.

Barb drove north to see him a few times but got lost every time. Don kept in touch, and later when he moved to his own place in the desert, some land where he was not just parking but living, he would send photos of the animals who trusted him and became his friends—the ground squirrels that danced on his head, the raven that would alight on his arm—and then, when it was all over, his sisters and friends would try to reconcile the image of the jackrabbits that gathered every morning for breakfast at the table Don had set for them in the sagebrush with the image of Don the cop killer, and it just didn't make sense.

Yet there was one thing that rang loud and true: Don knew the desert better than anyone, and the fact that he had been able to outfox a massive display of manpower and technology for an entire week confirmed what he had been telling everyone all along: he had learned the ways of the land and the animals that lived there and one way or another, in the way of all shamans—good or evil—he had shed a skin and disappeared.

Men with Guns in a Convent

A very happy Easter to you and great joy in Our Lord, my daughter. We should never open the doors of our soul to sadness. . . . The spouses of Christ shouldn't be sad but smiling serenely and without tears.

> —From Letter Number 13, circa 1925, by Mother Luisita, founder of the Carmelite Sisters of the Most Sacred Heart of Los Angeles, refugee, candidate for sainthood

WITH EVERY HOUR THAT A CRIMINAL IS ON THE LOOSE, THE chances of finding him diminish exponentially. By the morning of Day Two, a thousand cops and deputies had joined the manhunt. Some traversed the desert in quadrants, walking every cubic centimeter of its lonely stretches. LA County was sparing no expense on the search, which had morphed into exactly the kind of hydra-headed, Orwellian monster that Kueck feared—an overwhelming display of manpower, vehicles, food, searchlights, trailers, aircraft, mounted civilians, dogs, Andy Gumps, weapons, ammo fuel, surveillance equipment, and tracking gear.

At the Mount Carmel Retreat Center in Palmdale, Sister Mary Michael was taking a sunrise walk among the boulders and Joshua trees just after morning Mass. She gazed eastward, toward the Three Sisters Buttes, a mountain range in which three rounded peaks were the most prominent. The buttes are a well-known landmark to those who appreciate this rugged part of LA County, a marker of comfort and beauty that brings the endless desert expanse to a rolling stop, beckoning the pilgrim to slow down ever more and take stock. Was the formation first named by three sisters? What was it called when the ancestors of the Shoshone roamed its flanks, traveling up and down its trails as they headed westward, into the Mojave, and then crossing another mountain range to trade with their brothers at the edge of the Pacific Ocean? No one knows the answers to these questions, but the members of the order at Mount Carmel sometimes joked that it was fitting that they lived near the Three Sisters Buttes, a range that seemed to invoke their calling.

Mount Carmel was a convent that served the area's poor, offering daily mass and comfort, and providing a day care center for children whose parents worked the valley's orchards and fields. Knowing that there had been a deadly incident nearby and that the fugitive suspected in the killing could be lurking, Sister Mary Michael was somewhat wary as she strolled on the second day of the manhunt. Yet as she listened to the cactus wrens and their dawn exchange, she was struck as always by the land and sky and light, and reduced one more time to a state of sheer humility and awe. She offered up a silent prayer of gratitude for her blessed life amid the Old Testament scenery that looked like the birthplace of the savior, and as she reflected, a figure approached, closing in from across the sands. Something about the gait told her the person was a man. It wasn't unusual to see someone walking the desert at dawn, but it wasn't all that common either. She grew more suspicious and wondered whether the advancing figure might be the wanted man. He was big and tall, she noticed, and was heading directly for her. Reversing course, she turned back toward the convent while keeping an eye on the stranger. She now saw that he was wearing a dark suit. How strange, she thought. That's not what the radio said. He's supposed to be wearing a T-shirt and maybe some jeans. Does he want to hide in the convent? What about the children? She picked up her pace, but it was too late. "Sgt. Phil Guzman," said the man, extending a hand and now stopping her in her path. "Los Angeles County Homicide."

He was soon joined by Sgt. Joe Purcell, another veteran homicide detective. Both of the men were hoping to catch a break—maybe some desert rat would live up to the name and drop a dime on Kueck; maybe as Kueck got more desperate he'd surface somewhere. But Kueck had an edge. In his possession were his cell phone, rifle, Sorensen's gun—and the deputy's two-way radio. For some reason, he had not yet left the area, although he probably could have. While on the run, he was flipping through the frequencies and paying close attention to all of the police chatter. When a call went out for backup at East 200 and Palmdale Boulevard, he knew to head in the opposite direction. On another channel, he learned that Black Butte Basin Road was hot, so he backtracked. Guzman and Purcell believed that they needed to embed men where Kueck was hiding, and the convent was the perfect place.

The Carmelite order began in the thirteenth century, when a sect of hermits went to live in a grotto at Mount Carmel in tribute to the prophet Elijah. According to the Old Testament, it was atop this peak that Elijah battled with disbelievers in a test of faith, ultimately calling down rain in a time of drought. Decades later, the order dedicated itself to St. Teresa, the fifteenth-century mystic who was torn between the material and spiritual worlds, and battled with demons as she fled inward. During her journey, she underwent a series of miracles that happened after bouts of ecstasy in which she levitated and communicated with angels. Writing about her lifelong journey from adulation and glory to humility and devotion, St. Teresa called many to the life of the spirit, urging selflessness, fraternal love, and detachment from worldly goods. Down through the ages, warriors have represented themselves by way of insignia on their shields. Saints have symbols too, and Teresa's is a heart, a book, and an arrow. In pursuit of her teachings, the Carmelite order is what they call "discalced"—one whose priests and nuns go unshod or in sandals.

When Sister Mary Michael greeted Sgt. Guzman, she was dressed in the conventional garb of the sisterhood—robes and sandals. Just as she had wondered why a man would be wearing a dark suit on such a hot day, Guzman thought about what it must feel like to dress in dark robes in 100-degree heat. Although the pair did not discuss such thoughts, they formed a fast connection, rooted in the commonality of acceptance and both belonging to tribes on a mission—a brotherhood and sisterhood that people turned to in time of need, but shunned at other times. As the two cops and the nun walked toward the convent, Sister Mary Michael trod carefully past the cholla, cautioning them about spines that could "jump"—meaning affix themselves immediately to passing skin or fabric and instantly embed, probably the one projectile that could penetrate a bulletproof vest and then damage its protected flesh. Perhaps the sister thought about making a little joke of that but then stopped herself, for that may have been too forward. Learning a bit about LASD's desert mission, Sister Mary Michael marveled at the mysteries of the world. Here were two strangers who needed help, although not the kind that she or the other residents of the convent generally provided. She was not being asked for prayer, although that would unfold in its own way, and she was not being asked for food or water, although the sisters would soon offer it. As it happened, the strangers needed lodging, but not for themselves; the SWAT team needed a home in the desert, a place to camp while they mounted their search, until the wanted man was caught. When that would happen the detectives did not know. It could be within hours, Guzman explained, or several days. Although he didn't say it quite like this, LASD did not have any idea where Donald Kueck was at that moment. But they believed he was in the area, and they needed to start living where he was hiding. The convent was ideally situated, on 180th Street East, a main drag in Palmdale where cell phone reception was good and with plenty of wide open space around it, save for the intermittent creosote, Joshua trees, and rocks—not bad as a takeoff and launching pad for helicopters.

So later that day and in the following days the warriors came in from the battlefield and laid down their arms. Some of the nuns had met Deputy Sorensen when he first arrived in Lake Los Angeles and made a point of introducing himself to those in his jurisdiction. "If you ever need me, call me," he had said, giving them his cell phone number as he did with pretty much everyone. "I'm available 24/7." There was never any occasion that had warranted calling the local deputy, but the nuns were grateful for the personal introduction, and when Steve's compadres arrived to search for their brother's killer, the nuns may have feared for what was to come— after all, they lived by the credo that says to hate the sin but love the sinner—but they could not turn away and they cooked for the hunters and went about their daily tasks and callings, attending morning and evening Mass, which once or twice some of the men attended as well, divesting themselves of weapons and bulletproof vests, dipping a finger into the holy water at the chapel entrance, making the sign of the cross, genuflecting, praying to the source of all protection, and proclaiming the miracle of the resurrection.

Later that week, when a camaraderie between the cops and the nuns had developed, some of the cops gave the nuns a ride in a helicopter, the hulking Sikorsky 5, and the cloistered women whose mandate was to pray for the priests—the men in their order—experienced an intense proximity to men in another kind of uniform, in dire circumstances, a moment that was perhaps a latter-day kind of ecstasy that St. Theresa herself may have undergone during her own flights into levitation and visions, filled with whirring blades and swirling air and what were those strange scents—men on the chase? burning fuel? hot metal?—and to have slipped their earthly bonds in such an exciting fashion they were grateful.

NEW DEPUTY IN TOWN

Please Don't Talk to the Lifeguard
> —Song Number 98 on the Hot Singles list for the
> week ending August 3, 1963, sung by Diane Ray

MOST COPS HAVE CHOSEN THEIR LINE OF WORK BECAUSE THEY are
the kind of person who wants to make a difference. Some perhaps
have chosen naïvely, with little understanding of the way it is on the
streets, pursuing a dream of wanting to be a police officer or fire
fighter when they grew up. Others come right from the streets, a life
of petty or sometimes hard crime in fact, heading for a world of trouble. Someone turns them around and they become a cop because
they know how to talk to people who are falling through the cracks,
especially kids. (Or, in the old days, they were pressed into service
by frightened citizens, who sometimes hired outlaws as sheriffs. As
the noted cowboy scribe Frank Waters wrote, "With a tin star he
stood the chance of also wearing a halo of righteousness; without it,

a noose.") Then there are those who instinctively know that someone has to enforce the rules of society, and they feel hypocritical if
they don't walk the walk of the American credo: "We are a nation of
laws, not men." And yet others join up for the camaraderie, the pen-
sion plan, the good salary, or a combination of all of these things,
and then some simply fall into the gig because it suits their temperament—they are service-oriented, they feel comfortable in a world of
rules—and once inside the club, they know they have come home.

As far back as his friends can remember, Steve Sorensen wasn't
telling people about wanting to be a policeman when he grew up,
but it was clear that he liked to help people. Born in Pasadena, California, in 1957, he was the youngest of three children; in fact he
was at least ten years younger than the nearest in age of his two
sisters—an accidental or, to use a popular term of the day, "change
of life" baby to parents who were much older than the parents of
his peers. When he was eleven or twelve, the family moved to
Manhattan Beach, California, a then blue-collar community where
families settled so they could be near the ocean—it was better for
Steve's asthma, said a doctor. One of the first things his old friends
will tell you is that even as a kid, he was the neighborhood handyman, often carrying out tasks for people in the neighborhood with
or without being asked—and took pride in that role. These were
things he did throughout his life—carrying groceries for the impaired, landscaping for the elderly—the small acts of kindness that
often go unnoticed in the world at large, but without them life
becomes that much more cruel.

Steve's father was in automotives, and his mother was a home-
maker; by all accounts and to outsiders, his parents were loving—
after all, they had moved for his health—although not expressive
of their emotions. His mother, Rosetta, was a bit more attentive—
although perhaps because of the number of years between her and
her youngest child, the kind of attention she gave was sometimes
out of touch. With his blonde hair and blue eyes, Steve was emerg-

ing as a typical So Cal kid, classic in fact, and acclimating easily to life at the beach, where he had hooked up with a young surfing crew that was apprenticing to some of the older stars. But for his first Halloween in the neighborhood, his mother dressed him up as Tiny Tim—the strange, ambisexual man who was a regular on the *Johnny Carson Show*, crooning "Tiptoe Through the Tulips" with his ukulele to the delight of millions of viewers and a plethora of jokes. It was a curious way to treat a boy who was hanging around with the local surf gods, and although he would end up taking care of his mother years later, "Steve never forgave her for that," a childhood friend recalls. Shortly after that fateful Halloween, he ran away after slamming a pitcher of syrup down on the table and splattering it all over his clothes. "I hope he isn't going to school like that," his mother told a neighbor, "completely covered in syrup." The rebellion was short-lived, although not without impact in a family where drama was generally internal.

By the time he was a teenager, Steve was a hard-core surfer in this well-known surfing town, part of a crowd that included some of the best wave riders in the area, including figures who later became legendary, though not in time to cash in on the surfing boom that is now worldwide; to this day, some members of this pioneering crew are still living in shacks and pouring drinks to pay the rent, clinging to a reef like hermit crabs.

At the beach and in the lineup whenever the surf was up, Steve and his buddies were California golden boys, always tan and buff, and resented by other high school cliques for the way they seemed to slide through life. His mother wondered how he was going to make a living when the time came, even though Steve was not the stereotypical hard-core party surfer of Hollywood—"Hey Bud, all I want is some good weed and some tasty sets"—and he always had some sort of job, like working at the local liquor store or, what he really liked, being a lifeguard, where he would sit alone in a tower all day, watch waves, and rush into an emergency when called. "My girlfriends and I all had crushes on him," his next-door neighbor Julie Franks remembers. "He was the town stud."

In 1975, Kimberly Brandon-Watson, a sophomore at Mira Costa High, met the future deputy when he and some friends walked into a Christmas party in Hermosa Beach. "They were so cool they were scary," Brandon-Watson recalls from her graphic design studio nearby, "especially Mark Bowden," a surfing superstar who himself was friends with the local surf king, Mike Purpus. Kimberly still lives and works in the town where she grew up. On a fall afternoon, I spent several hours with her as she painted a portrait of her old beau, and through the window, you could see waves breaking offshore and rolling in as the Santa Ana winds carved perfect hollow sets—the kind of surf Steve and his buddies lived for. Although Kimberly did not know any of them before that night at the party, she certainly knew of them; Hermosa Beach was a small town, and pretty much everyone knew everyone else at least by face recognition only, even if they came from the adjacent beach towns along the south bay of Los Angeles. But she did not expect any of them to acknowledge her; in addition to the coolness factor, they were upperclassmen, and she was even a little leery as they made eye contact with her and then moved into the holiday swarm. Lingering inside Kimberly's orbit as his buddies made the rounds, Steve soon approached and introduced himself. Surprised that he was talking to her, Kimberly was nervous but quickly charmed and then felt that he was very nice. When he asked for her phone number, she gave it. The next day he called, and they were together off and on for the next four years, with Kimberly swept off her feet in a romance filled with adventure, old-fashioned courtliness, and the kind of teenage obsession that takes over your life, with Steve showering her with so many gifts and flower bouquets that Kimberly finally ran in the other direction.

In the beginning, it wasn't that they liked all of the same things, but they had enough in common to become a couple. Kimberly didn't surf, but she liked the beach and being in the ocean. She and Steve would play volleyball together and play on the sand, and it wasn't long before Steve withdrew from his wave-riding crew and gave himself over to Kimberly; in fact he was at her house almost every day—just twenty-two short blocks away—until an anguishing pattern of breaking up and reuniting was set in motion. An artist and seamstress, Kimberly would often design and make things for Steve, like his trunks and special logos for his shirts. They would go on surf trips to San Diego in his orange and red Datsun. Sometimes they went to Magic Mountain, listening en route to Rod Stewart, or alternating between her favorite, David Bowie, and his, Elton John. Once they went snorkeling at Catalina Island, a short ferry trip from the port of Long Beach but a long way from city life. It was early on in their relationship when the pair had proclaimed their feelings for one another. "I love you with all my heart," Steve wrote later after one of their separations. "'This is only the beginning of what I hope to feel forever,'" he continued, giving credit to the band famous for the line—Chicago—and then signing off.

But something else was going on, and in retrospect it's clear to Kimberly that her first boyfriend was deeply troubled. He would not discuss whatever was nagging him beneath the surface, even when it erupted in unexpected outbursts that would soon subside. But Kimberly Brandon-Watson was madly in love with Steve Sorensen, and he too was head over heels with the girl who once sat on a couch at a party, frightened by the in crowd. It wasn't until years later that Kimberly realized that her high school beau was tightly wrapped—as others would describe him throughout his life.

For example, there were little things, such as the fact that Steve had really bad vision. But he hardly ever wore glasses, Kimberly recalls, because he didn't want people to see him with Coke-bottle lenses. And he did not wear contact lenses, so for Steve, the world was often out of focus. "Things had to be perfect," Kimberly says, or as another friend recalls, Steve was "insanely prideful." Aside from concern about cracks in his physical presentation, there were more serious problems as well. Sometimes when Kimberly talked with other men, Steve would simmer and soon erupt. Kimberly would respond in kind, and on occasion Steve would do something like punch a hole in the wall and then calm down. Kimberly would discuss the relationship with her mother, who advised her not to respond to his explosions or his endless displays of affection, but to play hard to get—a common dating motto of that era and one that is periodically rolled out nowadays in best-selling self-help books. The ploy worked, and Steve always came back after long periods of no contact. "It seems when I don't call you for a while, you are more friendly, or you like me more," Steve wrote in a letter, marked by florid penmanship and occasional spelling errors, and similar in proclamations and regret to others that he sent to Kimberly when they were estranged.

I guess for you the old saying Absence makes the heart grow fonder is true. I am not trying to critisize you by saying for me it is a little bit true to, but for me when I don't see you I get lonely, not just for someone to talk to but to hear your voice and talk to you. One thing that I would like to do is ask for forgiveness for my jealousy. Sometimes it gets out of hand and it rules my actions . . . I now ask you to try and understand me. How I feel when I want to hug you or kiss you and you turn away it hurts because I am still very In love with you romanticly . . . there has been no dimming of the flame . . . I know sometimes I show my love for you buy buying you things, I know this angers you but I can't help it. I love you . . . P.S. Give me a call.

The pattern of breakups and reunions continued, and soon they both enrolled at El Camino Junior College in the nearby beach town of Torrance. Steve joined the water polo team, throwing himself as never before into the sport and becoming the team's star. Kimberly studied art. Sometimes they talked about career plans; Kimberly wanted to paint or go into graphic design, and Steve spoke of joining law enforcement or becoming a paramedic. It was becoming more and more apparent to Kimberly that beyond a love of the ocean, the two had little in common. Gradually the relationship lost steam. The gifts and letters ceased. The pair continued to see each other, but behind all the years of drama, she had already checked out. One day she told Steve how she felt. "He said, 'Fine,' and I was like, 'Wow,'" she says. The relationship had run its course and was over.

After the breakup, Steve immersed himself in beach life more than ever, becoming an LA County lifeguard. For six years he watched the beaches from San Pedro north to Dockweiler State Beach, a beautiful though noisy strip under the takeoff and landing patterns near the Los Angeles airport. People tend to regard lifeguards the same way as they think of surfers—partying airheads who put the word "dude" at the end of every sentence and not to be taken seriously because their office is outside and they plan their lives around the weather. For sure there was a partying crew among the county lifeguards. While Steve did hang out with them, he was not known to cut loose or get wasted. He didn't chase after women in a way that would be noteworthy, and he never had to get the last word or be number one. This is not to say that he wasn't your average jock and didn't take advantage of situations that presented themselves, but really, more than anything and in his heart of hearts, he wanted respect—at least that's how it seemed to LA County deputy sheriff Steve Propster as he looked back at the time when both men were lifeguards, before their paths diverged until they ran into each other years later, when both had joined the sheriff's department.

"Reality was messy for Steve," Propster tells me one afternoon in a coffee joint near the harbor patrol, which is now his beat. In many ways Propster was, and is, the opposite of Steve. A self-described man of the warrior-scholar tradition, Propster was a dope-smoking surfer in high school, then went to USC on an arts scholarship, influenced by comic books like the *Silver Surfer* and wanting to draw comics and write screenplays. Along the way, he was recruited by the Navy SEALS but didn't join because his girlfriend got pregnant. Having to get a job and finding out that it would take years to sell a screenplay, he enlisted in the Los Angeles Police Department. While perhaps at odds with the creative path, the job was really an affirmation of a family tradition: Propster's father—his hero—was a Green Beret in Vietnam and then a cop in the LAPD, working his way up the ladder to chief of police in the town of Gardena, a working-class suburb of LA known more for its grit than its gardens. "I became a cop because of my father," Propster says. Having grown up hearing stories of war, inside a family with its own share of rough-and-tumble characters, he was not surprised by the mean streets of Los Angeles. In fact, as a kid in Gardena, he knew plenty of gang members and why and how they got that way. As a cop, he "signed up to see the world at its ugliest," he says.

In his view, Steve Sorensen had little knowledge of the world he would soon enter; having grown up in a cloistered area, he did not have a sense of the way things really were—only of how they should be. "He wanted Camelot," Propster says. "He was Sir Galahad, he was Dudley Do-Right, he was the guy with the badge striding into town, ready to make things perfect."

It was 1984 when Steve became a lifeguard, the year when the Olympics had come to Los Angeles and So Cal icons became international stars. The smell of excellence was in the air and LA was feeling pretty good about itself. The golden dream was broadcast around the world, with images of breaking waves and palm trees swaying and the PCH snaking up the sparkling coast as the backdrop for the Olympic ideal of a perfect 10. It was a time for showing off and, yes, for having a good time, but really it was all about getting validation from the outside world, about how things looked—

not the fault lines that crisscrossed the region or echoed of personal turmoil beneath copper skin and fair hair and blue eyes. For foreign news crews, surfers and lifeguards were all the rage; while world-class athletes performed at venues around the city, correspondents headed for the beach, talking with real live wave riders and hoping to snag an interview with the water gods behind the black wraparound shades up in their towers, when they descended at sundown and walked among mortals until the sun rose again and they were called back. It mattered little that these men were often "hard to get," the dating ploy Kimberly's mother had offered; being up in a tower apart from and above the disturbances and pleasures of everyday life with an official job rendered them idols, conferring admiration on those who were just beyond reach but so very needed in an emergency situation.

To get Steve down from the tower, in a nonphysical sense, his friends called him "Stevie." But that was pretty much as far as the teasing went; Steve could not really take a joke and would rarely get down and dirty with this buddies. "He had been around us for years," Propster recalls, but he bristled at the rough guy talk and there were just certain things he would not discuss, rarely showing his cards. By all accounts, he was most content when surfing—a solitary activity in which communion with the water takes you out of the world and into the present moment—or on the job, for him, a place where you are untouchable yet needed by all.

During this period, Steve had been hanging around with a new girlfriend, a champion swimmer and lifeguard. The pattern was similar to the one with Kimberly, only this time, shortly after a serious eruption that puzzled his friends, he quit his job as a lifeguard and left the beach, left town in fact, and joined the army. It's not that he had never mentioned wanting to become a soldier; it had come up in conversations with Kimberly and, later, once in a while with other friends. There were no wars going on, and the promise of travel and various other perks was very real. More importantly, it was a way of getting experience for law enforcement. So while it wasn't a surprise that a member of the LA County lifeguard service would divert to the military, in Steve's case, his beach crew was surprised that he came down from the tower.

His next-door neighbor Julie Franks was sorry to see him go. She still had a crush on the good-looking surfer and would miss hanging out with Steve in her backyard, listening to the Stones, Aerosmith, and Led Zeppelin. One day, Julie looked across her driveway and spotted Steve on his front lawn, polishing his shoes. Later that day, he left for the army. He was twenty-nine years old and for the first time in his life breaking from home.

Steve was assigned to the 527th battalion and stationed at Kaiserslautern, Germany, a large base consisting of both army and air force military communities, including the famous centers of Landstuhl and Ramstein. Known throughout the military as K-town because it's easier to say, the base is near the northern edge of the Pfalz Forest, a scenic destination spot for tourists and hikers, and one of the biggest forests in Europe. From 1986 through 1989, Steve served as a military police officer—MP—and was fortunate to score living quarters in the air force barracks, which were nicer than the army's, with carpeting and only two men assigned to a room.

Dan White was his roommate during Steve's first year in the army and the designated driver for the guys in his battalion whenever off-base excursions involved drinking. He also provided the car, ironically coming to Germany with a German-made VW bug that he had bought in Arizona, driven to the East Coast, and shipped there. It arrived as it was, complete with some busted parts, and whenever the gang would take a cruise on the autobahn or head into town for *pommes frites* and beer at Rosie's Diner or dinner at Dutch Michael's, something would go wrong with the car. Dan was a mechanic and could fix most things, but Steve often volunteered for the job. For instance, in the winter, frost would form on the inside of the windshield because the defroster wasn't working, and he was the one who scraped it off so the crew could continue their journey. At the local pubs, Steve partied like the rest of his army buddies and was known for having a good sense of humor, Dan tells me on a phone call from his home in Holland, Michigan, where he has lived since his army days, after a trailer fell on his leg at K-town and he retired with medical benefits. He had not learned of Steve's death until hours before our phone conversation, in one of those strange moments that seem laden with messages in retrospect.

While watching the TV show *I Shouldn't Be Alive*, he had come across Steve's business card from the army. He decided to track him down, called the number on the card, found that it was not working, went online, and learned that he had been killed nearly eight years earlier. Stunned, he looked for more information and quickly found out the name of the pastor who had delivered the eulogy at Steve's funeral, John Wodetzki, now based in Cincinnati. He called John, whom I had met when I first began working on this story. After Dan and John had spoken, John let me know that Dan could fill in a few blanks about Steve's time in the army, and he put us in touch. Several hours after Dan had learned that his army buddy had been killed back in the States, he and I were talking about his memories of Steve. He recalled Christmas and caroling and painted a picture of how the ex-lifeguard Steve had come down from the tower and was apparently flourishing. "He loved his job," Dan said, "and took pride in his uniform." But throughout his time at K-town, Steve talked about the beach all the time, yearning for waves.

Before our conversation ended, Dan made a point of offering one more story. After his accident, Dan was hospitalized for many months when it turned out that the army had misdiagnosed his injury, and he had a blood infection that snowballed into something much bigger. Steve was the first of his buddies in the 527 to visit, and over the weeks he came back many times. On his last visit he brought him a copy of *Somewhere in Time*, a time travel movie starring Christopher Reeve and Jane Seymour and set on Mackinac Island in Michigan, Dan's beloved home state. Watching the sentimental film about a man who visits a bygone era to meet his soul mate helped Dan get through his painful ordeal, satisfying his own longings for his native turf—and echoing Steve's yearning for home. After Steve brought him the movie, Dan never saw him again. A couple of years later when he returned to Michigan, he filed Steve's business card in a box along with other souvenirs of K-town.

By 1989, Steve's army stint was finished. He returned to California, moved back into his old quarters for a brief period, and got a job as a driver for Rockwell, delivering top-secret documents to locations around the country. He didn't like the constant traveling and also was concerned about his parents, who had slowed down a bit more in the few years that he had been gone. Wanting to be near them, he quit his driving job and returned to the beach, securing a position again as lifeguard and then entering the Los Angeles County Sheriff's Academy in January 1991. During this period, he shared an apartment with Steve Kirchner, a teammate from his swimming years at El Camino. Back on his home turf, Steve surfed often and made frequent trips to Catalina. He didn't have many friends and the few he had, he chose carefully, Kirchner recalls. And beware the person who dismissed him—he would not stand for it and there was always a consequence. Yet, as always, you could count on him when there was a crisis, and inevitably someone would call with a problem or needing a favor.

To get away from things, both Steves would head out to an avocado ranch in Fillmore where the pair would shoot quail. It was a sprawling place, owned by Sorensen's sister Dixie and her husband, a wealthy man who was a petroleum geologist, active with his wife in the state Republican Party. Out in the chaparral, Kirchner got the sense that Steve wanted the kind of life his sister had, on a big piece of land with a suitable house and a family to go with it—a *Leave It to Beaver* scenario that Steve longed for, a perfect world where everything looked nice and you were supposed to color inside the lines, the thing he missed out on, having been born to parents who were too old to be June and Ward Cleaver. Even when they were partying and on the prowl, it was clear to Kirchner that Steve wanted to settle down. It wasn't long before he found himself in a whirlwind marriage to a friend's sister; the union was annulled a year later. "He was amazingly impulsive," Kirchner recalls, "always searching for some elusive thing." Soon after that, he met a woman on the beach, and there was an attraction. A few years older than Steve, Christine was British and divorced; she had a grown son and lived in nearby El Segundo. The two had a couple of important things in common: neither was a social butterfly and both were looking for a second chance. They dated, fell in love, and in 1991 went to Lake Tahoe and got married. By then Steve had joined the sheriff's academy, and it wasn't long before the pair moved to Lancaster in the Antelope Valley. Unlike others, Kirchner wasn't really puzzled by the move. His complicated friend was not cut out for "a major metropolitan area." He had "loner tendencies." And being the only sheriff in a remote area—dry though it may be—isn't that different from being alone in the water and waiting for waves or being up in a tower and watching them.

After Steve had met Christine, Kirchner didn't see much of his friend, except for a time or two that he went up to Steve's new place and they went four-wheeling in the desert. After that, the pair fell out of touch. Then, one August day, after completing a lifeguard competition in the South Bay, he emerged from the water and was jogging up the beach, feeling pretty good as he approached the finish line. "Hey man," someone said, "did you hear about Steve? It's all over the news." Kirchner was taken aback, shocked at the brutality of what had happened but not totally surprised. Years later, Kirchner and I are having a conversation on the telephone, and he recalls a moment that has come to mean a great deal. On the day Steve had moved out and headed to his new life in the desert, Kirchner helped him pack up his belongings. "He was a coffee addict before Starbucks," Kirchner says. "He brewed his own coffee and was packing his Krups grinder." "Oh no, you're taking the grinder?" Kirchner joked. Sorensen gave it to his friend, and he still has it, packing it up himself when he moved out of their apartment and into a new home with the woman he married a few years later. Once in a while, he uses it to make his own coffee, and it reminds him of the guy he used to swim with at El Camino.

When Kimberly Brandon-Watson learned that her high school boyfriend—the best boyfriend she ever had until she met her husband—had been killed, she visited a high school reunion website and listed all of the things she once loved about her late classmate. Steve Sorensen was

> not ever a slacker
> always on time
> always showed up
> always did the right thing
> he was a good person

To get back in touch with the man she remembered, Kimberly would travel to Catalina, revisiting its enchanted underwater kingdom, diving beneath the sea, looking as we all do to past moments when the inexplicable happens and returning with the question that many who knew Steve the surfer asked over and over: Why would a dedicated waterman forsake waves and head for the desert? Whatever it was, as Sheriff Baca would tell it later, in the drylands, in the beautiful, extreme, paved-over and wide-open Antelope Valley, it became Steve's mission to protect God's creation.

No Trespassing:
Welcome to Don's World

What are you looking for? . . . You're happy out there, are you? Eh?
Wandering? One day blurring into another? You're a scavenger,
Max . . . You're living off the corpse of the old world. . . . What burned
you out, huh? . . . See too many people die? Lose some family?

    —Pappagallo to Mad Max in *Mad Max 2:*
    The Road Warrior

IN THE SHADOWS OF THE VANISHED COMMUNITY OF LLANO,
Donald Kueck had pieced together his own desert utopia. Oh, it
did not have groves of palm trees or alfalfa fields or waterfalls or
even babbling brooks, and it was not pretty or particularly inviting.
Nor was it set up for others to live there—but of course that wasn't
the point. It was a utopia for one, a place where a man could be left
alone and not have to submit to the fetters of the world, to get

through the day and night in whatever way that might happen, to smoke pot or get high whenever he wanted to in the manner of his own choosing, to not get dressed in the morning or to get dressed for a while and then cast off the clothing if it suddenly caused an awareness and became constricting, to tinker and concoct and organize, to live like the animals and birds and trees had always lived, to dream uninterrupted. Yet there was a plan of sorts in the construction of Don's world—in fact he was very set in his ways (the German in him, he told friends)—and there were plans to make it better, and he had everything that a man could possibly need and, at one time, kept all of his possessions highly organized in boxes, compartments, and shelves, almost like a personal army barrack.

Don's first attempt at a desert paradise happened at the far end of the alphabet avenues, on a parcel near Avenue T. There he lived in a tent, paying a small amount of rent to the owner of the property, living on a monthly disability check from the government, which he had been receiving since he had incurred his back injury at his job in Long Beach before moving to the desert. His role in the local ecology was one of scavenger; he would traverse the sands, find things, trade them at local flea markets for other things, or sell them for small and occasionally large change. He was also available as a handyman, in the finest sense of the word; his mechanical skills and general knowledge of how things worked permitted him to fix and invent all manner of contraptions and devices. Sometimes at flea markets or through the desert grapevine, those in need of a service would come his way. He would head over to the customer's house on an old bike he had salvaged from a wash after a flash flood or in one of the old muscle cars he had rebuilt from spare parts he had found in some far-flung junk pile or another rusted out vehicle and get the job done in a way that would last for a long time. But outside his tent and over time, Don acquired a lot of junk, ultimately attracting the wrath of the landlord, who asked him to leave.

Coming to his rescue were his older sisters, Lynne Kueck, a career nurse in the navy, and Peggy Gilmore, a housewife in Pensacola, who purchased a one-acre piece of land not too far away from where Don was already living. In any direction, there was wide-open space, the mountains in the far distance, and then forever. It seemed like the kind of location that would crank down the chaos in anyone's mind and permit a state of grace for those who were open to the region's gifts. Lynne and Peggy bought an old trailer for Don to live in, and now, at 19100 East Avenue S-8, he could have the ultimate American dream: he could build a sand castle, literally, on his own land, and no one could tell him to dismantle it or complain about too much junk in the driveway. At its peak and before it began to crumble, before his own degeneration, his family and friends marveled at what he had eked out of nothing. "He was a brainiac," a friend recalls. "That's how he rolled."

The first thing that any desert outpost needs is water. At first, Don acquired some large blue drums in a trade or because they were just lying somewhere, and he cleaned and sterilized them. Then he strapped them on top of an old Lincoln, headed to a friend's house, filled them up, and brought them home. With a makeshift system of pulleys, he would crank and lower the drums into compartments he had dug in the sand. There the water would remain cool and free from dirt, and he piped it into a sink in his trailer with a homemade hand pump. He also rigged an outdoor shower and used it regularly, contrary to the perception that solitary desert dwellers are caked with dirt and haven't bathed in months or years. As the days passed in his new desert abode, he walked the land in every direction, studying its rhythms and ways, coming to know where there were outcroppings of certain plants or trees, which meant there was water nearby, depending on what kind of plants or trees they were, and discovering ancient seeps in the buttes to the east. He also watched which way the water flowed and where it went after the summer monsoons, and soon he was able to dowse the terrain. To get to the source, he would dig down until he found underground trickles and streams. He would mark these places with cement pipes that he had found along his desert treks, sinking them into the ground but leaving a portion visible so that he would know where the water sources were. Whenever he needed water, he would head to these wells and pump some out, filling up jugs and heading back to his trailer.

Over time, his gerrymandered way of living seemed to be boundless. Once, on a junk run, he found some abandoned solar panels. He hauled them back to his place, hooked them up to a battery, attached them to his trailer with duct tape, and used them in the winter to warm it. He acquired old cars, especially his favorites—Dodge Darts and Swingers, and at one time there was a Plymouth. At any given time there were several on his property, and he was working on them, switching parts around to make them run and selling pieces of them to anyone who needed a particular part. To move the nonworking cars around, he ran a pulley from the engine of a large lawn mower to whatever vehicle needed to be moved, turned the mower on, and began the operation. It was an efficient method of getting the job done, and visitors marveled at how one man could maneuver the cars across dozens of yards of desert gravel. In addition, he kept a vast store of automotive information in his head; he knew which car had already yielded what parts, how many valves remained in a particular engine mount, how many miles of gas each working car could get by the gallon on a paved desert highway, assuming you were driving the speed limit, which friends say he generally did. Whenever he drove anywhere, he would calculate the exact amount of gas he would need based on the mileage and driving speed, and fill up accordingly. Quite simply, he was a man on a budget and did not like to waste things.

This view applied to his manner of sustenance as well. Generally he lived on a diet of canned sardines, tuna, mackerel, beans, and quantities of peanut butter, which he bought in bulk at local big-box stores. He liked to bake, often surprising the occasional visitor with his homemade bread fresh from a small iron oven in his trailer that was powered by propane. It was a simple recipe—flour, baking soda, and water—and guests all remember it as the best bread they ever ate, a surprising offering in a harsh place, manna from a hermit's heaven. In addition to this bit of homemaking, Don was trying to grow fruit. "An orchard," he once joked to a visitor, perhaps harking back to the long-gone apple and almond fields that flourished at the old commune, or perhaps it wasn't a joke but a grandiose statement about what he was up to, which was cultivating a pear tree near his trailer.

The tree came from a cutting that Don had acquired in a trade. He planted it in the dirt and rigged a perpetual irrigation system. This consisted of four holes he dug around the tree, into which he inserted black pipes, each about three feet long. At the top opening of each pipe, he placed a one-gallon wine jug upside down, piercing the bottom with small holes so that moisture would gather inside the jugs and drip down through the pipes, directly feeding the roots of the tree. To protect the tree from animals, he arranged chicken wire around it. After a while, the tree yielded some pears; Don had become an Adam in his own garden, never finding or looking for an Eve, partaking of his own fruit, tempted and succumbing on his own to the many snakes that lived all around him, some of which were now residing in his trailer.

He had befriended other animals and birds in his strange domain and was taking care of what may have been one of the last families of ground squirrels in the Antelope Valley. It was a time of drought and scarcity in the western Mojave, a situation that had been unfolding for years. Wildlife was under siege as tract housing edged closer to remote areas, taking out groves of Joshua trees, barn owl populations, and other animal tribes. The Mojave Desert ground squirrel had long been listed as threatened under the California Endangered Species Act, although a small and scrawny population remained, pressed deeper into remote areas such as

Llano during the years Don lived there. To help them along, and add to his band of friends, Don dug a hole in the floor of his trailer and, through that, ran a plank into a small tunnel he had hollowed out, creating a burrow for the animals. He attracted them with peanuts; then he brought them inside and ran them down the plank under his trailer and into their new quarters. Every day, he would open the trap door, and they would emerge for a meal.

Although Don did seem to prefer the company of animals, he did not create a situation that precluded daily contact with people. Outside his trailer he had hooked up a large antenna, and he used it to receive signals on the radio that he kept on a shelf next to a cot inside it. Usually the radio was tuned to the police scanner. He had a television, but because of its age and the fact that he really wasn't all that interested in watching it (his sisters had given it to him as a gift, on the off chance that the mechanized diversion would help him in some way), it was able to receive just one frequency. This was the Home Shopping Network, and toward the end of his life, he watched it often, purchasing loose gems on *The Gem Show*, trying to acquire something that he could pass on to his daughter and her children. There was one more way for him to connect with the outside world should he feel the need or have an emergency—a cell phone—another item his sisters purchased for him. In the end, it would play a large role.

Exactly when Don put up his "No Trespassing" sign we do not know. There's a funny thing about those signs in the desert, and there are many: the land they are warning you off—actually, to be precise, the property—is not always inviting. In this part of the Mojave, the westernmost segment, the altitude and sunlight and rainfall have contrived for a terrain that is sparsely populated with cactus and flowers and that great signpost of the Mojave, the Joshua tree. But the people who live behind the signs are serious—as the old saying goes, "as serious as a heart attack." Head past these signs in the desert and you are at risk; in Don's case, an interloper was entering a world whose king had spent years alone, marinating in the sun, exploring the nooks and crannies of himself and the desert, cultivating a philosophy based in part on God, Buddha, Native American mythology, and search-and-seizure law—his own version of the old commune's mix of watchwords and homilies, one that he would expound on when the opportunity arose and refine and chew on in the solitude of latter-day Llano.

You see, Don loved to read, and he relished the thinking and simmering that happened because of it and spilled into his other endeavors. While living in Llano, he had assembled an amazing library of works penned by some excellent writers, picking up the obscure and best-selling books and magazines and pamphlets at flea markets, or finding them strewn across the desert, nature's very own, always-open, perpetual learning annex. The collection tells us that Don studied American history, war, weaponry, geology, living off the grid, space travel, time travel, the environment, inner dimensions, and aging—and his family and friends confirm that these subjects and concerns informed much of his thought and conversation over the years. But there was more than that; as we shall see, the knowledge and insight he gleaned from these works factor into his last days as a fugitive. Here are some of the books in his collection:

Saudis: Inside the Desert Kingdom by Sandra Mackey
Gun Digest, 33rd anniversary 1979 deluxe edition
Black Holes, Quasars and Other Mysteries of the Universe by Stan
    Gibilisco
Geologic Guidebook: The LA Aqueduct System
American Indian Archery by Reginald and Gladys Laubin
Radio Fundamentals TM 11-455 War Department Technical Manual
All About Telescopes by Sam Brown
Modell's Drugs in Current Use and New Drugs, 37th edition, 1991
Saddam Hussein and the Crisis in the Gulf by Judith Miller and
    Laurie Mylroie
Analysis of Electrical Circuits by Frederick F. Driscoll

The Complete Guide to Growing Marijuana
Escape from Corregidor by Edgar Whitcomb
A Sand County Almanac by Aldo Leopold
The Log from the Sea of Cortez by John Steinbeck
Trial by Tom Hayden
Pathfinders: Overcoming the Crises of Adult Life and Finding Your
   Own Path to Well-Being by Gail Sheehy
The Planetary and Lunar Nodes by Dane Rudhyar
The Buddhist Tradition in India, China, and Japan
The Second Ring of Power by Carlos Castaneda
Reunions: Visionary Encounters with Departed Loved Ones by Ray-
   mond Moody, MD

A man with such an extensive library ought to have a good
place to sit down and enjoy a book. Like many a conventional man,
Don had one; it was a Barcalounger, or a lounging chair in that category, an old one which he probably found in a junkyard or perhaps
scored while bartering some of the loose gems from the Home
Shopping Network. The Barcalounger was in his living room, which
in his case was the outdoors. It was facing the east, sunrise, and
there he would sit and look across his kingdom, watching and reading, in the shadows of the Three Sisters Buttes, his favorite place in
the Mojave, the selfsame formation that provided comfort to all
who gazed in this direction, including the nuns at Mount Carmel.
During the last two years of his life, it was in his Barcalounger, with
the grace of the mountains and the sage-dotted land before him,
that he turned to two particular books, seeking a way out of an existence that had become increasingly painful and filled with fear and
anger and doubt. The first book was *The Second Ring of Power* by Carlos Castaneda, the thirteenth in the trail-blazing series that helped
to usher in the counterculture, telling the story of the Yaqui Indian
shaman named Don Juan who enters Castaneda's life and forever
changes it, guiding him through portals to other dimensions where

he gains wisdom from plants and animals, returning to the here and now to use it. The second was *Reunions*. Its author, Dr. Raymond Moody, is a highly educated man—brilliant, according to some; a crackpot say others—who chairs the Department of Consciousness Studies at the University of Nevada at Las Vegas. He has written several best sellers about encounters with the dead. As it happens, he has much in common with Don: he hails from the deep South, his father was a military officer, and for many years he was drawn to astronomy, psychology, and philosophy.

It was while reading Plato's *Republic* that Moody learned of a warrior named Er. Thought to have died on the battlefield, Er suddenly sat up and told of entering another world, returning just before he was about to be cremated. The story convinced Plato that there was an afterlife, and years later, when Moody's mother was dying, she roused from her deathbed and spoke of a visit to the next dimension, where her ancestors awaited. Coupling the two stories, Moody was convinced that the living could contact the dead, and it became his mission to contact his mother when she died. He has devoted his life to helping others contact the departed, and his book *Reunions* provides details on how to reach across time and do so. The method is called "psychomanteum" or "mirror gazing" and involves a mirror and a variety of elements, such as music, hypnosis, and nature. Following a series of instructions, the person who seeks contact gazes into the mirror until the reunion has occurred.

Sitting in his Barcalounger, Don would page through *Reunions*. It was not an ancestor with whom he sought to make contact. Nor, as far as anyone knows, was it his great-grandparents or his grandparents. And it was not even his father, who had died in 1992. It was his son, who had preceded him in death, the thing that every parent fears, even those who have had little or no contact with their children, and it was this event that propelled a torqued-out, once brilliant, and now degenerating hermit from the land of illusion to desperation, murder, and flight.

THE LOST CHILDREN
OF THE INLAND EMPIRE

*My heart is broke
I have some glue.*
—Nirvana, "Dumb"

THEY HAD NAMES LIKE LIZARD AND PARANOID PAM, AND THEY were in bands like Let's Go Bowling and Nazi Bitch. They hung out at a place called Spanky's, a punk dive across the street from the Mission Inn in Riverside, California, the history-infused hospitality headquarters for presidents, foreign dignitaries, and well-heeled tourists. A lot of these kids were products of what were once called "broken homes," but broken didn't begin to explain it, and their stories spoke of a wreckage across the suburban lands of their home turf, the Inland Empire, that strangely named California region that is a corruption of a vanished real estate dream—the

Orange Empire!—and has engendered all manner of jokes and disparagement—Conquer this!—and that no one can quite figure out the boundaries of, but most agree that it begins where greater Los Angeles bleeds into San Bernardino and Riverside counties and then the whole thing ends where a warehouse runs into the desert and people go shooting.

One day in 1989 ninth grader Chris Smallwood was walking through this region, down La Sierra Street in Riverside, where he lived with his mother and sister, heading to school. He met a kid named Chuck, aka Charles Donald Kueck, who had just rounded the corner from Doverwood, where he lived with his mother, her boyfriend, and two sisters, one from his mother's first marriage and the other from her third. Chuck was tall and skinny and dressed in black—black T-shirt, black leather jacket, black jeans, black boots—and he was pushing a ten-speed bike. He was a bit embarrassed about his impaired vehicle situation and later, by way of explanation, added some information about his family, off-hand comments that to an outsider would sound an alarm: "My mother's wasted and so's her old man." But not here in this working-class neighborhood of small one- and two-bedroom homes, where the mothers were beleaguered and the fathers were broken, often absent because of divorce or jail time, or at home, barely hanging on, drowning in booze or drugs, lashing out at their wives and kids, at ghosts, trying to shake off a legacy of poverty and violence that dated back to the clan rivalries of their Scots-Irish forebears, some of whom came to America as indentured white slaves. On the day of that first encounter, the boys formed a quick bond, mainly because of the neighborhood that they lived in and the mutual knowledge of what that meant. As they continued on to school, they discussed matters of the day, discovering their shared love of certain bands—Black Flag, Social Distortion, the Dead Kennedys—and spoke of their own musical aspirations. From then they on were buddies.

A few weeks later, a kid named Rande Linville was standing outside the window of a liquor store in downtown Riverside. It was 1:30 in the morning and he was about to break in. But he heard the sound of skateboard wheels on pavement and turned to look. "There were these two guys on boards," he says. "I was surprised to see them because there weren't very many skateboarders then. And most of them looked like me, blonde, clean-cut, with surfer hair. These guys were wearing black leather jackets and looked like punks." They were Chuck Kueck and Chris Smallwood and along with Rande they were about to become a close band of friends who called themselves The Three Amigos—a reference to the John Landis movie with Chevy Chase, Martin Short, and Steve Martin, in which three actors who play gunfighters end up in a Mexican village where they actually have to fend for themselves.

As they stood in the parking lot on the night of their first encounter, Rande asked, "What's up?" He was wondering if he was going to have to fight two people off for the swag from the liquor store, especially because there appeared to be a serious tribal difference if you judged the situation by clothing alone. And then came the response: "What's up?" For a moment there was a standoff, and then Chris decided to end it, reaching into his crotch—to Rande's alarm—and pulling out an American flag. "Dude," Rande said, "whaaa?" Chris explained that they were out stealing flags and were on their way back to Chuck's house to burn them. The news was startling and hilarious, and Rande cracked up and then they all started laughing, and then Rande explained his break-in plans. Chuck and Chris approved and Rande picked up his skateboard and smashed the window. Chuck dove in and then the other two boys followed, returning with candy, cigarettes, and beer, and then they jumped on their boards. Instead of heading to Chuck's, they cruised back to Rande's apartment, a small, three-room unit he shared with his mother and sister in a nearby Section 8 housing project. Inside Rande's bedroom, they cracked open a six-pack and started to drink.

"Dude," Chuck said as he looked around the room, "you like Black Flag?" He was referring to a wall poster and he was impressed. Then Chris joined in, noting a flyer for the Circle Jerks, and high-fiving Rande. Surprised that the surfy-looking guy would be into punk rock instead of metal, Chuck and Chris exchanged a look, and then Chuck turned to Rande. "I play bass," he said. "Chris plays lead. We need a drummer. Do you—?" Before he could finish, Rande was in— as it turned out, he was a heavy metal drummer transitioning into punk, and he had been playing for a long time. Soon after that they formed their first band, named one night after Chris and Chuck had seen the Oliver Stone movie *JFK* and Chuck, recalls Chris, "was all, 'Dude, dude, dude,'"—mimicking his friend—"Oswald was set up, we gotta call our band Oswald's Revenge and I said, 'Dude, that is so right,' and from then on, that was our band."

Chuck was now part of a world that was getting some serious attention; it included bands like No Doubt and the local outfit Voodoo Glow Skulls, regulars at Spanky's and famous all over the country. In fact, amigo Rande Linville's best friend was a member of the Glowskulls, the most revered band in the Inland Empire. Because of the association, Linville became a sought-after drummer, and his crew—Chuck, Chris, and all of their musician associates— assumed a high profile in the Inland Empire, their fame only adding to their street cred. When Gwen Stefani was in town, they could go backstage, and a couple of times they partied with one of their idols, Henry Rollins, along with his seminal OC band Black Flag. Along with outlaws like William Burroughs and Charles Bukowski, Rollins was a serious inspiration. Rollins looked and dressed like a skinhead, but he was anything but. Chuck often quoted from his book *Pissing in the Gene Pool*, with one passage holding particular relevance. "I've got a roach crawling on my hand," it went. "Should I kill it? . . . I don't know, let me think. It was the first thought that popped into my head. I raised my other hand to crush it but all of a sudden I stopped dead in my tracks. I thought about all the people who think of me the same way I think of this roach. All the people who see me as a filthy crawling piece of vermin that should be destroyed. Hah! The roach is my brother and long may he prosper!"

Heartened by kindred spirits and part of a flourishing nation-wide scene, Chuck and his friends were in demand as musicians, playing gigs around Riverside and once or twice at clubs in Los Angeles. After a while, Oswald's Revenge became other bands, as bands have a way of doing, but the three amigos were always in them, adding and subtracting other personnel, and they were always together, in spirit or in person, bonded forever by the fact that, as Rande recalls, they were "three fully abused kids who loved the same music." In the annals of rough upbringings, this was not an exaggeration; they were indeed fully abused, but underlying that was a theme that ran through their lives, which could be summarized by way of one question: Where's Dad? In the case of Rande Linville, he confided to his friends that his father—long gone by the time the boys had met—was a heavy drinker prone to violent outbursts directed at his mother and the entire family. After one especially bad episode during which his mother was roughed up and the cops were called, the father left for good, and it would take years for his mother to right herself, ultimately returning to college and graduating with a degree in nursing.

Rande was five years old when his family collapsed, and by the time he met Chris and Chuck in the liquor store parking lot, he had been out of control for a decade. But even before that, at the age of twelve, he was selling large quantities of pot and sacks of speed provided by relatives in a nearby town, smoking a lot of marijuana himself, and becoming involved in various scrapes and run-ins with unsavory characters and the law. In sixth grade he was also facing the kind of bad luck that seems to plague people, especially kids, who are already in trouble—his school bus crashed and he incurred a broken femur, resulting in years of pain which he sucked up, already quite adept at hiding his feelings. Through it all, he found solace and grace in rock and roll, reveling in it when he would visit his grandparents, a country act called the Conways who had settled in the high desert town of Joshua Tree. Out there amid the creosote and sage Rande would join in when they sang the old bluegrass standards, learning harmony and how to play the guitar, knowing from then on that music was an escape route, although he wouldn't fully follow it for years. By the time he was nineteen, he was busted for dealing large quantities of marijuana. He did a two-year stint at the Banning Correctional Facility in Riverside County, coming out angrier, stronger, and—after years of street fighting, skateboarding, and snowboarding—more buff than ever and ready to take on the world. His strength and youth would serve him well, for the three amigos would soon find themselves in an epic battle involving a very big and very bad man who had a starring role in their lives. By then, they were all rough and ready.

The situation involved amigo Chris Smallwood, fatherless in a way that could never be fixed; his father was killed in a bar when the husband of a woman he once had an affair with walked in and shot him in the head. At the time Chris was thirteen years old. His younger sister Amanda was twelve. But even before Donny Smallwood died, Chris had felt his absence. A Vietnam vet who had served on the *USS Hector* in the navy, he returned and was wracked with nightmares, unable to shake the effects of war—in his case, bringing men home in body bags. So he started drinking and he was running around, running really, and he didn't hold down a job for more than two weeks and then one day someone put a stop to all of it. The children were bereft and destitute and their mother was stunned; she knew her husband was tormented but certainly was not prepared for his death, let alone a violent one. She had been working for years as a dental assistant after putting herself through school with a job at Montgomery Ward, and she could hardly afford to quit now in order to minister full-time to her kids. Coming to Virginia Smallwood's aide in the aftermath of the killing was a friend of her husband's—a three-hundred-pound man with a swastika and an eagle on his back. For the purposes of this story, we'll call him Al. At first he seemed harmless enough, a physically huge knight to the rescue who consoled mother and children, fending off other comers and hardships. To get away from everything, Virginia had decided to move her family to Kentucky, where her parents lived. En route in Phoenix, the U-Haul broke down. Al had been driving them and called a family member who lived nearby. As the truck was being repaired, Virginia looked around. "I thought hey, this looks pretty nice," she tells me on the phone. "Let's stay here." They did, and for a while things were OK. Al liked cocaine; it mellowed him out, unlike the effect it had on others, and it was usually available. After about a year, proximity to some especially gnarly neighbors forced a move, and Al and Virginia and the kids headed for Las Vegas. It was difficult to score coke there and things started to get bad. Al began to take control of the household, issuing rules about organizing the kids' clothes by way of color and permitting one hour per day of television. The rules seemed acceptable at first, but he displayed frightening outbursts if they were broken. The situation degenerated when the kids were at school. Al became destructive and violent, hitting Virginia, breaking things, throwing large pieces of furniture across the room. When the kids came home, they would notice that their mother was bruised. "One day," Virginia says, "he grabbed me and put a knife to my throat." Cops were called and things settled down, until they boiled over again, and Al would get violent. Finally, there was an escape route: a friend was visiting, and Virginia asked him to take Al to a casino. While they were gone, she packed up the kids and left, heading back to California. They stayed with friends in Norco, a rustic town where to this day people ride their horses to the store, and soon they moved back to Riverside.

In 1928, the Daughters of the American Revolution commissioned a series of monuments called the Madonna of the Trail.

There was one in each state along the National Old Trails Road, which extended from Maryland to California—twelve in all. The idea was to commemorate the pioneer woman whose strength and courage helped conquer the wilderness and make a new home in the Promised Land. Wrought from granite, the towering sculpture portrays a bonneted woman in full pioneer dress, baby in her arms and youngster at her side. She is in mid-stride, resolute, clutching a rifle. On February 1, 1929, the second to last of the Madonnas was dedicated in Upland, California, at the corner of Foothill Boulevard and Euclid Avenue, a few miles from Riverside, where the first white trappers had entered the Golden State by land. The women who soon followed had not been acknowledged in such a way until this unveiling. "They were just as brave or braver than their men," President Harry Truman had said at the ceremony for an earlier monument. "In many cases, they went with sad hearts and trembling bodies. They went, however, and endured every hardship that befalls a pioneer."

Over 150 years later, little had changed on the frontier. Yes, it was modern and crowded, but still brutal, with women trying to hold the line. Amid a world of violence, on LaSierra Avenue in Riverside, Virginia Smallwood maintained a safe place—not for her, as it turned out, but for the kids who gathered there. You see, Al had returned to California, to stay with his own family and seek the company of Virginia. After a while, they reunited, and Al moved back in with the Smallwoods. It wasn't long before the same problems erupted. Yet even while sometimes bruised and visibly battered, Virginia was everyone's mother, or in the words of her daughter Amanda, she was "the community mom"—a comparatively stable parent with a steady job (she had resumed working as a dental assistant), a person who liked to take care of others, not so she could receive foster care payments from a government agency (as some who abused the system, and the kids in it, were known to do), but simply because she felt so inclined. Sooner or later, in this

land of want and need, the children who wandered the malls looking for their own kind, or just drifted through because that's where
the trails led, made their way to the Smallwoods' house, gathering
'round the table for dinner on any given evening, nurturing their
weary bones with the burritos or chorizos and eggs cooked up by
the generous Mrs. Smallwood, stretching her small salary to feed
an army of haunted kids.

There was one kid who seemed a bit different, more trouble-
some, a tornado really; as soon as he started coming home with
Chris, Virginia noticed that his energy was more chaotic and yet
very intense and everyone seemed to fall under his spell. He was
living with his mother at the time yet sometimes stayed on the
streets, or at the homes of other kids, and soon, as always, his good
looks, wit, and explosive charisma won the day, and Mrs. Smallwood permitted him to become a member of her household and
move into her garage. Over time, she and the other members of
her family learned the details of his personal story, and it was one
of the worst she had heard, becoming more harrowing with every
revelation, confirmed eventually by relatives and friends who had
already fallen into his orbit.

Who can say when the trouble began? Certainly the fact that
his father had walked out of his family's life was a factor, opening
up a fissure that would not come together again in spite of attempts
by both father and son to reach across it after not having seen each
other for over ten years. There were other factors too—a mother
whose troubles were a mystery to outsiders and her involvement
with a strange man whom Chuck and his friends came to call
Ranch Dressing Rod, after his fondness for slathering food with
this particular condiment. And by all means, we must consider ge-
netics, which now show that nearly all aspects of personality, seemingly, are hard-wired (though susceptible to refinement in one way
or another), and certainly we must acknowledge the general
malaise that prevailed in the late twentieth-century cities of the In-

land Empire, where the natural world was fast becoming a dream, replaced with such things as the Stringfellow Acid Pits, a rock quarry that was used for years as a dump for toxic waste, then named as the first Superfund cleanup site, one of the biggest hazmat episodes in modern history. It was a sad fate for the region; where once the scent of orange infused the air, now Riverside County was one of the most polluted areas of the country. On any given day, you could not just see but taste and feel the particulate smog emanating from the diesel trucks that plied the freeways; it was a presence, obliterating what had come before, especially during the summer months, when the heat would trap it and cage it up like some foul entity that needed to be exorcised from the land. Soon some locals—kids mostly—started to call the place Rivercide, and it was popping up on top ten lists for "highest rate of meth use" in the country or "cities with the worst smog," and it was running out of jobs and possibilities, and as always in America, the old saying prevailed—the rich got richer and the poor got drunk or, more accurately at this point, high, wasted, or tweaked. A new vocabulary was upon the land; words like "rehab" and "OD" were in common rotation, becoming strange badges of honor, providing an identity for many who otherwise would remain unknown, conveying a life story instantly, to the listener and the bearer, a thing to hang on to, with echoes of street fights and trouble with cops and bands you admired, signifying that you belonged to a tribe, and that tribe was everywhere with no place to go, except the next party.

As to what exactly contrived to make Charles Donald Kueck an alcoholic by the time he was twelve we cannot say—not that the problem was noticed, by anyone other than Chuck—far from it, in fact. It seemed that all of those times he fell out of the tree while playing at his grandparents' home in the working-class suburb of Lynwood were viewed as the product of a young boy's rowdiness, even the time when he hit his head and passed out for a while. As he later told an uncle, he wasn't accident-prone or "not being careful," he was blasted on Martini and Rossi. That this could have been a lie to win affection must be considered, for the boy was a con man, a good one, and his uncle blamed himself and cursed his family and thinks he may have given Chuck some money to make up for the oversight, money that of course went right into a drug purchase, but many years later, when the boy's friends and relatives were able to put his story together—all of the near-misses, the illnesses, the roller-coaster ride with spills and thrills for those who came along—it was all of a piece, and by then everyone knew that Chuck was a hard-core junkie and, in the way of all good junkies of the era, was on his way to Seattle.

He was nineteen or twenty at the time and had some serious chops—major cred as an addict and rocker on the punk scene in Riverside, by way of early training in Huntington Beach, where he lived as a preteen with his mother and stepsister before they landed in the Inland Empire. At the beach, he had gotten involved with skinheads, dressing the part, an angry kid in combat boots and leather. For him, skinheads were a form of protection against a cruel world and also a bulwark against a stepfather who was a violent disciplinarian. Not that they intervened, but he was comforted by their presence; they were a ready-made brotherhood for a kid who didn't have one. He was doing acid then, causing mayhem around town, and his mother tried the tough love approach, sending him to Phoenix House for a twelve-month stint in the early 1980s. Phoenix House was one of the country's first addiction treatment centers, forming alliances with law enforcement agencies everywhere as the drug problem erupted across the land, making arrangements with courts and parents to keep kids in rehab lockdown as an alternative to actually going to jail. When Chuck emerged, nothing had changed, other than the fact that he was one pissed-off kid, and more determined than ever to make his mark.

To get away from the skinhead scene at the beach, Chuck's mother took the kids and followed a time-honored trail that led to the Promised Land; although for her it was west to east, still into the desert, to the city of Riverside. It had the amenities of an urban center, she reasoned, and with all of the wide-open space out there, her kids would have room to breathe—and live. But the desert is a trickster sometimes, a blank slate on which many a projection is made and thought to be confirmed, even when it calls from a distance and the dreamer has not yet paid it a personal visit. The endless vistas with the still and frozen plants and the post-rainstorm flower and frog surprises and the granite mesas you can lie across and soak up the warmth from when it's hot are the one true thing that calms the restless soul, asking not for a reaction but a submission, a letting go, if only the dreamer can do such a thing. Perhaps, for a little while—in retrospect, for Chuck and his family, maybe it was a few hours or days or weeks possibly—it seems that they did so. But as it happened, there were skinheads in the desert—all over So Cal, actually—and one day Chuck would find himself among them again, long after he had been following a different path.

It's not that he calmed down in Riverside—far from it. Inside Chuck's head there was a lot of static. It came out via music and in all manner of raging. At the time America was involved in two desert wars. One was far away in Iraq and Kuwait, the Gulf War. But on the home front, there was a siege involving poor kids who lived in areas dependent on income from members of the military who were stationed at nearby bases and shopped in local cities and towns. Many of these soldiers and Marines and members of the Air Force were deployed, and the American desert was bereft of income. There was little money flowing through the pipeline of gas stations, fast food joints, bars, and other establishments that depended on the men and women of the US military to drop a lot of cash every other week on payday. The situation created a lot of stress in homes across the region, and hit hardest were the kids, many of whom had found themselves in various battles since they were born. Now, the violence in their homes spiked, and they acted out accordingly.

In terms of who had what role in the platoon of lost children, Chuck Kueck was always the first in. Diving through a broken window at the liquor store was just one example. Another one occurred during a family reunion in Laughlin, Nevada. Chuck's uncle had brought some fireworks to celebrate the rare occasion. On the eighth floor of a hotel, Chuck lit a bottle rocket, sending an elderly woman to the hospital. Then there was the thing that happened one night at a show at Spanky's. The place was packed, and there had been a number of hot bands playing—punk, ska, maybe some metal. In the middle of a particularly intense set, with action at the mosh pit in full effect, the music suddenly stopped—or at least it became barely audible. When a high is interrupted, especially one involving hundreds of pumped-up, tweaked, and blasted teenagers packed into a small place with few lights and poor ventilation, anything can happen—and did. Projectiles were thrown at the band—cans, bottles, hammers—someone stormed the ticket guy, and then he was trampled; the mosh pit erupted into a free-for-all with a tier of kids piling up as some screamed for air.

Watching it all was a thirteen-year-old named Fritz Aragon, a regular on the scene; he had seen some kid with a Mohawk unplug the electrical cord for the band's amps and then leap into the pit of moshing fans. The next day when he was walking to school on La Sierra, he spotted a lanky boy with freaky hair on the other side of the street. He was heading toward Fritz. "Oh my God," he thought, "that's the kid who unplugged the show." It was Chuck Kueck. They struck up a conversation, decided to skip school, and headed over to Chris Smallwood's, where Chuck was then living. For the rest of the day, they played music. But before they jammed, Fritz noticed something strange. "What's up with this old guy?" he thought. "Why is he here?" "He" was Chris, on lead guitar. At thirteen, the boy had gray hair; the kid with the murdered father had grown up really fast.

And so had Chuck: as he told his friends, after his own father had walked out, his mother had remarried. His stepfather had treated him with cruelty, and his mother was plagued with her own problems. Although she was now divorced and had a new boyfriend, the damage was done and escalating; no wonder he was swallowing pills and guzzling booze and, soon, jamming smack-filled needles into his arm. It all came out in their music, and it wasn't long before Chuck and Chris and Fritz were playing in a new band called Falling Sickness, after the archaic name for epilepsy; none of them had it, but for sure they were all falling down—wasn't everyone?

But behind the label, trouble was brewing, and one night it all erupted at Chris Smallwood's house. Chris and Chuck and Rande had been out waging mayhem, their own brand of urban terror. For kicks, they used to set off gopher bombs at Stater Brothers and other large stores in the area. Gopher bombs are incendiary devices sold in many places, used to wipe out small animals such as moles, voles, ground squirrels, gophers, and so on. You light the fuse and drop the lit end of "The Giant Destroyer" or whatever device you purchase into the animal's burrow. Once lit, the item becomes a smoke bomb, sending sulfur into the tunnel and smothering small creatures that live there. But the bombs can start fires or, if dropped into air vents, emit foul odors into crowds, setting off smoke alarms and sending people into the streets. It was a successful night of local vandalism for the three amigos, with bombs going off in several places and various citizens confronted with foul odors, smoke, and general disruption of activities.

When the boys returned to home base in the morning, Virginia had just gotten off the phone with Al. They had been arguing. Wearing her characteristic muumuu, she greeted Chris and Rande and went outside to pick up the newspaper. Suddenly a green Jetta screeched across the lawn, driven by Al. He was heading for Virginia, trying to run her over. She jumped away and Al slammed on the brakes. Flying from the vehicle, he lunged for Virginia, who was trying to flee. Meanwhile Chris had ripped through the screen door and was running toward Al. Unbeknownst to Al, the three amigos had been keeping an ax handle covered in duct tape stashed away in case of a self-defense emergency. In fact, they had been preparing for months, lifting weights and doing push-ups, as Rande recalls years later, "We were eighteen and ready." Chris's sister Amanda ran for the ax and handed it to Rande. He rushed out with the weapon and Chris grabbed it, attacking Al and subduing him with serious blows. Rande piled on and they both returned the years of violence with their own amped up kicks and strikes as Virginia kept calling "Stop!" It was a bloody and prolonged battle for household supremacy, but the boys won. With a black-and-white racing towards the scene, Amanda chucked the ax in the brush behind the house. Al was severely battered and appeared to have broken bones. When the cop asked what happened, he said the boys had attacked him and he didn't know why. But the twenty feet of skid marks and the general situation said otherwise. Chris and Rande explained their story and Virginia backed them up. There were no arrests and Al was taken to the hospital. As for the Jetta, no one remembers.

The cycle of violence inside the Smallwood house had come to an end, and Chris's mother was grateful. But the battle would reverberate for all of them, for years. And it also cemented their bond; including Chuck, they were now the three amigos forever. As Rande Linville describes it years later: "It was fuck you and your perfect family. We never had one."

Yet trouble has a way of hanging around, and its favorite was Chuck. On the last day of summer school after his junior year, he took six hits of acid, stole someone's tricycle, and was riding erratically through downtown Riverside wearing his leather jacket. Was he acting "trippy"? Did he do something that seemed out of the ordinary, such as have a conversation with a door or tree or parked vehicle? We do not know, but because of the stolen trike, an APB had been issued, and he wasn't hard to spot, given his general demeanor and foot-high Mohawk, recently spray painted by his friends. We do not know who said what first, or exactly what Chuck was hearing, but when the cop stopped him, he went for his gun. There was a scuffle and it was over quickly. Chuck was cuffed, arrested, and thrown in the Riverside County tank—in particular, a cell filled with local skinheads and Nazis. Although they were once his presumed protectors, this was no longer the situation. His friends were now a wide range of cosmopolitan people who were making all sorts of kick-ass music, and they were drawing from reggae and ska and acid rock and punk—a rock and roll drift net that was sweeping up kids across the land and saving them from all manner of riptides at home.

To further bind himself to this world, Chuck had asked a friend for an anti-Nazi tattoo, and the tat artist obliged him. In jail, he was covered up in the requisite orange jumpsuit. That doesn't mean your cellmates don't find out what's on your skin; in fact, one of the first things that happens is someone will ask you to roll up your pants so everyone can see your tattoos. This was not something Chuck wanted to do, but he was forced to. The sight of an equality sign—a circle bearing the letter *E* on Chuck's forearm—with a KKK figure hanging from it by a noose enraged his cellmates. They were amped up even more by the "Fuck off Nazis" inscription beneath it. "I got worked," he told his friends when he was released, and they could see from the bruises and wires in his jaw that he wasn't kidding. "The racist cop threw me in with the skinheads, and they rearranged my face."

From then on, his anti-establishment fervor spiked and so did his paranoia, and he vowed never to return to jail. Years later, it was a vow his father would make after his own time in the slammer, their lives an echo of one another, even intertwining during the years they had no contact, father and son on a strange downward spiral, both heading to the same place.

As Chuck's nosedive escalated, so did his fame. With his jail-house stint, he was now an ex-con, as new war stories added to his chest. Girls were drawn to him more than ever, hoping either to rescue the bad boy, to be bad with him, or for a combination of both. One of these girls, a regular on the junkie circuit of kids that stretched from the California deserts into the northwestern cities of Portland and Seattle, began supplying Chuck with heroin. He liked it and began using regularly. Among other things, it made him feel close to Kurt Cobain. Like a lot of kids, he idolized the grunge king and found himself in the anguish of his songs. Soon he would head to Seattle and enter Cobain's orbit. But there was another junkie he admired as well. This was Sid Vicious, who had recently OD'd and become more famous than ever with the release of the movie *Sid and Nancy*, which told the tale of his descent into addiction and the strange murder of his girlfriend in Manhattan's Chelsea Hotel, where they were living. Chuck wanted to live like that, deciding at some point in his heroin haze that it was time for a change. His friends in Riverside weren't really hard-core enough; they were drinking and doing acid, maybe some other things, but not shooting smack. By then he was dressing like Sid Vicious, wearing a padlocked chain around his neck. To wipe out his old identity he changed his name to Jello, telling people it was after Jello Biafra in the Dead Kennedys. But really it was an old nick-name he had gotten from the amigos while swimming in a pool filled with gelatin. "That's when I knew Chuck was done," Chris re-calls years later. "When he told everyone to call him Jello."

But it would take a few years to finish the job. First he wanted to reconnect with his father. He knew that Don was living in the desert, and he decided to head out and see him. One of the first things he did when he got there was tell him about what happened in jail.

MAY I HAVE THIS DANCE?

Take my license 'n' all that jive.
    —Sammy Hagar, "I Can't Drive 55"

ON JUNE 6, 1994, AT HIGH NOON, DONALD CHARLES KUECK
and Deputy Steve Sorensen had their first fateful encounter. As it
escalated, both men became resolute and angry, and then frightened. They acted accordingly, becoming involved in a series of
rapidly cascading mistakes and bad reads. In this encounter dark
seeds were sown and they would flower nearly ten years later in a
nearby pocket of the desert.

Sorensen was heading west in a remote area on Avenue J in his
1990 red Toyota pickup, on his way to the North County Correctional Facility, or Wayside in cop parlance. He was stationed there
as a guard—part of the mandatory work for all new recruits in the
Los Angeles County Sheriff's Department. In front of him was a '71
Lincoln, two, maybe three lengths ahead. Suddenly, Sorensen told

police, the Lincoln slammed on its brakes, causing him to brake in order to avoid a collision. Thinking that the driver of the Lincoln had been trying to avoid an animal, he fell back to about eight car lengths and then accelerated, trying to pass the vehicle again. But between 130th Street East and 122nd Street East, the Lincoln braked two more times. At 121st Street East Sorensen tried to pass once more. But when he approached the rear of the Lincoln, it moved into the eastbound lane, causing him to swerve left to avoid a collision and head across the road onto the shoulder, with the Lincoln still in the way. Thinking that the driver was trying to force an accident, Sorensen reached for a pad and pencil that had fallen to the floorboards when he braked, retrieving it to write down the vehicle's license plate number.

From his rearview mirror, Kueck saw the deputy bending over and reaching toward the floor on the passenger side of his truck. As the truck veered closer to the Lincoln, Kueck became concerned that if the driver did not look up, there might be a collision, so he accelerated. Sorensen followed the Lincoln for another five hundred feet, until it stopped and the driver exited, walking quickly toward the pickup. "Hey motherfucker," Kueck yelled. "What do you think you're doing? I don't tolerate this kind of shit!"

Concerned that Kueck was about to harm him, Sorensen took out his badge and Beretta, identifying himself and pointing them both at Kueck. "You ain't no real cop," Kueck shouted. "And that badge don't mean shit." He continued to advance, and Sorensen told him to stop or he would shoot him. Kueck stopped, turned around, and put his hands behind his head. Sorensen then told him to lie down on the ground. "Fuck no! It's too hot, man," Kueck said, and put his hands on the Lincoln. At that point, a man in a truck in the westbound lane noticed the car with an open door on the side of the road and the pickup parked nearby. Thinking that the car had broken down and someone needed help, he turned around and saw that a man was standing there, with a gun aimed at another man near the back of the Lincoln. Sorensen told the motorist that he was an off-duty deputy and asked him to call for help. He contacted police on his CB radio and wondered if something awful was about to happen. "He ain't a real cop," Kueck kept yelling, refusing to stand still, jumping around and making several moves toward Sorensen, and then backing away like he was going to run. "I don't have to listen to you 'til I get a lawyer," he said to Sorensen, still pointing his gun at Kueck. Within minutes, a chopper landed in the adjacent alfalfa field, and a deputy emerged, ordering Kueck to lie down. Again he refused, lowering to his knees. At that point he was handcuffed and placed in the back seat of an arriving patrol car as several additional police vehicles converged on the scene.

Statements were taken from Sorensen and Kueck, and they differed. Kueck explained that he hadn't slammed on his brakes but was tapping the brake pedal to keep Sorensen from tailgating. He also said that when both vehicles had stopped and he got out of his car, Sorensen was already out of his truck, yelling orders and pointing his badge and gun. He claimed that he was the one who flagged down the motorist and had been following Sorensen's orders all along, even though the deputy kept yelling, "I'm going to do you." When an investigator asked him why he kept watching the truck in his rearview mirror and tapping his brakes, especially when he could see that the victim was not looking at the road, Kueck spun out a strange story about his car having fiber-optic cables that pointed toward the driver and lit up when the brake lights were on. When he finished giving his statement, he was released.

He got back into his Lincoln and headed to a doctor's appointment. A traffic incident report was filed, with statements from Sorensen, Kueck, officers on the scene, and eyewitnesses. At first, investigators found the report puzzling. Sorensen was on his way to work in a remote area, and there had been plenty of room to pass Kueck. There would have been no reason to tailgate. As for Kueck, he wasn't speeding—the usual problem on far-flung desert roads—so something else was going on, as both men had said. Moreover, Kueck couldn't have known at first that Sorensen was a cop; he was in a pickup truck and off-duty. Any driver might have been reluctant to pull over and face the wrath of a stranger. On the other hand, Kueck did appear to be driving erratically. Why was he obstructing a man in a truck behind him? What was the big deal about just letting someone pass? The deputy wasn't trying to pull him over; he just wanted to get in front of the vehicle, until it became clear that was not going to happen. So what was the problem? Was Kueck tweaking? One of the passing motorists thought so, judging from his apparently manic demeanor. But maybe he was on edge for another reason. Only hours before his run-in with Steve, his son had told him about getting beaten up in jail, placing emphasis on having been set up by the guards. He might have been worked up about the story and taken it out on anyone who approached, especially when he found out that they were a cop. Not that his motivations mattered; for cops, traffic stops are the deadliest kind of police action, next to domestic violence calls, and anyone who causes trouble during one generally incurs the full force of the law.

In the end, eyewitness accounts backed up Steve. Kueck had been obstructing Sorensen's vehicle, nearly causing a collision and forcing the deputy off the road and onto the shoulder. His strange story about fiber optics might have entertained people at a party but not members of law enforcement.

But Kueck viewed himself as the victim. In the days following the incident, he had been calling and visiting the sheriff's station and the district attorney's office, seeking assault charges against the deputy. Finally, several months later, he himself was charged with assault with a deadly weapon—his car. At that point, he embarked on a letter-writing campaign, sending a statement about what happened to Sheriff Sherman Block (then head of the LASD), the Internal Affairs Bureau, his Congressional representatives, and the FBI. "I most definitely will not resist arrest under any circumstances," he wrote, probably alluding to his behavior during the encounter with Sorensen. "All my life I have had respect for our countries [sic] enforcement personel [sic]. I find it difficult to believe what these investigators are doing. I cling to my hopes that the system will correct these perversions of justice." When the incident was finally adjudicated, he pled guilty to a reduced charge and was told to report regularly to a probation officer. What recipients of his letter made of it we do not know. It reflected an ongoing aspect of life for many solitaires in the Mojave, some of whom had probably waged their own similar campaigns against law enforcement. Yet evidence of such battles rarely remains. Years later, when a copy of the letter was found in Kueck's trailer after the deadly encounter with Sorensen, it cast the episode in one more mysterious light.

PERSON OF INTEREST

I got myself into a situation here.
    —Marlon Brando, *The Fugitive Kind*

As the second day of the manhunt was coming to a close, Donald Kueck had still not been officially named as the suspect in Steve Sorensen's murder. He was a "person of interest"—a vague though widely used designation for someone who can't be named as anything more because there's not enough evidence. The tag angered some of Steve's fellow officers, especially local cops, who knew him personally. After all, witnesses had actually heard the murder—the shots being fired at Kueck's place—and then had seen Kueck pacing around Sorensen's vehicle and retrieving items from it shortly after the deputy had been asked to make sure the squatter was gone. In addition, law enforcement had located and identified Kueck's car, the one he had used to drag Sorensen's body away from the scene of the crime. What was everyone waiting for?

"This was the most bizarre murder of a sheriff I have ever seen," recalls Detective Joe Purcell in a phone call shortly after the incident. A vicious cop killer with an automatic weapon was still on the loose, and the search rapidly expanded beyond the sheriff's department. In 1873, the bandito Tiburcio Vasquez eluded a mounted posse in this very region for a year; nearly a hundred years later, another desert thief killed a cop in a traffic stop near Victorville and then outran military and police hunters for weeks. Now, two centuries later, Donald Charles Kueck was contending with an arsenal developed for modern warfare. A few miles from the crime scene, air traffic control at Edwards—one of the world's largest Air Force bases—picked up the news and passed it on to the pilots who fly over the desert every eight minutes on maneuvers. In the hours following the murder, deputies had learned that Kueck had a cell phone. Now, on Day Two, the FBI dispatched a C-130, a super high-tech signal-tracking plane that would pinpoint Kueck if he used it, picking up the signal as it bounced off local radio towers. By the end of the afternoon, as backup poured in from other desert towns, Lake Los Angeles had become the Gaza strip—no one was getting in or out without showing ID; every parolee in every trailer park and tattoo joint in the Antelope Valley was hauled in and questioned. Officers from all over Southern California combed Kueck's property and the surrounding desert, looking under every rock, behind every Joshua tree, deep into animal lairs and wrecked muscle cars and down ancient gullies and washes. But there were no signs of the man with the Fu Manchu; Donald Charles Kueck had vanished.

At 5:15 that afternoon, from somewhere in the desert, he placed another call to his daughter. All day long, television reports had been carrying the news of Sorensen's death, linking her father to it, and broadcasting his mug shot. It had been taken two years earlier when he was arrested for assault; the guy who once looked like an Eddie Bauer model now looked like Mephistopheles. In the phone call with Rebecca, Don sounded calm, almost nonchalant. She now knew why he would not be "coming over on Monday," and confronted him about being linked to the murder of the deputy. "Oh that," Kueck said. "Yeah, I know." He then asked how he looked on the news. It was a strange remark coming from a hermit, yet everyone wants to go out pretty. But beyond that, cops theorized later, it was evidence that Kueck wondered how much he'd have to change his appearance in order to fade away. Would he finally cut his hair, the one physical thing that represented being wild and free? As she hung up the phone, Rebecca pondered this and other related matters, and longed to see her father again. And she also hoped that no one else would be killed.

DAY THREE

HERE COMES THE CAVALRY

No man in the wrong can stand up against a fellow that's in the right and keeps on a-comin'.
    —Texas Ranger creed

IN 1965, AFTER A SERIES OF COP KILLINGS IN LOS ANGELES, THE Los Angeles Police Department developed SWAT, which stands for Special Weapons and Tactics, the paramilitary unit quickly adopted by law enforcement everywhere. It was first deployed in 1969 against the Black Panthers, in a raid at their South Central headquarters at Forty-First and Central. The raid led to a street battle before a gathering crowd, and it was broadcast on the evening news. Along with two other simultaneous raids, the assault led to the arrests of three high-ranking members of the Panthers, as Matthew Fleischer reported years later in the *Los Angeles Times Magazine*. But SWAT had been tactically unprepared for urban warfare with highly trained soldiers in their own army, and the team headed down to Camp

Pendleton for further training with the Marines. Six years later, the
situation would repeat itself on the streets of Los Angeles. This
time, SWAT was up against a strange crew of California prison veterans and middle-class radicals, deployed to rescue a kidnapped
heiress who seemingly had gone over to the other side. Although
the deployment happened by necessity, the location was right: the
city where glamour and power meet and then reign supreme was
the right frame for an elite group of fast and fit men in uniform at
the height of their powers, a paramilitary outfit that could muster
quickly and flush out increasingly sophisticated snipers, bank rob-
bers, and hostage takers, a team with a sonorous name that rolled
off the tongue—why, it could have been dreamed up by Hollywood, and in a way it was.

Its original proponent was controversial LAPD chief Daryl
Gates, who ran the department from 1978 to 1992, overseeing in-
vestigations of such notorious criminals as Charles Manson and the
Hillside strangler. He became infamous for his extreme positions
on drug use (casual users should be "taken out and shot") and choke
holds (suggesting that they were not really an excessive use of
force, but that cardiovascular conditions predisposed black people
to succumbing quickly to the tactic). His career ended with the
Rodney King riots in 1992, after LA erupted in violence when a
jury acquitted four white cops accused in the videotaped beating of
King a year earlier. But by then his enduring legacy as "the father of
SWAT" was established, and units modeled after his pioneering
teams in Los Angeles were being deployed by law enforcement
agencies across the land, locked in the endless and oldest battle
there is—good guys versus bad guys, with one side or the other always seeking and gaining an edge and a few guys in a uniform
standing between them.

Gates himself was an LA creature through and through, a man
who grew up on its streets, under the false shade of its palms, those
palms with their froufrou fronds that everyone thought were so

pretty, lulled into a sense of safety by the graces of Los Angeles—
the soft quality and tone of the light during certain hours and seasons, the perfume of the night-blooming jasmine, perfect and
hollow sets rolling in at the beaches. With his rough upbringing in
the form of a violent father, Gates never bought it. He knew about
the rest of the postcard, the rats that lived just beyond view, and
where he came from, it was him or them, and as the place got
weirder, so did he, and then one day, he ordered up a new piece of
equipment, an urban tank with a battering ram, a sexy new piece of
armament that could take on the baddest of the bad, better than
any unmarked Crown Vic or fully loaded chopper. In 1975, he
rolled it out to take down the Symbionese Liberation Army, a
bizarre, self-trained paramilitary unit that outfoxed law enforcement for over a year as the nation watched and wondered how the
taunts and violence and killings would come to an end.

The SLA was a small, radical group of upper-middle-class
white kids led by an escaped black convict named Donald De-
Freeze, who had been meeting with Berkeley-based prison reform
advocates while he was in prison for armed robbery at Vacaville.
Hiding out with some of these advocates in Berkeley, DeFreeze began calling himself General Field Marshal Cinque and, with the
others, cooked up plans to foment a revolution by ending racism,
monogamy, and the prison system, among other features of a capi-
talist society. DeFreeze—or Cinque—was not the first graduate of
the notorious California prison system to have been made over
into a hyperviolent man, nor would he be the last.

The SLA's first act was murdering Marcus Foster, the Oakland,
California, school superintendent who was targeted because he
was in favor of an identification system for students. Although he
had backed off of it by the time of his murder, the SLA had apparently not gotten the message. Its members went on to kidnap
newspaper heiress Patty Hearst, issuing an "arrest warrant" for the
young socialite shortly after the abduction and demanding that

Hearst's parents set up a program for distribution of food to poor people in the area. When that was done, ransom demands for millions of dollars followed; as the negotiations unfolded, Patty, who was being held in a closet, was transformed into a person called Tanya—in an echo of DeFreeze's own journey to Cinque while he himself was in prison. Two months later, she surfaced in a San Francisco bank robbery with SLA members, wielding a rifle as the others snagged $10,000 from a teller and within hours issuing a statement referring to her parents as "pigs." Law enforcement lost track of the group until two members were caught shoplifting in Los Angeles; from outside in the getaway car, Hearst fired shots, and the trio fled. On the following day Chief Gates deployed his new tank for the first time. It carried an LAPD SWAT team to a house where the group was hiding. In a fierce gun battle that raged for hours, the SLA deployed its own arsenal until finally the LAPD fired gas canisters into the house and then rammed the bungalow where Hearst's kidnappers were making their last stand. The house exploded, and across America citizens sat before the television hearth and watched the oldest show in the world—flames—and the fire raged for hours, consuming the hideout until it finally caved in on the notorious renegades, killing them all.

At first it was thought that Hearst was inside the house, but within days cops received a communiqué from surviving members; along with the rest of the country, they too had been watching the bonfire—from a motel room near Disneyland. Patty Hearst was with them, still a captive. Several months later, the group was back in San Francisco, staging another bank robbery in a nearby town and killing a bystander in the process. Shortly after that, the two surviving members of the SLA were arrested, along with Hearst and a recent recruit. Hearst described herself as an "urban guerrilla" and was charged with armed robbery. Her family hired F. Lee Bailey to defend her in a trial that was the media circus of its day, with the noted attorney laying out the story of her confinement in a closet for two months, with little food and water, and how that experience stripped away the layers of Patty and turned her into Tanya. She was sentenced to seven years, and after serving twenty-two months, her sentence was commuted by President Jimmy Carter. From then on she was always with a bodyguard; months later, she married him, had children, and faded back behind the drapes of San Francisco society.

With the stanching of this prison-fueled rebellion, SWAT teams quickly became part of the repertoire of municipal police departments across the land—and calls for reform of the California prison system continued to go unheeded. By 2003, Los Angeles County's own SWAT team—different from the team that was part of the city's police department—was regularly deployed in high-risk situations, such as serving arrest and search warrants to individuals who might be heavily armed, carrying out hostage rescues, and subduing people who are barricaded. The hunt for Donald Kueck involved two of these three mandates, in addition to a range of other tasks.

A standard view of SWAT teams is that they are a kind of beef council, comprised of muscle-bound men who receive orders and hit the ground running and that is all. But as always, the conventional wisdom fails, with much more to be added to this profile. For instance, take Gold Team member Bruce Chase. A wiry and agile man in his forties who favors dark, wraparound shades and Hawaiian shirts during his downtime, he generally steers clear of the sun because of his fair skin. You might not take him for a cop, let alone a member of SWAT, because in Southern California, if someone is fit and minus a tan, somehow little else matters. You also might not take him for a man whose code has been deeply shaped by books, simply because of the above-mentioned beef-related assumptions. Yet he is one more character in our story with a serious involvement in literature. In particular, during his formative years and beyond, it was the books of the well-known western scribe Louis L'Amour. Although the author died in 1988, his celebrated novels

of the West live on—*Hondo* and *Flint* and *Down the Long Hills* among
the nearly one hundred reprinted many times for his endless parade
of fans, his life's work never appearing on "best of the century lists"
or any part of the literary canon but to this day a signpost on the
path for who knows how many, the thing that says, "Turn here."

When Bruce Chase was a young boy, more than anything, he
dreamed of the Wild West. He played cowboys and Indians in the
Virginia woods, where he spent his childhood years, and then one
day he started to read the works of L'Amour, and that's when his
dreaming began to get serious. L'Amour took him into the great
American dreamtime, a world of red rock and mesas and pretty
horses, a world where a man does what's right simply because in his
heart of hearts he knows what needs to be done. And one day, after
his family moved from Virginia to California, the boy would follow
in his older brother's footsteps, in the footsteps of his beloved
Sackett brothers, the L'Amour characters who headed west and became lawmen, signing up for the thin blue line via an agency whose
very name—which included the word "sheriff"—recalled another
time. Over the years, he would advance through the ranks and become part of the Los Angeles County SWAT team.

Strangely, there was a L'Amour book called *The Lonesome Gods*
that took place in the California desert and happened to be one of
Chase's favorites. It told a story of good and evil in the drylands,
and months later, when the hunt was over and we talked about his
role in a similar and epic battle in the latter-day desert, he went to
his garage and retrieved the book from a collection he had stored
away years earlier. Then he sat down and read the book again, and
it became part of our conversations about this story, for I happened
to know it myself. You see, I too had a L'Amour phase, not to dis-
parage this master, and rereading it, I could see how this particular
novel had pointed the way to Chase's life's work and continued to
inform it over the years.

In particular, there was a passage about a team of men riding to right a wrong, five against twelve, heading into the desert at night under skies lit by stars. There was cool air, there were hooves that clicked on stone, and as the men galloped up a hill, there came the creaking of saddles. These men had all endured trouble in their lives, but beyond that there was no comparison. Now they headed into battle under a flag of courage, L'Amour wrote, "loyal to the last fiber of their being, and strong with the knowledge that if men are to survive upon the earth there must be law, and there must be justice, and all men must stand together against those who would strike at the roots of what men have so carefully built."

THIS PRESENT DARKNESS

All shadows whisper of the sun.
 —Emanuel Carnevali

IF STEVE SORENSEN COULD HAVE WAITED, HE MIGHT HAVE HAD a career as a lifeguard. "When he got back from the army," recalls his old roommate in Manhattan Beach, "he wanted to go full time. But there were cutbacks, and he was impatient." In January 1991, after he had been married for about a year, Steve entered the LA County Sheriff's Academy, a member of class 271. At the age of thirty-three, he was older than the other recruits, and during the four-month training period, he became a role model of sorts for some of the other guys. One in particular was Deputy Bernard Shockley, whom I met during a visit to headquarters for the Special Enforcement Bureau in East Los Angeles, where the SWAT team is based. As I was talking with Sergeant Joe Williams, the canine handler for SWAT during the manhunt for Kueck, Shockley overheard

our conversation and joined in. Ten years younger than Steve, he choked up at the memory of his classmate and said that he had looked up to the ex-surfer for his quiet and helpful ways. "I knew him at the beginning of his career, and I was there at the end." With their names close alphabetically, Shockley sat next to Sorensen in the academy. "Steve was a mature guy," Shockley says, recalling someone who was beyond the antics that are typical of a bunch of guys in their twenties who are supposed to take orders from someone else in a classroom.

In the early days of training, the two trainees quickly bonded over insider beach knowledge. Shockley had grown up in Santa Monica and Venice, and he and Steve would talk about lifeguard stations 25 and 6, known for being a certain kind of surf break and hangout. But beyond that, there wasn't much small talk with Steve. He was a serious student, a fastidious one, and never got into trouble. For instance, Shockley recalled, unlike some of the other guys, he never had to write a five-page paper about having a thread hanging from his clothes. In addition, he was quick to spot and warn his classmates about slacker behavior that could get them into trouble. "He was the first to say, 'Your briefcase isn't locked.'" Yet his concern went beyond rules and regulations. "When he said, 'How are you?'" Shockley recalled, "he meant it."

When Steve graduated from the academy, his first assignment was the same one given to all new members of the LASD: working in detention as guards. The idea is that everyone has to deal face-to-face with men behind bars, rather than simply arresting people, testifying at trials, and then never seeing them again. The assignment took Steve from the Pitchess Detention Center in Castaic (or Wayside) to Mira Loma in Lancaster, the largest penitentiary in the county and one that housed a number of men who were in the United States illegally. This was probably where Steve learned firsthand about problems that plagued Hispanics. Later, as he settled into his new beat in Lake Los Angeles, he would take up the cause of Hispanic locals in a battle that reached a fever pitch shortly before he was killed, with Sorensen filing a defamation lawsuit against several members of the town establishment and announcing that he feared for his life.

After putting in his time at county jails, Steve followed the trail of the beginning deputy, assigned to ride-alongs at the Temple and Santa Clarita stations, which took him into a gritty and racially mixed part of Los Angeles and a mostly white suburban area with more wide-open space. At that point it was on to patrol training in the Altadena station. Next to Pasadena and abutting the San Gabriel Mountains, which separated LA proper from the Antelope Valley to the north, Altadena is a beautiful enclave known for its tree-lined streets and Craftsman cottages, including the home of Zane Grey, now a local landmark where the noted writer penned some of his best works, stories that continue to bring young boys to the west, just like L'Amour's. The town is residential and equestrian-zoned, but under the iridescent jacaranda blooms and on certain thoroughfares there is also a notable gang presence—and the Altadena station had more action than, say, Malibu or Topanga Canyon.

Sergeant Rob Hahnlein, his partner during that period, recalled Steve as a cop who was driven and conscientious, generally wearing a tight uniform—a preference that might have made him look more muscular than he already was and given him an edge on the streets. He was often the first to volunteer for extra work and would use his old Toyota pickup when he was undercover. His main worry was that someone would steal it. That didn't happen, but there were plenty of drug busts on this busy beat, primarily on the notorious Squiggly Lane—a haven for local dealers. Once, Hahnlein recalls, at the corner of Glenrose and Harriet, there was a particularly gnarly episode in which he, Sorensen, and several others went to break up a drug sale. As Steve arrested a suspect, the guy bit him on the bicep. Sorensen refused medical treatment, and the man was charged with aggravated assault. "On a scale of one to ten," Hahnlein says, "everything was a ten for Steve. There were times I would tell him to relax, but it was always go go go. He was a superman who did not want help."

In 1999, word came that the Lancaster station in the Antelope Valley was looking to fill a new and first-of-its-kind resident deputy position. The beat was Lake Los Angeles. Already living in the area, Steve applied, was interviewed, and got the job. In March 2000, he began his patrol, immersing himself in the community, introducing himself to local business owners, pastors, town council members, and other residents, getting to know a broad range of citizens. By all accounts, he liked the solitude of the desert and was thriving on his new assignment. He and his wife adopted a baby, and the ex-surfer from Manhattan Beach sank roots deep in the Mojave, becoming the ultimate citizen, buying groceries for poor people, doing yard work for seniors whose limbs no longer permitted it, bathing the infirm when they went off their meds and no caretaker was in sight, investigating Section 8 real estate scams, brokering deals between minor scofflaws and offended parties when others might have hauled the small-time crooks off to jail. Many locals considered Sorensen a godsend, and some in the community literally thought he had been sent by God to carry the cross of goodness into a parched desert wilderness of evil. Among those who held that view were two residents, Connie Mavrolas, an Antelope Valley native and reporter at the *Lake Los Angeles News*, and John Wodetzki, a pastor at the Twin Lakes Community Church. Sorensen had met them shortly after he began to patrol his patch of the Mojave, and together they soon formed a tight trio of community crusaders who wanted more than anything to clean up the Antelope Valley, purging it of tweakers, bikers, Section 8 troublemakers, and squatters, and also to do right by the valley's often ignored Hispanic population, including those in the country legally and illegally.

Although not welcome by many in the town's establishment, at the time of Deputy Sorensen's murder, Hispanics comprised 65 percent of the population in Lake Los Angeles and owned a portion of its small businesses. Not all of the Hispanics were in the country legally, although some had been in the Antelope Valley for years, working in the fruit, vegetable, or alfalfa fields, or local restaurants and other establishments. Steve's tenure in Lake Los Angeles had begun before 9/11, when laws regarding immigration and migrants were not as stringent as they are now, and the issue of who has a right to live and work here and who does not was not as heated. Nevertheless, in California, which has a large Hispanic population scheduled to overtake the white majority by the year 2025, the issue, if not front and center, is generally just below the surface. In the Antelope Valley, with its cities partly the result of white flight from LA proper, some in various communities had no desire to share a zip code with Hispanics, documented or otherwise, while others were simply adamant about following the rules and acquiring citizenship through normal channels, as their forebears had done decades earlier.

In the years before 9/11, Sheriff Baca, an iconoclastic guy among heads of law enforcement agencies and part Hispanic himself, did not want his department to operate as an arm of ICE, the federal Immigration and Customs Enforcement Agency, which was later subsumed by the Department of Homeland Security. In other words, it was not the mission of the LASD to track down, arrest, and deport undocumented workers. That didn't mean that immigration laws weren't enforced, but LASD's attitude was different from, say, LAPD's, which was operating under the more stringent Special Order 40, which meant that if a Hispanic-seeming person were arrested, he or she could be asked to prove citizenship.

While Steve was a stickler for rules, he knew that often enough rules were outdated or didn't make sense in some way, or were arbitrarily followed and, when they were, would cause undue problems for people who were holding on but just barely. In Lake Los Angeles, Steve had gotten to know various Hispanics on his beat, and received a quick course on their history in the region, meeting a farmworker who was a colleague of the late César Chávez, and friends of this man who themselves had eked out a living in the fields and later at their own small establishments—feed and dry goods stores—in the high desert. One of them, José Gomez, owned a store in Lake Los Angeles called The Hitching Post. It had been in business for over a decade, and many ranchers and equestrians depended on it for supplies. The store was also a way station for residents en route to other errands; often they stopped in just to catch up on local goings-on and chat with José and his wife, Nellie, who welcomed strangers and friends into their store as if all were members of their family. The pair could make small talk with anyone, even though they didn't speak much English. José was quite the vaquero and loved most of all to talk about horses. He had one, and he and Steve instantly hit it off, mostly because of José's animal, who had been trained with Spanish commands. The deputy didn't speak much Spanish but began to pick it up as he watched José interact with his horse, and soon Steve took to the horse, one more animal he had a kinship with, communicating easily with the big bay and the bay responding. One day José offered Steve his beloved steed. Steve was embarrassed by the generous and unexpected offer, and refused it. But José persisted. Why did he live in the desert if he didn't want a horse? José asked. After a while, the deputy relented and one day José brought the horse over and from then on it was Steve's and he called it Cinnamon. José was a frequent visitor, teaching Steve to ride, often arriving on his own horse, and sometimes the two of them would head out into the desert for an afternoon jaunt, but often enough Steve would head out on his own.

Some long-time white locals were surprised that the blonde, blue-eyed surfer would take up the Hispanic cause. But Hispanics got little respect in town and Steve took it personally. As much as he couldn't stand to be teased or take a joke during the old days on the beach, he didn't like it when people ragged on those who couldn't defend themselves—or risked it all when they did. With his heightened sense of right and wrong, and propensity to take offense when either he or his friends were disrespected, the path became clear as he found out about something that was going on in Lake Los Angeles: an attempt to shut down some Hispanic-owned businesses because of their failure to comply with an ancient county code having to do with outdoor lighting after dark. It wasn't that they were being targeted for being Hispanic, but they happened to own the establishments that were in violation, and some in Lake Los Angeles were happy to see them go. But in a town where people still rode their horses to the store, hitching them up while they shopped for supplies and groceries, the attempt to suddenly enforce the ordinance made little sense. "Why has Regional Planning suddenly decided to attack the honest business owners of Lake Los Angeles?" José Gomez wrote in a public letter with the help of a more accomplished English speaker. "Perhaps I should open a liquor store. The County seems more than eager to grant operating permits for these types of businesses. I say this because there are three locations in town where you can buy hard liquor, beer and wine. However, if the County has its way, you will not be able to buy feed for your animals or get your car fixed. Please stop by the Hitching Post and sign your name to the petition I am circulating concerning this issue."

At the time Steve became resident deputy, there were two newspapers in town—*About Town* and the *Lake Los Angeles News. About Town* was the predominant periodical, and, recalls Connie, "the editor had a weird hold on the town." That was about to change, as Steve came to the defense of José and other business owners who had been cited, entering a cauldron of small-town politics and turf battles, with the two rival newspapers fighting over who would get the first exclusive interview with the new resident deputy and, in doing so, appear to have him in their corner. Connie got the scoop and it was the beginning of an unlikely alliance, with Steve enlisting Connie's aid in a campaign to restructure the way business was done in Lake Los Angeles.

Perhaps it was to be expected that Connie Mavrolas would become involved in such a battle. The daughter of migrant farmworkers in the region's onion fields—the very fields Joseph Wambaugh memorialized in the title of his classic book about the murder of two cops in 1985—Mavrolas had grown up in a two-bedroom house in Palmdale, sharing one of the bedrooms with her five siblings as her parents slept on the other side of a thin wall. The house was on Avenue M between Thirtieth and Fortieth Street East near the Rockwell testing grounds. For shade in the relentless summer sun, the family planted an oak tree; it's still there today, along with the house, as well as an old petroleum tank next to the living room window. To Connie's parents, the house was a palace. They had grown up in a small pueblo in Chihuahua, Mexico. Her father came to the Antelope Valley when he was fourteen, working as a ranch hand and also in the alfalfa fields, sending the money back to his family. Several years later, he went back to Mexico, married, and returned to the valley with his bride. They had children and continued toiling in the onion fields—for twenty-five years, in fact. During the 1960s, the fields were being sprayed with pesticides, and Connie's mother started a boycott. "When the planes showed up to spray," Connie says, "my mother told people to walk out." She was fired and blackballed, though with her onion field wages she was able to buy a fifteen-person passenger van where workers could be housed during certain times of the day. She was ultimately hired back by the farmer.

Connie and her brothers and sisters also worked in the fields. "You'll work here so you'll never come back," Connie's mother would tell them, wanting her kids not just to have a better future, but to appreciate where food comes from. Today, Connie's mother is disabled. But the children are not working in the fields; Connie excelled in the local public school system, graduating with honors and then attending Antelope Valley Community College. Her dream had been to become involved with civic matters and to write, especially about what was going on in her hometown. In 1995, she joined the staff of the local paper, as well as the chamber of commerce, and it wasn't long before she began speaking up for the valley's Hispanic population, some of whom were still working in the region's fruit orchards, vegetable fields, and vast plains of alfalfa. But others had become business owners, running mini-marts, feed stores, and restaurants, and by the time Sorensen had become the resident deputy in Lake Los Angeles, the town's commercial establishments were about 65 percent Hispanic-owned. By then married with kids, Mavrolas was often covering events and nursing with a notebook in her hand. In the desert, people are often known for their gigs—Twentynine Palms has "Water District Judy" for instance. In certain parts of the Antelope Valley, energetic and high-spirited Connie became known as "the reporter with the kids."

As she made her rounds, it wasn't long before she met Pastor John Wodetzki, who had recently bought a house from Steve Sorensen in Lake Los Angeles. Pastor John had just moved to the area from Colorado Springs, arriving with his wife and three children on the day before Thanksgiving, just a couple of months after 9/11. It was a time of great purpose in the Antelope Valley, home of Edwards Air Force Base and a region where many veterans and active members of the military live. Their service is honored across the valley: in downtown Lancaster there are murals honoring pilots, a Walk of Fame with sculptures of Chuck Yeager and Jimmy Doolittle amid a beautiful desert garden, a Stealth bomber parked at the corner of Avenue K and the Sierra Highway—a frank and stunning monument to power. Now the country's military was revving up for what has turned into our longest war, and with downtown Manhattan still smoldering, the urgency was palpable. Eight months prior to making the move to Lake Los Angeles, John and his wife felt that God was telling them to move back to California, where he was from. A graduate of Fullerton Seminary in Pasadena, he applied for a job at the Twin Lakes Community Church in Lake Los Angeles but was turned down. After 9/11, he reapplied and was hired, moving with his family into a rented house while scouting for a home to buy. "Have I moved to Egypt?" John thought when he first arrived. Although he had grown up in the Mojave, in a small mining town called Eagle Mountain near Joshua Tree National Park, this was different—more spare, more urgent somehow, perhaps a kind of Old Testament trial. In the wake of the attack on America, his wife, Tish, a member of the Air Force, was deployed to Addis Adaba. John soon found a suitable home on 171st Street, and he bought it. As it turned out, the seller was Steve Sorensen—a man whom he would tearfully eulogize months later. Their initial meeting suggested no such connection.

One day after purchasing the home, John spotted Steve in his SUV on the corner of 170th Street and Avenue O, where he often parked so people could stop and talk to him. For Lake Los Angeles, it was a busy intersection, with mini-marts on the corners and a steady stream of traffic. John introduced himself through the driver's window and Steve extended a hand. "Would it be okay if I moved in a bit early?" he asked. It was ten days before the closing. "My wife was just sent to the Middle East, and my kids and I are really cramped where we are now. It would really help if we were in our new house." Deputy Sorensen said no—and in a way that was direct and off-putting. Surprised, John walked off and wondered why the resident deputy was such a prick. They would not become friends until a year later, and soon Steve explained his refusal to have the new buyers take early possession of his house: he was concerned about an early move-in, lest the new owners wanted to change things or decided not to close—or worse, refuse to move should a dispute arise. By then, he and John were allies in a greater battle—and good friends. John completely understood Steve's position. But at the time, one thing was clear to the new pastor in town: the local deputy was a man who did things by the book, and if you didn't like it, too bad.

In the months prior to Steve's death, some members of the Twin Lakes congregation were reading a novel called *This Present Darkness*. Written by Frank Peretti, the book was first published in 1986, and by the time Steve became resident deputy in Lake Los Angeles, it was a monster of a best seller among evangelical Christians across the country. Several years after his death it became a musical on Broadway. It tells a suspense tale of spiritual warfare in a small town plagued by the never-ending duel between angels and demons. In this case, a local reporter and pastor take on New Age figures who are bent on seizing control of the town. They are aided by prayers from concerned citizens, whose supplications bolster the physical strength of those who are fighting against evil. The title of the book derives from Ephesians 6:10–12 in the New Testament; in the English Standard Version, it says this: "Finally, be strong in the Lord and in the strength of his might. Put on the whole armor of God, that you may be able to stand against the schemes of the devil. For we do not wrestle against flesh and blood, but against the rulers, against the authorities, against the cosmic powers over this present darkness, against the spiritual forces of evil in the heavenly places."

With the arrival of Steve, the soon-to-become-epic battle of good and evil was validated by the novel; here was law enforcement coming to the rescue as if in answer to prayers, and together the three allies saw themselves as carrying the cross of goodness across a parched landscape of ill winds. Indeed, the alliance was all the more astounding for the friendship between Connie, a Catholic, and John, a Baptist; members of the two communities often

find themselves embroiled in an ongoing dispute over the interpretation of biblical matters, and John and Connie themselves
were astonished as their bond developed. As the three found
themselves in the midst of a time-honored battle, there was a keen
sense of urgency, fueled by people who tried to undermine them
by publicly accusing Steve of asking for protection money from
the businesses he defended. The battle played out in local newspapers, in bars where people gossiped, and at heated town council
meetings where members of the local establishment fought for the
status quo against the three upstarts who were trying to reform an
old process, opening it up to long-time Hispanic residents of Lake
Los Angeles In the early months of 2003, the issue became so
contentious that over 700 people attended one of the council
gatherings—a huge turnout in a town with about 12,000 residents.
To the cheers of many, José Gomez addressed the crowd, along
with other locals who were under siege, including business owners
Oscar Espitia and Manuel Magana—fellow members of a group
called Latinos Americanos in Acción who had coalesced around
the trouble in Lake Los Angeles. Pastor John and Steve also made
statements, and Connie reported it all in the *Lake Los Angeles News;*
the trio was marching on through the desert.

While Steve wouldn't have described his mission as religious,
it certainly was righteous, and in the manner of the driven, he did
not let up. Along the way, he acquired a variety of enemies—those
who thought he was a gung-ho cop and out to prove something,
including some valley bikers who were not pleased with his zeal-
ousness, unlike others who cleaved to him, to this day painting a
picture that recalls Christ or the saints walking with lepers, only in
this case it was a man in a Los Angeles County sheriff's uniform
who was blazing a path behind a badge and a wall of will.

From day one, he had been available to those in his jurisdiction, and sometimes even outside of it, every minute of every
day—the quintessential beat cop as Captain Carl Deeley of the

Lancaster station, Steve's reporting agency, would describe him at his funeral. Many locals had his cell phone number—and used it, for all manner of requests. But now, his job seemed to consume his entire being. A fair number of the calls he received were from residents complaining about neighbors who lived in Section 8 homes. "Section 8" is a federal program in which landlords can rent designated properties to low-income tenants at a reduced rate, with the government picking up the difference between the tenants' payment and the rent specified in the owner's contract with the government. During Steve's tenure in Lake Los Angeles, the housing market was at an all-time low. "Investors and local realtors were buying properties like crazy," Connie says, "and making them into Section 8 housing. Section 8 was paying land-lords the same rate for low-income renters as they were in other parts of LA County. For a 1,200-square-foot house in LA, the landlord could make $1,400 a month, with the renter paying around $200 out of pocket. In Lake LA, where renting was only around $600–$700, the landlord would bring in the same amount, even though the house wasn't in the same market. So it didn't matter that the renter low-life was thrashing the place, selling drugs, or lowering the standard of living in the neighborhood. The landlord was making bank, and the check was being sent to his house from the county." Steve, Connie remembers, went after this "like a dog with a bone." At one point he found out that a local real estate office was sending flyers into welfare offices in Los Angeles and Pacoima. "One-way free U-haul service to Lake LA for Section 8 housing," the flyers proclaimed. "Steve was furi-ous," Connie says. "He started a crackdown on the trouble spots in town and went after the landlords, and the criminals living in their houses."

As Steve's campaign escalated, people seemed edgier than ever, and "sometimes even we were worn out," Connie recalls. Some locals who opposed them began to refer to Steve, Connie, and Pastor John as "the toilet paper gang." Steve took the epithet and owned it, giving the band a motto—"to wipe the slate clean"— and at the height of their battle, commissioning special T-shirts for the group, bearing the logo of a hand wielding a plunger pushing through a roll of toilet paper. Those on the other side of the battle did not take kindly to the reference that they were something to be cleaned up. Strange things happen in the desert, but as the battle for the soul of Lake Los Angeles escalated, such episodes seemed to come more quickly. In fact, within several weeks, there was a cascade of omens. Cat heads on poles appeared outside the Carmelite convent in Lake Los Angeles. "We took this as a response from the Wiccans," Connie says. "Then my dog was poisoned." Pastor John's door was shot at, and animal carcasses were strewn at the church door. In the face of such things, some might have called it a day and left town. But the trio was not backing down, and in the days preceding his murder, Deputy Steve Sorensen filed a lawsuit against some Lake Los Angeles locals, stating that he feared for his life. But his job as resident deputy trumped all, and no one was going to run him off his beat. "Looking back on the whole thing," one resident remembers, "I now understand the urgency. I see why Steve was in such a rush for us to do so many things. He didn't have much time."

CITY OF LIZARDS

Ask the dust.
  —John Fante

ACCORDING TO AN LA LEGEND, THERE IS A STRANGE SYSTEM OF tunnels that was constructed 5,000 years ago under what is now the downtown library. In this ancient system, there was once a kingdom of Lizard People. Do you think it's strange or funny when people traverse the sands with metal detectors, hoping to find lost rings, coins, or buried treasure? If you happened to have been walking the streets of downtown Los Angeles in 1934, you might have seen a rugged-looking man in a jacket, jodhpurs, knee-high boots, and a fedora, seated on a folding chair and tinkering with sensitive instruments wedged into the ground. This was G. Warren Shufelt, an educated version of the pilgrim with the magnetized trident, a geophysical mining engineer who was looking for minerals in the netherworld below LA. After driving a 250-foot shaft into

the seams of Los Angeles and then taking X-rays, he was in for a serious surprise. For he had detected not just minerals but tunnels. Upon further studies across an area stretching from the library on West Fifth Street to the Southwest Museum at the foot of Mount Washington, our engineer became ecstatic, believing he had located a sophisticated arrangement of tunnels. He mapped the course of the tunnels and found that there were large rooms along the tunnel route, catacombs and vaults, as well as deposits of gold. For a time, he pondered the meaning of his strange discovery. One day, the story goes, there came a meeting with Little Chief Greenleaf, a Hopi medicine man in Arizona, and Shufelt recounted his discovery. The medicine man knew instantly what the engineer had found in the bowels of the city of the queen of the angels. According to an ancient Hopi legend, there were three lost cities on the Pacific coast. One of them was in Los Angeles, and it was dug 5,000 years ago by the Lizard People. This feat occurred after the great catastrophe—"a huge tongue of fire that came out of the Southwest, destroying all life in its path." To survive future catastrophes, survivors headed underground, building a sophisticated city.

They did this by entering the underworld through the ocean and using powerful substances to burrow tunnels without removing earth. They lined the tunnels with a cement that was stronger than any used in modern times. The system they built was well-planned and complex: there were several layers of tunnels, and every day the tide passed in and out of the lower tunnel portals, forcing air into the upper levels, providing ventilation for city dwellers, and cleansing the basement structure.

Like all lost cities, the underground city of Los Angeles was fabulous. There were large rooms inside the tops of hills above the city, labyrinths where 1,000 families lived on separate floors just as they would today inside skyscrapers. To guard against the next catastrophe, there were vast stores of imperishable food such as herbs that sustained life, healed wounds, and grew in underground gardens. But it was not just herbs that were stored below. The people who went to ground harbored an elaborate kingdom of riches, maintaining their records on golden tablets of precise measurements, as they always are in disappeared capitols. In this case, they were four feet long and fourteen inches wide. Inscribed on one of the tablets, as it always is, was the story of the origins of the human race. Shufelt tried to excavate the room that was said to house the critical tablet, but the endeavor was doomed. Worried about a cave-in beyond 350 feet, officials shut down the dig, and the vault was never to be penetrated again.

But this is much more than a tale of elusive treasure and a fruitless attempt to cipher a great mystery. For the purposes of this story, the most telling feature of the lost city underneath Los Angeles is its shape. You see, the Lizard People had not just burrowed underground like reptiles; their entire city was laid out like a lizard.

According to the Hopi legend, its tail lies to the southwest, below Fifth and Hope streets. Its head is situated on the northeast, in the direction of Dodger Stadium. The key room is directly under South Broadway, near Second Street, and that's where the directory to the city and its golden tablets can be found. It was in tribute to the reptile that signified a long life that the underground city was fashioned, and also in prayer; the ancient people of Los Angeles had chosen to live in the body of a lizard to escape the next great fire. Scoff not, for fires were frequent then, as they are now; prehistoric residents of the LA basin referred to the region as the Valley of Smokes, after the seasonal eruptions of flame. If they had to, our legend goes, they could burrow deeper into their subterranean universe and slither away, crossing the reptile door.

Amid a flurry of publicity when his dig was shut down, engineer Shufelt vanished from the record. There seems to be no mention of Little Chief Greenleaf in tribal records. There is, however, mention of a Lizard Clan that traveled to the Pacific from the Southwest and back again in Hopi migration stories. What they left behind we do not know, and perhaps it is only this strange story of survival and transformation, a tale that is discovered from time to time, whispered and repeated in esoteric gatherings when Los Angeles is on fire, and when it is not. And decades later, the story has resurfaced, cast in a different light: some say there is a tunnel system beneath the Mojave Desert, one that resembles the infamous Cu-Chi tunnels of Vietnam, used by guerrillas during that war as living quarters, supply routes, emergency rooms, weapons caches, and a communications hub. The United States mounted a concerted campaign to take out the tunnels, at first sending B-52 bombers over the area to drop thirty-ton loads of explosives and later deploying 8,000 troops from four divisions to root out the enemy. But the campaign failed, proving how comparatively simple tunnel systems with trap doors that were camouflaged, and sometimes rigged with explosives, can outlast sophisticated orchestrations of warfare.

The tunnel system of the Mojave Desert is said to function like the tunnels of Cu-Chi, serving as an escape hatch for those who find themselves in the never-ending war against civilization, finding refuge in a sprawling city where people—lizard-like perhaps—are said to flourish. Tales of this system wax and wane, and sometimes people say that the system is linked to the one found under the library by the defrocked engineer. It was during the manhunt for Donald Kueck that such tales would reach a fever pitch, reverberating across the Antelope Valley and in Internet chat rooms and on the general grapevine that seems to come alive whenever there is a fugitive in our midst. Had Don himself—a devotee of shamanism, student of desert plants and rocks and creatures and ways—molted and gone to ground? Had he crossed the reptile door and entered the secret labyrinth of Los Angeles County?

THE HERMIT VANISHES

There it is. Take it.
—William Mulholland at the opening of the Los Angeles
Aqueduct, 1913

AS DAY THREE HEADED TOWARD THE AFTERNOON HOURS, THERE was still no sign of Kueck. On the ground local cops who had known Steve were especially frustrated. Since the first day of the manhunt, they had been squeezed out of the operation, after some had swarmed and entered Kueck's trailer, attempting to mount their own search, as LASD SWAT was about to mount theirs. "They do fight or flight," a member of the SWAT crew told me months later. "And we don't." The situation caused chaos on the ground, and now no one was telling them what was going on. Not that that was strange in an operation of this magnitude; locals were often shut out when headquarters took over. Still, Steve was not just a cop but their friend, and they wanted some answers.

Looking to the sky on the third day, they saw one, and knew that something critical was underway. Throughout the manhunt, Deputy District Attorney Brian Berger, a longtime AV local, had been keeping a blog. "Lake Los Angeles is not far from Palmdale Airport's Plant 42," he wrote, "home to, amongst other things, Skunkworks—the top secret aeronautical research and development center. We are used to seeing strange things flying above us. Well, we started seeing a low-flying C-130 overhead. It made too many passes over too long a period of time to be anything other than a hi-tech surveillance plane." Berger and his associates were right. After searching Don's trailer on Day One, investigators had found some of Kueck's letters and personal papers, learning the names of his family members. They contacted them that after-noon. A sister of Don's, Peggy Gilmore, provided important infor-mation, including the fact that they had bought Don a cell phone, hoping he would stay in touch and use it during an emer-gency. They had also learned that Don had a daughter who lived in Riverside; on the day after Steve's death, they converged at Becky's apartment just moments after Don had called, attaching a tape recording device to her telephone. They also gave her a cell phone—a direct line to cops. Although she was worried about en-trapping her father, she also wanted to see him come in, alive, on his own volition, and she thought she could help. Now, as local deputies watched the skies, they took heart in this new phase of the investigation. It wasn't just the plane they noticed; there were three Chevy Suburbans with government plates circling the area beneath the C-130's flight pattern. Each vehicle was top-heavy with antennae. The plane and the cars with the listening attach-ments were the sign of one thing only, and that is what's known in law enforcement as a trap and trace operation. In other words, cell phone tracking had now intensified. It worked by making use of the pings, or cell phone signals, that were bouncing off cell phone towers that crisscrossed the Mojave. If surveillance is picking up pings from one tower, that means the pings are in line with the phone's action. If the pings are coming from three towers, that means they are in the area of use. The areas of use—or effect—will intersect in the general location of the cell phone, but the exact coordinates cannot be ascertained. As Berger knew, use of this surveillance meant that now the FBI and Justice Department had joined the hunt, since they are the agencies that have to sign off on the operation. "It was only a question of time before we would capture Kueck," he wrote.

But where was he? There were no signals coming from his phone, and there were no sightings. As the heat-seeking tentacles of law enforcement continued to probe every fissure in the Antelope Valley, cops squeezed Kueck the old-fashioned way. An old mug shot had been broadcast and plastered everywhere, and it proved all too familiar to certain locals, who called in to report sightings of the guy with the demented gaze, the defiant Mojave ponytail and Fu Manchu, the collapsed speed-freak face—someone had seen a man running down the Southern Pacific tracks in Llano; there was a guy with a sword near the dumpster at the mini-mart; someone just stole someone else's rifle. In a furious attempt to bag the killer, cops in black-and-whites and SUVs raced all over the Mojave, only to find the sad truth of the American desert: another ex-con with no place to go, lying facedown in the sand, blasted on Yukon Jack.

At the Saddleback Market in Palmdale, everyone had a theory. "Maybe he flew out of here in one of those ultralight planes," said one local chick, sucking hard on a Marlboro. "I hear he's in Mexico," said a guy in a T-shirt that read "Show Me Your Tits." Someone else ascribed Sorensen's murder to secret army experiments up in the buttes, suggesting that Kueck was set up, while another theorized that Kueck had floated down the aqueduct to Los Angeles. This last theory was fairly credible. The Los Angeles aqueduct ran 419 miles from Inyo County to the north right through the Antelope Valley and into Los Angeles—from where airplanes, buses, and trains were going everywhere and leaving any time, a perpetual exit door through which countless men and women running from one thing or another flowed all of the time. The aqueduct's route through the Antelope Valley was especially scenic, its turquoise trail winding along the white Mojave sands and providing a counterpoint to the relentless pounding of the heat and light as only water can. Perhaps the place was not landlocked, it suggested: Jump in and I'll wash away your fears and police record, or I'll just give you a ride outta here. . . . The messages it whispered must surely have been heard by our hermit, who lived nearby the aqueduct and had studied it well. From one of his books, he had learned about its geology and construction. He knew how it flowed and when it flowed at its highest peak, along with its intake patterns as it came down from the higher elevations, carrying replenishment out of the Owens Valley, which it had sucked dry so long ago. He also knew how many miles per hour it traveled. It didn't look like it flowed fast, but that was deceiving; at peak flow, it traveled at 4.8 feet per second, and every now and then, in the old days when he had first arrived in the AV, he would take advantage of the twenty-four-hour font and paddle down the aqueduct in an old kayak, or maybe just float in a tire, entering it at Fort Tejon Road in the town of Littlerock, where it ran parallel to the Old Butterfield Stage Road, and then floating down to Avenue S, where he hopped out as it headed under the freeway and then south to Los Angeles. Now, while looking to escape, he could make a desperate repeat of his old course, running south from the place where he had dumped his car, trekking across the desert and back through Llano, down into Largo Wash, the arroyo that nurtured the old commune after the rains. Inside its flanks, he would have been difficult to spot, and he might have headed across the ancient animal pathway and then zigzagged down Black Butte Basin Road, past the compound belonging to Frank Baker, whose phone call had triggered the fatal visit from Deputy Sorensen and where there were a couple of ultralight and small craft airports.

In fact, on Day Three, someone reported that a man bearing a rifle and matching his description—six feet two, 180 pounds, brown hair—was running across the railroad tracks nearby and heading for one of the hangars. A couple of black-and-whites raced to the location, but no one was there; perhaps they had missed him by seconds. From the airport on Black Butte Basin, he would have kept running south while possibly tracking east, into the Theodore Payne Wildlife Sanctuary, a 320-acre preserve at 235th Street East between Avenues U and V, a little-known and neglected county preserve where the wildlife has mostly vanished. There, on the side of Rock Creek Wash, he might have employed his years of studying desert creatures, quickly digging out or appropriating a burrow belonging to another animal and crawling inside it coyote-style until the passing aircraft finished their latest sweep of that lonely quadrant. At that point, he would have been close to escape. All he had to do was cross Highway 138, the one that runs right past the old ruins at Llano and then make his way to the aqueduct, just yards away. Slide down an embankment, and you're gone.

Yet if he hadn't done so already, he would not be able to do it now. Cops knew that Kueck was probably thirsty and at some point might head for the aqueduct—not just an escape route but a drinking fountain, the very thing that the engineer William Mulholland, a man whom Kueck admired, had designed it for. Just like in the old West, when lawmen waited at a water source for outlaws to come in, along with other predators waiting for prey, cops had staked out positions along certain embankments. In addition, self-appointed vigilantes were listening to police scanners and mobilizing on foot and horseback at the slightest hint of suspicious activity. Everyone knew that not only was Kueck desperate, but he needed water. For the seven days of the manhunt, during daylight hours and especially at midday and throughout the afternoon, the temperature was over

100 degrees. It hadn't rained in weeks. There was little shade on the floor of the Antelope Valley and few easily accessible sources of water. Quite literally, the place was baking, and so was everything and everyone in it. Even when a man is walking under such conditions—and not fleeing the full force of one of the world's largest law enforcement agencies—staying alive is difficult. "Of all the survival environments," writes Rory Storm in his essential work, *Desert Survivor's Guide*, "the desert is the most demanding in terms of requiring speedy decisions and quick reactions. You don't have the luxury of pondering the best course of action. Without water, you will last at best five days—and that's resting in the shade! If you try to walk out, you'll last one day."

We do not know at what point Don began to dehydrate. It had to happen at some point. He might have been able to refill his jugs at one of his water caches once or twice after filling up on the first night at his buddy's house, but it would have been difficult to continue accessing them without attracting attention, and it would have been hard as well to keep running with large water jugs. Perhaps at some point, Don had even jettisoned the bottles. There are many ways to get water in the desert and Don knew them. If he could get to the buttes, there was water in the hollows of certain rocks—natural tanks that had been in use for thousands of years. Inside a junked or abandoned car, there might be water in the windshield reservoir or radiator, provided that the vehicle had been recently left there and the water hadn't evaporated or been consumed by others. We can imagine our hermit, coming across such a fountain, ripping it open with a nearby crowbar, swilling down the liquid, slathering his face with grease from the engine to protect it from the sun, then instantly realizing that the water was filled with deadly additives—and knowing that the desert had thrown him another black queen.

On the other hand, perhaps there was no such succor available. There were still other methods of water extraction. For instance,

with a wide temperature range between day and night, condensa-
tion forms on things like metal sheeting. The desert is a metal
graveyard, littered with engine parts and the dregs of glider wrecks,
dismembered trucks, camper shells—a treasure trove of spare parts.
On the run, Don may have availed himself of the condensed moisture, drinking it on the spot or mopping it up with a rag or his own
T-shirt, wringing it into a container and saving it for later, when—
as he well knew—he would be going mad from thirst.

An average man—say 165 pounds and five feet ten—needs
about three liters of water per day. Don, at six feet two inches, was
a bit taller than average and weighed 180 pounds. Recall that at his
friend's house on Day One, he had filled a couple of water jugs before he fled into the night. We do not know what size the jugs
were, but whatever he consumed at the time and until the bottles
were empty was probably enough to keep him running and on the
run for another twenty-four hours or so. Additionally, he would
have tolerated some water loss, according to the Army Study
Guide's chapter "Water Use in Desert Operations"—a book that
pertains to the task at hand. The body has a small reserve of water
and can lose some of its high water content—about 60 percent for
the average man—without any adverse effects. However, "after a
loss of two quarts, which is about 2.5 to 3 percent of body weight,"
the book explains, "effectiveness is impaired. Soldiers/Marines may
begin to stumble, become fatigued and unable to concentrate
clearly, and develop headaches. Thirst will be present, though not
overpowering. . . . But as dehydration continues, the effects will become more pronounced." Heat cramps, heat exhaustion, or heat-
stroke can set in. Cramps would be the first sign of a problem.
While on the run, the first place Don would have felt them would
have been in his legs, arms, and abdomen—the muscles doing the
most work. The symptoms would be shallow breaths, dizziness,
slurred speech, stumbling, and vomiting.

Yet with all the odds against him, there was something big in Don's favor. It wasn't just his deep knowledge of the desert but the fact that he was used to it. "It takes about two weeks for the body to fully acclimatize itself to the temperatures of the desert," Storm writes. "This is why troops are inserted into the arena of war well ahead of any planned battles in order to get accustomed to the heat before they engage with the enemy." Given this information, you could say that Don had a two-week edge on the men who were chasing him, except for the fact that they were there in numbers that increased almost hourly, tightening the ring of fire that was now encircling Don.

As Day Three wore on with still no sightings, sergeants Purcell and Guzman received a tip. There was a strange guy in the aqueduct at 170th Street and Highway 138. Dozens of tips had been pouring in, and they were trying to follow up on the ones that sounded credible. This one did. From their command post inside a large LASD bus on Palmdale Boulevard, they sent out a call to SWAT at the convent. Two deputies were dispatched immediately, jumping into a black-and-white, racing south on 180th street, turning onto the highway, and heading for the aqueduct. At 170th Street, they fanned down the embankment, coming face-to-face with three local cops who were already there, waiting for the fugitive. But he was not there, and as far as they knew, he had not been there earlier; the tip was an error or maybe a prank, phoned in by a local, maybe a friend of Kueck's, who had been watching the manhunt on television and rooting for Kueck's escape. Or possibly it was just an error—there was somebody in the aqueduct at that location, but not the wanted man. Or perhaps, once again, Donald Kueck was right there, withering away in the heat, his brain starting to sizzle, desperately needing a drink, just yards away from freedom.

Even as he fought to fend off dementia, he knew that sooner or later the searchers would leave and all he would have to do is wait. Stay quiet and wait, just like the creatures who lived there—all of the four-legged and scaly and winged ones who were his friends, teachers, and allies. As afternoon faded away and the ever-so-diminishing temperature began to coax animals from the lairs that protected them from the heat of day, so too did our hermit emerge from wherever it was that he was hiding, perhaps popping his head out like one of his beloved ground squirrels, testing the atmosphere for threats, or even realizing that the coast was clear for a split second in the scheme of things and fully standing up—safe to do from the lower elevation of a wash—so that his head was just a bit over its edge, and he could see and hear things, like a jackrabbit with its big antennae-like ears, listening for the distant whirr of chopper blades or something closer, like the breath of another man or men, for that is how attuned the longtime dweller of the desert becomes, particularly one that has become preternatural. Detecting no threat, our hermit retrieved his cell phone from a pocket. It was 6 PM, dinner time, and across the countryside families were gathering around the table. Some would issue a prayer of thanks for the bounty before them. Others would dig right in. Yet others would have a fight, and somewhere someone would get killed. As the horses of the sky pulled sun's chariot ever westward, the urge for evening contact and succor—whatever was driving it and however it played out—affected all living things, and Donald Kueck placed another call. Once again it was to his daughter. "I'm in the desert," he said. "My phone is losing power, but don't worry, the sheriffs will never find me."

Rebecca asked him if he had killed Steve Sorensen. "No," he said. "A couple of tweakers broke in while I was out shooting snakes. They stole my car." He suggested that they were the ones who killed the deputy. Rebecca was concerned for his safety and asked if he was planning to give himself up and explain what happened. "No," he said. "They'll blame me." "What are you going to do?" she said. Her father told her that he was planning to leave the country—and there the phone call ended.

The desert continued to cool, and as darkness fell across the Mojave, all manner of night hunters were traversing the sands and the skies—hawks on the prowl for lizards or mice, ravens looking for rabbits or young tortoise, bobcats and coyotes on the hunt for small animals, and then of course there were members of law enforcement, who had listened in on Kueck's latest phone call with the device they had installed in Rebecca's phone the day Don had killed Steve. The announcement that he was leaving the country was strange. Was Kueck serious? To do that, he'd have to change his looks and have a lot of money stashed somewhere. Moreover, he'd have to get it. Did he have it? Were friends helping him? Was he taunting cops, knowing that they were recording his phone calls to his daughter and realizing in his bones that there was no way he was getting out of the Antelope Valley? Did he secretly want to be caught in a showdown? No one knew the answer, but cops were taking the threat seriously. Now news choppers were circling the desert, breaking into network programs with live coverage of the manhunt. As Don's friends watched the saga unfold on television, they figured if anyone could outfox a desert posse, it would be the man they had visited many times in his far-flung, makeshift abode.

"Dad . . . Dad . . . are you there?" Rebecca had said as her father's phone crackled and then faded out, and then she too turned to the news to see if anything had happened. She had grown close to her father in the past few years; after the death of her brother—Don's son—Kueck had clung to her tightly, trying to maintain the connection, even as he was spiraling down. She had begun to count on him for protection and safety—the kind of things that fathers provide—and she felt that he had done so, albeit in a nonconventional, erratic way. He sometimes showed up with toys for his grandchildren that he had scrounged from the desert—playthings discarded by desert families living off the grid and possibly on the run themselves—but also arriving on occasion with guns, tweaked on various visits, once offering to kill an abusive boyfriend and take the body into the desert, and other times just wanting to hang out, talk, eat, and sleep. The phone calls from Don—three so far—were beginning to make Rebecca feel weird. She was used to his unpredictable behavior; there was even a routine to it. A month before he killed Sorensen, he had visited Rebecca for the last time. "He almost ran over some guys who were working on the driveway," she says months later. "I knew he was doing speed. He slept for a couple of days, and then he was all right." Before he left, he took a few hits of speed from his nasal inhaler. "He was like Charlie Chaplin," she says, recalling her final image of her father. "He was running around and breaking things." But Rebecca figured she'd see him again soon. He needed her, and she needed him; it was a connection between two people who were trying to hold on. And now it was all disappearing. On Day One, when Don called, she didn't know what had happened to Steve Sorensen. On Day Two, she had seen the news and wasn't sure if her father had killed him. She wanted to believe him when he said he didn't because what daughter wants to believe otherwise? By Day Three, she knew he did it—and she knew why. He was never going back to jail, he had told her and others many times, joining a macabre and frightening chorus of graduates of the California prison system, one of the most notorious incarceration operations in the world.

"It was all very weird," she would later say about her communications with her fugitive father. "One day I'm talking to my dad, who's supposed to protect you, and the next day I'm talking to a killer." It would be three days before he called again, and that would begin a series of calls that became Don's final statements.

TENDER GOODNESS

Sit in the mud, my friend, and aspire to the skies!
—Ivan Turgenev, "Enough"

FOR TEN YEARS OR SO, DON'S FAMILY HAD NO CONTACT WITH him. There were occasional letters but that was it and they grew concerned, especially as word of his son's plight began to reach them and they enlisted the aid of a cop to try to track him down. Finally they were able to find him in his tent in the Mojave, and from then on they were back in his life. As much as they tried to keep Don afloat, there was not much anyone seemed to be able to do for his son, Jello. It was clear to all concerned that the teenage boy was in big trouble, sinking deeper into his drug use, enduring a violent household, and finding refuge either on the streets or in the homes of others, such as it was. There was a summer during which Lynne and Peggy had brought Jello to Mobile, Alabama, their hometown, so he could get away from everything, spend time with his grandparents, and possibly learn that things didn't have to be so hard. Of course such knowledge is not acquired easily, and during the period he was visiting his family, it became clear that there was only one way to fix this boy—his father.

But could two broken people save each other? It had happened before, just as prison inmates are coupled up with abandoned dogs or wild horses and then remake each other and form a new kind of union. It would take some coaxing on the part of Don's sisters; he had not seen his kids in ages. Told to stay away by his ex-wife, figuring that they were being taken care of by her new husband, and quite possibly okay with not having the responsibility of being a parent, he had not really tried to make contact. At some point, with his daughter Rebecca's help, the idea of a reunion was broached. It happened at Bob's Big Boy in Riverside, the town where the kids were living; considering that Don was on a budget and that kids love burgers, it was a natural choice.

But it wasn't just the burgers that made the place a favorite for kids; there was the Big Boy himself, a giant-sized icon with big blue eyes and tousled hair, wearing red-and-white checked overalls and carrying a cheese-topped double-decker on a platter, presiding over the entrance to every Big Boy in the chain, Bob's or otherwise, ever since 1936, when the enterprise had been dreamed up, reportedly in response to a hefty six-year-old who would sweep the floor at what was then called Bob's Pantry in exchange for giant burgers. Goofy and embarrassing or ironic and collectible by today's standards, the cheerful sentinel served an era well, welcoming all the hungry souls who dined under its shadow and providing giant platters of burgers and fries that led to a moment of satisfaction. And too, there were other delights, such as the Scrammy Hammy, which appealed to families on a budget, and items such as ice cream sundaes and shakes were favored by children, and it wasn't unusual for families across America, during a certain time in our history, if they were within range of a franchise, to have a weekly outing to Bob's Big Boy, or a Big Boy restaurant attached to another name, an event that was a gift from parents to kids and one that is remembered by children who once went there—now grown-up with children of their own—with a certain amount of yearning, and who sometimes post their memories in chat rooms and other forums, lamenting the lack of a Big Boy in their communities, planning reunions at ones that still exist, trying to return to a warp in which the tender goodness listed on Big Boy menus conjured not just desirable food but a state yearned for by all, perhaps defining what went on in certain families or at their own dinner tables, wherever and however those happened to coalesce—and always they return and happily they dine, if only for a moment, under the big eyes of the ever-smiling and contented child who stands guard at the entrance.

In 1992, at the time of the reunion, Jello was eighteen, and Rebecca was twenty. To them, the statue was probably a joke—and one that was especially laugh or cringe-worthy if you were tripping, as Jello often was: "Dude, I looked up and Bob looked evil. . . . His eyes were dripping blood, and I thought he was gonna kill me. . . . Then I went in and ordered eighteen double-deckers. . . . When I couldn't pay, they called the cops." On the other hand, strip away whatever reaction the kids might have had to the place, and you are left with one thing only: both of them needed a father in their lives, and not just any father, but one who would be kind. Their mother accompanied Jello and Rebecca to the reunion. We don't know exactly what the boy thought while sitting there with a father he barely remembered. We do know that he was a pissed-off individual, beyond the usual anger that teenagers harbor and nourish; it was who he was. Given that he was well versed in the literary and poetic rants of his time—Henry Rollins, Kurt Cobain, his friends who poured out their own feelings in lyrics and art and inky glyphs of truth on their own skin—he might have sat there in his Mohawk and leather and chains, cagey behind it all for he was a player, and thought, "You motherfucker, why have you forsaken me? Do you have any idea what my life is like?" And although he did not say those words, his father knew them—although not all of the details, not every episode of abuse and childhood alcoholism, and early encounters with heroin—and it's a fact that he also knew his son's heart and had read his body language right away; he had already been briefed by relatives that his son was a chip off the old block—handsome (a younger twin, really) and charming and funny, and pretending that everything was fine. He made small talk and spoke of his love of rockets, to which the son immediately responded, in a most positive fashion, as boys generally would.

And nor did the daughter say exactly what was on her mind for such moments are fraught—especially for daughters and fathers, so much is riding on them, so unfamiliar is each party with being face to face with so much hurt and betrayal. Yet there they were, in a round booth no less, whose very nature broke down barriers because it was not a square, and she may have hidden behind a menu anyway (for they were large), and she may have made her own kind of chitchat (she remembers only a few details of the encounter), telling her father about boyfriends, accomplishments, plans for her life, possibly holding back tears, pretending like her brother that everything was fine, talking over her brother or at the same time as each hoped and vied perhaps for a crumb of attention from the man they feared might vanish again, and as the attempts at connection were essayed, missed, sort of made, throughout it all, the three of them—father, daughter, son—had a moment that would connect them for the rest of time. And when the heaping platters of tender goodness arrived, the reunited trio ate happily and heartily, although the girl soon lost her appetite, tightening up inside and suddenly vanishing inside of herself.

Other families had gathered around the booths, partaking of Big Boys under the bright lights. At some point, plans were made—

"I want you to come see me in the desert," Father said, or words to that effect. "We'll build rockets. You'll meet my friends the ravens," and then he laughed and spun out some information about the beautiful and brilliant birds, like everything you would want to know and then some, such as information about their wing span and their ability to remember people and places, and how they knew how to make and use tools, and it was clear that they were among his associates. "The desert is an amazing place," he told his kids. "Really, you gotta check it out." Or words to that effect.

The waitress in her cheerleader uniform stopped by and said the dessert specials, and then Father might have told the kids, "Go ahead, get the banana boat! You won't break the bank! Seriously!" and then he flashed a wad of bills, not to impress his children but to show that the meal was not an undue burden for him, for it had been mentioned —or he feared that it was common knowledge inside his family—that he was only working odd jobs and living off a small government check from his disability and that meant he was a pauper, and he did not want to alarm his children. And so they ordered gobs of ice cream and Father did too, for he craved sweets as a result of various drugs that were coursing through his system, and then the waitress delivered the treats, the exclamation point at the end of the sentence, the thing that would seal the deal for all of time, and later, after the coming together of the long-separated threesome, the children would talk about it a lot, but on that very day, when the son had rejoined amigo Chris Smallwood, in whose mother's garage he was then living, the first thing he said was, "Oh my God, dude, I just met my father."

"Hey, dude," Chris replied. "At least you have one."

As it happened, there was another boy, about eight years old, who dined at Bob's Big Boy every month with his family, always looking forward to the adventure—it was a big outing—always ordering a vanilla malt to go with his double-decker and fries, and while it cannot be said for certain, chances are good that he may have been sitting with his mother and father and sisters and brothers at a booth close to Donald Kueck, perhaps even adjacent to, on the day that the Mojave pilgrim treated his son and daughter and ex-wife to a meal. This was Bruce Chase. Now grown up, the slight hint of a smile crosses the lieutenant's face as he recalls his family's weekly outings to the place whose menu offered "tender goodness"—a subject that happened to come up during one of many conversations we had on the patio of a harborside restaurant in LA during the years I was working on this book. For a quick moment, he was back at Bob's, far away from the sheriff's department and the never-ending battles with liars and gangsters and hard-core killers, a young boy again, behind the wraparound shades. And then the conversation returned to other matters, such as the manhunt and the twists and turns on life's road and how it is that some people end up on the side where all the trouble is and how some of them make it worse. "There is such a thing as evil," Chase tells me. "And I believe that in the murder of Deputy Sorensen, it was everywhere."

SHERIFF'S STATION, LAKE LOS ANGELES

Shane, come back.
  —Little boy, *Shane*

THERE COMES A TIME DURING THE COURSE OF A STORY, IF YOU work on it long enough, that information you hadn't expected comes your way. You might have wanted something along the same lines, and possibly had even tried in various ways to get it, whatever "it" was, yet try as you might, it is not to be had, and that's all there is to it. And then one day, things fall into place or you say something that makes someone think of the thing you had been wanting to know for years, only they didn't know you wanted to know it, and there you are, at one more fork in the road.

For some time while working on my book, I had wanted to visit Steve Sorensen's house—not just drive down the unpaved and

remote road in Lake Los Angeles and stop for brief moments of reconnaissance, as I had done at various times since I began working
on this story years ago, but go inside and see where he lived and
worked, walk in his footsteps, get a feel for that part of the Antelope Valley. After all, Donald Kueck had lived nearby, and I wondered if there was any sense of that just from looking south toward
Avenue T. All I knew so far was that the house was a sprawling
Bonanza-style compound fronted by a barrier of oleander hedge and
hurricane fencing, with pine and juniper trees in the front yard.
Not so different from other desert hideaways, but behind the brush
there was much to be learned. I had considered venturing up the
driveway and knocking on the door, but that's something I rarely do
in my work, unless I've been invited or as a last resort. As it turned
out, thanks to a mutual friend, I finally received an invitation from
the woman who had recently bought his house—unsellable and
vacant since shortly after Steve was killed. "A lot of things are just
like they were when Steve lived here," she said when we spoke, and
instantly I was out the door and heading north from LA into the
desert, then east on the 138, aka the Pearblossom Highway, the one
that David Hockney made famous in his desert collage, the two-
lane that is known among some locals as Tweaker Highway.

I looked north as I headed past the ruins of the old commune
at Llano, and wondered if anyone or anything might be hunkered
behind the remaining walls, hiding from the high desert winds and
perhaps preparing to stay for awhile. I knew that beyond that was
Kueck's place, and I wondered if anyone had moved in, maybe a
homeless crew that was drifting from one encampment to the next,
or a squatter who had donned the old size 11 Nikes I had seen
there on one of my trips and then decided to stay awhile. Slowing
down for a few moments, I spotted a couple of dogs making for the
ruins, heads down, panting, crossing the highway shoulder as the
gusts riffled their coats, made nervous by the passing big rigs, wary
like all desert outcasts, moving away from civilization and into

safety. In my rearview mirror they vanished, and then I approached a popular pit stop, the Country Mart in Pearblossom, where Kueck bought his propane, a classic Mojave store that stocks tat mags, sleds in the winter, motocross goggles, and all manner of packaged jerky. I thought about stopping in to purchase an egg salad sandwich (the best ones ever made), but I needed to get to Steve's house, lest the current resident change her mind and cancel my visit. You never know. People get nervous, wonder about letting a stranger into their homes, whether or not what you write will be fair. So I cruised along, skipping food and refreshment, remembering a ringtone I had once heard inside the Country Mart while waiting in line at the cash register. It was "I Drink Alone" by George Thorogood, and a guy in a mullet answered his phone as the lyric "Me and my buddy Weiser" trailed off into the store chatter. It was the best ringtone I have ever heard and one that you would never hear at the lower elevations—a surprise moment of grace and humor that echoed my desert beat and the lives of many who lived there.

Kristie Holaday heard my car as I turned into the dirt driveway, and opened up the gate. I drove in and parked behind a man who was off-loading bales of hay from a pickup for horses in a nearby corral. To my left I immediately spotted a playground in the front yard—a swing set, a slide, and jungle gym—under a towering floodlight that could cast an intense and frightening glow in the dead of night. Months before my visit, I had heard on the grapevine that Steve had readied his front yard for the arrival of his adopted son, setting up the equipment well before the day when the boy could use it. I also knew that as resident deputy, Steve was based in his house, dispatching himself from his own office and protecting it accordingly. But he was also a security freak and increasingly so, since locals in Lake Los Angeles had threatened his life after he tried to shake up the status quo by siding with Hispanic shop owners in their licensing dispute with the county. The front-yard floodlight looked like something from a penitentiary, an odd indicator in a field of child's play that something was amiss. Yet the rest of the yard told a different story, which Kristie had noticed as well when she bought the house in 2004, a year after Steve had been killed. She had been living in Tujunga, a rugged part of Los Angeles but still part of it nonetheless, on the city side of the San Gabriel Mountains. She had been running a rescue center for feral black cats, taking them in for spaying and then releasing them back into the wild. But she yearned for more space, and when her parents left Los Angeles and returned to their native Kansas, she felt a new kind of freedom and found herself longing for horses, which she had had at other times in her life. Every weekend, she would meet with a real estate agent in the Antelope Valley, hoping to find the right place. "The first time I saw all those Joshua trees," she says, "it reminded me of being on the moon." Yet still, she was intrigued and wanted to answer the call, but after looking at houses all over the valley, hadn't found one that she wanted to live in. Just as she was ready to start exploring other areas, the agent reluctantly suggested a big house zoned for equestrian use on an unpaved road in Lake Los Angeles. She was having trouble selling it, she said, and then in general terms explained why. She also explained what Kristie might like about the property—its size (six acres), its house (2,500 square feet with three bedrooms and three bathrooms), its views (wide-open space on all three sides). So Kristie thought she'd take a look; by then, she was mesmerized by that part of the desert—"living here is like being in love with a bad boy," she tells me—and when she saw the property for the first time, with its corrals and scenery, she knew it was a good match. "It was animal-friendly," she says, as we walk the grounds, "and I felt free." It was a feeling that superseded her initial trepidation about living in a house whose owner had been murdered, even though the incident had happened elsewhere.

All around her was wide-open desert land, dotted by creosote and the occasional Joshua tree, running all the way to a vertical expanse of buttes to the east, where the ancients had carried out their ceremonies and sheltered. At the time of her first visit, there were ten dogs living on the property. Christine and her son had moved out shortly after Steve's death, and a family friend was looking after the animals. These were dogs Steve had rescued, finding them during his rounds and taking them in. There was also a goat Steve had saved after a domestic violence call. "When Steve got there, the goat was tied to a tree," Kristie tells me. "He was in bad shape. They were gonna roast him." Four of Steve's dogs are still residents on the day of my visit: Bandy (short for Bandit), a beagle/basset mix who takes off whenever someone is using tools; Dottie, a little Aussie who had been abused; Delta, a shepherd chow mix Steve had found lying in an arroyo; and Lucy, a Queensland Heeler, a desert stray who hopped into Steve's SUV while he was parked near an abandoned meth lab. Bandy and Dottie follow us around the yard, as Kristie points to the cherry, apple, and peach trees Steve had planted, just starting to bear fruit now, in late spring; an old wood-burning stove Steve had placed under an olive tree in the front yard, one of those pieces of desert flotsam and jetsam that make for found art when displayed respectfully and in beauty; a hand-painted sign that said "free weeds—pick your own," and even a few dead trees that had been there for who knows how long. "Steve wouldn't cut them down," Kristie says. "He left them where the birds could land."

Steve and his wife had lived here for a little over two and a half years, buying the large, ranch-style house for $80,000—a desert mansion purchased for a song. From the moment they moved in, Steve had been adding on, remodeling it for Christine up until the time he was killed, installing new cabinets in the kitchen, repainting each wall of the spacious home, shoring up the two fireplaces, finishing everything except for the final touches on an electrified fence, the last security measure in a house whose twenty-seven points of entry he had wired with an intricate alarm system. To this day, Steve's handwritten list of the alarm setup is taped to the pantry door. His handwriting hadn't changed at all since the days when he penned love letters to his high school girlfriend; as a member of possibly the last generation for which legibility was prized, he still had that quaint characteristic known as "good penmanship." The alarm list includes "number 08 Matt's Bed window"—a reference to his son's bedroom. The elaborate alarm system had little to do with Kristie's interest in the house. When she began to get serious about purchasing the house, Kristie was asked to fill out a security questionnaire. "I didn't mind," she tells me. It was common knowledge around Lake Los Angeles that after Steve's death, Christine Sorensen had been getting threats and was careful about whom she might be letting into her life by way of a real estate deal. After Kristie was cleared, she and Christine met at the house to discuss her offer. Because of the improvements, the house was worth much more than what the Sorensens had paid for it, although, because of its history, it was still inexpensive, even by the desert's standards. "I told Christine I wanted to start an animal rescue," Kristie says, "and she was happy that I would keep the house the same way."

It takes time to get used to living alone in a remote area, no matter how much you think you're prepared for it, especially if you are not a hermit, and even if it seems that all of your life, this is where you were headed. But Kristie settled in easily with the four-legged outcasts that came with her new home in the desert, soothed and nurtured by their presence. Once in a blue moon menacing local characters ranged by—meth freaks, drifters, grim pilgrims of one sort or another—and Kristie was thankful to have the dogs as guardians. She quickly added to the ark, taking in cats and parrots, rehabbing a baby owl that had tumbled from its nest, and soon rescued horses joined the family. Her dream of using the corrals that Steve had built was coming to fruition. "These mustangs needed me," she says, pointing to the animals, each with its own story of abuse and neglect. "I know what it's like to hurt."

We continued to walk the grounds, and my heart soared as all manner of doors began to open. "Do you want to see Steve's studio?" she asked, stopping outside a weathered wooden portal and trying to open it. "Yes," I replied, and watched her jimmy the knob, understanding that the story was now writing itself, and thanking whatever spirits were guiding me. "It's locked," she said. "Or broken. I haven't opened it since I moved in." As she went to find the key, I realized that the unexplored studio was like the list of alarm point entries—one of those things having to do with Steve that Kristie could not bring herself to alter; as for why, often such things are not apparent until some time later, if at all, and when the moment of contact does arrive, no words can explain the rite. A few moments later, Kristie returned with a ring of keys, followed by Dottie and Bandi. "These dogs have saved me from being bitten by snakes," she said. "Sometimes there's a Mojave green coiled out here. They bark, and I know something is up." After a few tries, one of the more rusted out keys worked, and in we went, to Steve's world. It was a two-room studio, made of stone, an original part of the structure. The first room was a workspace, with nicely constructed shelves topped with cans of paint thinner and wall paint. Each can was labeled, and hardly any had dripped, although you could tell that they had been opened and used. It was the kind of workroom found in many an American home, and it reminded me of a particularly crowded workroom, a few miles away, in a neighborhood that was more heavily trafficked. Along these suburban routes, the men could generally be found at their respective hobby areas, usually on weekends, laboring on one project or another, retrieving drill bits of varying sizes from carefully maintained lockers, revving up power saws, checking the readings on a level. The particular workroom I was thinking of was labeled "asshole's garage"; the self-deprecating and large sign had been placed on the

guy's garage door, probably by his wife, and whenever he opened it
up, there it was, and there was the guy, fixing one thing or another,
making something better, and judging by the way his house was in
a state of constant renovation, with nicely done embellishments at
that, the guy was hardly an asshole—although perhaps difficult to
deal with after he had polished off a six-pack on a hot summer day
while putting the final touches on a new tool shed. Did Christine
Sorensen chide her husband for maintaining a geeked-out workspace? Why did she leave it in place after Steve's death? Most
everything else was taken, Kristie explained. Yet here was a part of
his legacy—Steve the guy who puttered around and made stuff.
Steve the builder. Steve the Cave Man, after all, not unlike the
ancients who once lived in the mountains to the east, themselves
decorating their dwellings with glyphs and symbols whose mean-
ings we do not really know.

Yet there was more to be learned inside Steve's studio. There
was a second room, and it too had many of his belongings, right
where he had left them. In fact, this was the room where he
worked as a cop, quite possibly the very spot where he had received the final call for help from the man in Llano who was concerned about a local squatter. The call could have come in on his
radio, which was on top of an old cabinet; this was the unit he
would receive dispatches on. Next to it there was a window with a
view of the corrals and the acreage to the east and north. "He
liked being out here near the animals," Kristie said. "And the
land." Every dawn he would come here to watch the sun rise over
the desert. It was indeed the kind of new-beginnings view that
only the desert delivers, the one that's visible only in the timeless
time, and now, in the mid-afternoon, we both admired the vista,
yet one more Mojave wonder in which the sun played across the
rocks and the sand and the creosote in a way that would never
leave you. "I don't know why I haven't used this studio," Kristie
says, and then she left to tend to the animals. I paused to try to

understand the moment, and realized that I was now inside Steve's tomb—without the physical presence of the man who belonged here—but with certain sacred objects of his life. I had seen the things that linked him to the act of building, an elemental activity that is so visible in the wide-open expanse of the desert, with its housing tracts emerging from the womb on the horizon and men in their driveways hammering and sawing. And now, here was more evidence of Steve's desire to ruminate, kick back (to the degree that a man like him could do such a thing), and let something else take over his body.

And then, as I stood and soaked up the feeling of the studio, there came the thing I was looking for. Actually it was the thing behind the thing, for I did not know that it existed. Against a wall in the carefully kept hideaway was an old hotplate with a coffee warmer on top. The warmer still had signs of use, desiccated coffee rings on the bottom, perhaps from coffee that Steve had made on the morning of his last call. I didn't see a grinder like the one he had left with his old roommate in Hermosa Beach; I figured that he ground his coffee in the kitchen, from beans that were kept in the refrigerator, and then brought the fresh pot to this studio, where he placed it on the warmer. On a shelf above the hotplate there were six or seven mugs—a few were cracked and they too had coffee rings. There was a chair at a small worktable, and I sat down and took in the view through the window, as Steve did every morning according to friends, a stunning sight in which the giant rock formations to the east filled the sky. I imagined the vanished deputy drinking his brew—"cowboy coffee" it was now called by purveyors of the old West—as he surveyed his kingdom, his beat. The formations were the Three Sisters Buttes, a region in the Antelope Valley known primarily to geologists, local pilots and hikers, and other aficionados of the terrain, including the sisters at Mount Carmel and Donald Charles Kueck. I now realized, as I looked south, that he lived several hundred yards away, if that.

Each morning, his friends and family members had told me long ago, he gazed at the buttes too. Over the years, as I followed this trail, I realized it was the same sight as the one beheld each dawn by Steve Sorensen. Don himself had three sisters, and in his last few years, they had come to his aid, and no doubt the name of those rocks had particular resonance for him, although we do not know if in fact that name had registered for him in such a way, and in any case few among us would not have been taken by the extreme beauty and the sacred thing that they manifested and conferred. On the day I visited Deputy Steve Sorensen's house, I sat in his chair and gazed at the buttes, and imagined that quite possibly, on the very morning of the fatal encounter, both men might have contemplated those buttes and their splendor, for each loved every elemental aspect of the desert, especially as it became a new place with every infinitesimal turn of Earth's axis and the ensuing shift in light, each perhaps raising a cup to his lips at the same time, savoring a favorite beverage, home-brewed or water from a spigot caught in cupped hands, and perhaps as the sun's rays spilled across the holy vista before them, each was filled with gratitude and awe as they prepared to embark on their fateful day, even as they were entangled in notes of a minor key and beyond shaking them off.

On the day that the house sale was completed, Kristie remembers standing at the front door as something unspoken passed between her and Christine. "The person who was responsible for the whole thing had been murdered," she says. "Now I would be the caretaker. It was very emotional." Christine handed her the keys and then got in her car and prepared to drive away from the house that Steve had renovated for his new family. Her son, Matt, was in the car's baby seat. "Where's Daddy?" he was saying, as Kristie had heard him say on other visits to the house. "Home?" Christine went to comfort her son and then drove away, not looking back or waving, torn up about leaving the animals behind, and heading out of Lake Los Angeles.

Ghost on a Bike

"So you never wanted a regular life?"
"What the fuck's that? Barbeques and ballgames?"
—Vincent Hanna and Neil McCauley, *Heat*

ON THE EVENING OF THE THIRD DAY OF THE MANHUNT, THE SKY
was clear, and the waxing three-quarter moon, eight days away
from being full, cast a bright light across the Antelope Valley, illuminating the Joshua trees and the greasewood and the cholla in
a way that defined them well. If you were sitting on top of the
Three Sisters Buttes and had a good eye, you would have spotted
a man on a bike. From the way it wobbled, the bike appeared to
be rickety and old, or maybe it was just because the man had difficulty pedaling. He was heading east, across a dirt road, toward
the buttes, then turned north and headed toward a group of dilapidated sheds. Next to the sheds was another house, a well-kept,
single-story, wood-frame house, with a driveway that was swept

clean, a basketball net over the garage door, and some kids' toys in the yard. Between the complex of sheds and the main house was a tree, a mesquite tree, noteworthy because few trees grow in this area, and this one was large and flourishing. There were lights on in the house, and inside it was a family, a Hispanic couple and six of their nine kids. The mother was a cleaning lady, employed at the thrift shop of the Twin Lakes Community Church, the one where Steve's friend John Wodetzki was the pastor. She knew Steve well; he frequented the thrift shop and purchased household items such as toasters and fans, redistributing them to needy residents of Lake Los Angeles. She was aware of the fact that Steve had been killed earlier that week, although she did not watch television regularly and had not seen all of the ensuing coverage. At 10 that evening, the man on the bike pedaled up toward the sheds and hopped off, laying the bike down or propping it against a wall. She recognized the man as an associate of C. T. Smith, who lived in one of the sheds on the property. He was carrying an assault rifle. Afraid, she stepped away from the blinds. For the second time that week, Donald Kueck walked into his buddy's place and asked for a favor. "Man, I'm hungry," he said. Then he gave Smith $10 worth of food stamps. "Get me some food, would you?" he asked, and then told his friend to put it in an old bus in the sands nearby. Smith agreed, and then Kueck asked for water. A little while later he picked up the rifle and left, riding into the night, pedaling hard, we can imagine, riding faster, alive with H_2O, faster now, taking off, imagining that he was levitating, out of sight, and even out of mind he might have thought—his own mind, his own joke, *Fuck off world, I'll see your manhunt, and I'll raise you with this*, now entering the jet stream and flying through the night, vanishing like a raven.

DAY FOUR

ROCKET BOYS AND THE ANARCHY VAN

We stand today on the edge of a New Frontier—the frontier of the 1960s. . . . Can we carry through in an age where we will witness . . . a race for mastery of the sky and the rain, the ocean and the tides, the far side of space, and the inside of men's minds? That is the question of the New Frontier.

> —John F. Kennedy, nomination acceptance address, Democratic National Convention, Memorial Coliseum, Los Angeles, July 15, 1960

There is nothing wrong with your television set . . . We will control the horizontal. We will control the vertical . . . You are about to experience the awe and mystery which reaches from the inner mind to . . . The Outer Limits.

> —The Outer Limits, opening narration, 1963–1965

Sometime after their reunion, Don began visiting Jello at the Smallwoods' house in Riverside, driving in occasionally and staying overnight, joining the castaways at Virginia's table and partaking of the loaves and fishes that Mrs. Smallwood always managed to provide. One day she convinced Don that it was time for him to be a grown up; Jello needed his dad and after all, although Jello called her mom like everyone else did, she wasn't his parent and it was time for them to live together as father and son. So Don took Jello back to the desert, and a week or two later Jello returned. He missed his friends, he said, and really, the whole scene. But the connection took in some way, for a few months later, he decided he wanted to spend more time with Don, and he headed back to Llano. He got a ride from his friend Mike Cazares; at seventeen Mike had recently started driving and, to commemorate his new mobile status, had fixed up his truck. The two had met in high school, although given the tribal nature of things, they were not a likely pair. Mike was different from the others who populated Jello's circle. He was not a punk or a metalhead or even a surfer. He was a rude-boy reggae guy, he recalls, the only reggae guy in town. He rode a Vespa. He called himself Rough the Mike, and he had a band called 96 Degrees, after the hit song recorded by the well-known reggae outfit Third World. With his ability to play bass, melodica, and percussion, Mike soon became a close friend of the three amigos. He jammed with them at gigs around town or in the Smallwoods' garage, where they put on shows and charged a small fee, and Chris Smallwood's younger sister, Amanda, served as a personal roadie, helping them with publicity, sound checks, and beer runs. Jello had told Mike strange and grand tales about his father. There were fables about his time in San Francisco during the hippie years, and one of them involved ingesting the crystal ball used to make the acid that Ken Kesey wrote about in *The Electric Kool-Aid Acid Test*. From then on he had seen only patterns, and that was why he had to live in the desert. There was another story about Don being a rocket scientist from NASA. Everybody was accustomed to Jello's overblown stories, but they were also part of his charisma. In this case, since they all had to do with his father, and few of Jello's friends had one, they were excited about the prospect of one of their own forging such an alliance, especially with a father who sounded like a larger-than-life version of themselves.

On the day Mike drove Jello out of town, they piled into his truck along with Mike's girlfriend, intrigued by the idea that they were about to meet a mythical figure. They traveled west on the 60 leaving Riverside and then hooked up with the 15, the route that takes you through the desert and toward Barstow and its vast discount shopping dungeons, and beyond, into Baker—home of "the world's largest thermometer"—and then Las Vegas. At some point Mike noticed a foul odor. "What's that onion smell?" he asked, and then looked over and saw Jello holding his arm out the window. Mike realized it was Jello's armpit. The boy hardly ever bathed. "Dude, that's nasty," Mike said, and Jello laughed and shrugged it off. Jello's friends were used to his poor hygiene, and they knew that the slovenliness was part of his general shtick. Sloppy rocker, the boy your parents hate, punk. And it worked; the kid was a serious ladies' man, often hooking up with strippers, models, older women, all manner of babes. They got high with him and gave him money and drugs. They took care of him and got to hang out with a bad boy. Regardless of his stench, or maybe because of it, Jello had that thing that women wanted, and to this day, his friends are amazed. "I thought he would have cleaned up for his father," Mike says now. "I don't know why I thought that. He didn't clean up for anyone." And there he was, heading for the high Mojave, in his Mohawk, leathers, and Sid Vicious padlocked chain.

The friends turned off at the Cajon Pass, a heavily trafficked mountain throughway that was once an old Indian trail. Then they drove west on the 138, past a stunning formation called Mormon Rocks, so named for the pilgrims who had followed a prophet's call and trekked into the San Bernardino Mountains, looking for the Promised Land. Following directions that Don had given to Jello at the reunion, when they got to Palmdale, they turned at Avenue T and followed it until it became dirt and then continued into territory that was marked by a certain rusted-out truck from the 1950s and then a particular mailbox where you were supposed to make a right. They drove around in circles for awhile and then finally found a camper shell on blocks and some old vans. It was Don's home.

It was late in the afternoon, and Mike, Jello, and Mike's girlfriend got out of the truck and began walking toward the camper. Mike immediately noted a strange thing: Don was sitting "Indian style" in front of it, meditating. There were squirrels on his body. "Dude, there's a squirrel on your shoulder," Mike thought, and then Don got up, realized that his son was among the trio, and started to weep. "I haven't seen you," he said, embracing his son. After the awkwardness of the moment had passed, Don showed his guests around, happy to welcome Jello and his friends into his desert kingdom. As they walked the land, Don pointed to the things he had built. There was a well a few yards from his trailer. And there were many others, scattered across the desert. "See," Don said, pulling back a plastic sheet on one of them. It was about fourteen feet deep and you could climb down on a ladder. At the bottom pot plants were growing. As they continued walking the desert that day, and over time, on other visits, Don talked of distance in clicks—military terminology. "He'd look at the mountains," Mike recalls, "and tell you how many clicks away the wells were."

During that first visit, Jello told his father he wanted to stay with him. It was a decision he had been considering for awhile now, but when Jello caught the lay of the land, it was a done deal. Out there he could do all the drugs he wanted. He could live for free and make music. Maybe even get to know his dad. Don, a man used to living alone and valuing his privacy, was torn. Could he handle having a full-time resident on his property? Beyond that, could he handle his son, who was clearly having problems? But behind the trepidation, he was elated. Out in Llano, the two of them could get to know each other. He could make up for lost time, maybe even be a good father. There were things he wanted to teach his son, and now here he was, ready to learn. Or so it seemed at the time.

So father and son agreed and the kid made the move. By then Don was living on the new property his sisters had purchased for him. There was an old primered van and Jello moved in. It was parked over a well, about a hundred feet from his father's. Father and son fixed it up, hanging curtains on the windows and rigging a shower area outside. The shower had a curtain and a bag of water that was warmed by the sun. On one side of the camp, they installed an outhouse. Jello began calling his new pad "the anarchy van," painting the word on the outside and hanging a black flag. The word was very much in vogue then; in fact it came right out of his scene—all of the artists and musicians and renegades who were shaking things up in places like Riverside, Portland, and Seattle, taking on modern empires and raging against the machine. The philosophy dovetailed nicely with the way Don lived and thought, a dressed-up (or down) punk version of "No trespassing."

Among Jello's friends, the anarchy van became infamous. They would come and hang out in it, pulling the curtains in the hot sun, tilting the radio downward into the well and then climbing a ladder to the bottom. With the music blasting, they would align themselves with the curvature of the well and lie there for hours, drinking wine and consuming other substances, taking the high up or down. "It was, 'Fuck you, this is my hole,'" Mike Cazares remembers. On several occasions, Don would join them, although since he was over six feet, there wasn't all that much room. Once down there, he would get high too, generally on the pain pills he

ingested regularly. Many times Jello was down in the well by himself,
steering clear of the extreme heat, playing the guitar all day long.

As the weeks went by, Jello's friends continued to visit, enchanted by the strange kingdom Don had conjured and learning
more about the man himself. If you were in or near Don's pad,
there was static and chatter and codes coming from the police
scanner, which was always on. Sometimes he used it to communi-
cate with friends. Every now and then a biker would come by,
and Don would meet him at his mailbox. Mike would think,
"Whoa, look at this rocker." He figured Don was picking up a
speed delivery, but it was never discussed. Sometimes he was ex-
ceptionally dressed and carrying a bottle of wine. "I'm going to
see this lady," he'd say. "She does exceptional metal work." It was
a classic desert ID, not meant to be cryptic, offered to tell the
truth by way of what was important without invading anyone's
privacy. But no one ever saw Don with "this lady," or any other
woman, or if Jello did, he never mentioned it to his friends. They
figured there must have been a girlfriend somewhere, at some
point, because Don—progenitor of Jello—was himself charming
and attractive and, unlike his son, clean and neat. He bathed regularly and made a point of always keeping his Fu Manchu rolled up
and tucked under his chin. His camper shell wasn't exactly a chick
magnet, but it was orderly and without dirt or grunge, reflecting a
resident who cared about how things look. For a man who shunned
company, Don was in fact kind of vain. At some point, it turned out
that he did have friends—male ones at least. A couple of times Don
took the boys to meet them. For instance, there was a guy out in
the desert somewhere who had two double-wides parked side by
side. Between them was a chair suspended by wires from a ceiling.
Don would climb up into it, cover his eyes, and trip, hanging there
for hours. There were also some musicians—gnarly old hippies—
who lived in a compound nearby. One day Don and the boys went
to hang out, and they jammed all afternoon. Don was proud of his

son, the musician, and happy to introduce him to friends. Yet having round-the-clock company, and a land-mate no less, soon made him feel cramped and trapped, aggravating his general condition and amping up weird behavior.

For all of Don's meditation and communion with nature and dedication to being a free spirit, he was often hyper and intense, and it seemed to some of Jello's friends that something else was always on his mind. To Mike, it was as if he felt hunted, or haunted maybe, or both. Occasionally he talked about a cop and some past history, and he complained about a squatter who was hassling him. At his place on Avenue T, he had constructed various subterranean hideouts—one of which cops had found on the first day of the manhunt. All around the edge of his land was a labyrinth, largely consisting of burrows, about five feet deep and four to six feet wide, with entrances of about three feet in diameter. Some of them were linked, and had adjacent rooms with their own entrances and exits, and one of them led to the airstrip on Black Butte Road. Inside some of the tunnels were blankets, and you could stand up inside them. One of them had an air duct vent, and another had a periscope made out of rocket parts. With its attached mirror, it provided a 360-degree view of the desert. The burrows reminded Mike of the holes in the river washes of Riverside where the wild boar lived, emerging every now and then to freak out derelicts who lived there too, sometimes ending up as their dinner.

However unconventional the scene, together Don and Jello were becoming little boys again, running around in the open space, having deep talks, watching the stars, exploring the land, building things, and blowing them up. True to Don's invitation at Bob's Big Boy, they made and launched rockets together, and pictures of the two of them together at that time portray a happy father and son, admiring their latest creation—a three-foot rocket ready to blast off right in their own backyard. For Don, being in the desert and making rockets was a lifelong dream, having come of age with the country's space program, imprinted with dazzling moments of exploration and adventure. For him, the moon walk wasn't a Michael Jackson dance but a monumental thing that happened in 1969, when an American spaceship landed on the moon and astronaut Neil Armstrong stepped out and uttered the line that marked an era: "One small step for man, one giant leap for mankind." Friends say that Kueck was well-versed in the history of space travel, having followed it since he was seven years old, when the Russians became the first of nations to enter space, or "outer space" as it was then called, in a rocket dubbed *Sputnik*. The gravity-defying vehicle broadcast its signal around the world, and in classrooms across America, children sat and listened to the eerie static and high-pitched wheeees and other assorted odd sounds that were coming through from another dimension.

In a way, the dream of flight started with dry lakebeds of the desert, those great prehistoric wastes that seem to issue a challenge: "Hey you!" they call. "Come have a party! Fly me!" For America, from the beginning of the twentieth century through the present, many private citizens and a parade of military institutions have come to see the wide-open space of the west, and in particular the Antelope Valley, as a place where you can test limits. In fact the Antelope Valley has long been known as Aerospace Valley. In 1902, an early Antelope Valley pioneer set the first of many land-speed records on Rosamond Dry Lake by whizzing across the sands on a sailboat with wheels. From 1926 to 1933 new records were established there by trailblazers piloting rocket-like capsules on four wheels. Later, through a series of land acquisitions, Muroc Dry Lake—backwards spelling for Corum, the family that first homesteaded there—became Edwards Air Force Base, the second biggest such base in the world. From there, in October 1947, Captain Chuck Yeager broke the sound barrier when he flew the Bell X-1 rocket research airplane at a speed of Mach 1.06, after it was dropped from a B-29 mother ship over the Mojave. Yeager and the other flyboys of the desert came to be known as having "the right stuff," and it was a thing that was fueled by wide-open space. Over the years there would come many more aerospace feats and break-throughs above the sands where they were dreamed up, and many of the men and women who worked to make those dreams a reality came to live in the Antelope Valley city of Lancaster—later, the command center for Deputy Sheriff Steve Sorensen and his remote desert outpost, and the place where his loss would be mourned by thousands.

Other than the fact that Kueck didn't have a college degree, couldn't hold down a regular job, and wasn't interested in working for anyone, he fit right into this region of engineering geniuses. Quite simply, he loved rockets, and one of the things he did in the desert was build them, set them off, and track them. It was a thing he prided himself on, a trait he cultivated, a way that he tapped— perhaps unconsciously—into his Teutonic heritage, and connected with his family; after all, his grandfather had served with Kaiser Wilhelm's army, and it was Werner Von Braun who had invented the rocket, the V-2 for the German army in the 1930s, before sur-rendering to the Allies and employing his signature skills in the development of America's space program. Out in the Mojave, Don had deployed his own method of space exploration, making so-phisticated projectiles out of desert treasure, with Jello and his friends serving as apprentices. For instance, he would find hollow metal fenceposts at various locations across the desert, some at the many piles of flotsam and jetsam that were wedged on the sides of washes, deposited there by flash floods, along with all manner of other junk—old refrigerators, old sofas, scrapbooks, pots and pans, the remnants of who knows how many lives that had been swept away long before the weather took what was left. Sometimes the fenceposts came from old homesteads built during the Depression, their perimeters still bearing that rare item of value that attracted desert scavengers, something made of metal that could be sold or traded, or hammered out and flattened into a patch for a leaky roof, pressed into service as a pipe or funnel, or just something that was shiny and dressed up a pack rat's trailer. "I collect fence posts. Why I don't know" would not be an unusual comment for a local to make, and his or her brothers and sisters might keep it in mind, knowing where to go if they ever needed a post for whatever reason. Don had acquired a number of these posts on junk runs by himself or with Jello, and whenever he wanted to launch a rocket, he'd add wings and tips and make other adjustments, and then he and his son and sometimes Jello's friends would pile into the Lincoln and head to a launch site.

Once there, they'd load the rocket with fuel, arming it with a homemade mix of propellant or attaching M-80 firecrackers. The fuel might be a concoction of sugar, sulfur, potassium nitrate, and water, or sometimes Don would use sulfuric acid or nitroglycerin, which he probably got in trades with friends and associates; the desert is one big Kmart—whatever you need is there, either out in the open or through the right person—and whatever Don required to construct his own space-bound capsules, he found. And ever the innovator, sometimes he tried unconventional recipes, such as mixing a fuel of peanut shells and some mystery fluid, lighting the liquid with a blowtorch, and then standing back to watch the rocket take off from El Mirage dry lakebed and soar toward the next county. These launches were sophisticated, mind you; he kept elaborate maps of where his rockets were launched, noted wind-speed measurements (critical for any launch but especially in the Antelope Valley, where the winds often gusted up to sixty or seventy miles per hour, shifting direction and speed at higher elevations), wrote down where each rocket landed (they had self-deploying parachutes so they'd return safely), and studied all of the charts later, making adjustments in his rockets and type of launch accordingly. Like any dedicated scientist, he saved the records, and they had a special place in a certain compartment in his trailer, stashed away where they would be difficult to find, lest a fellow scavenger enter his pad when he was gone and make off with all of his secrets. Interestingly, gripped by the same fear, von Braun made sure that the blueprints for the top-secret V-2 were not destroyed by the SS at the end of the war, hiding them in an abandoned mine shaft in the Harz Mountains of northern Germany.

This connection with serious science was a thing Don was so proud of that he made a point of telling friends and relatives that he was out there hobnobbing with local engineers, comparing notes on rocketry and attendant matters. To some of these friends who had seen him in action with his inventions and those selfsame engineers, he seemed at his happiest in those moments, never more so than when he was designing and launching his own vehicles, from his own personal test sites in the nether regions of the Mojave, sometimes right at the perimeter of Edwards Air Force Base. Perhaps the launches near the base were a joke, a way to tell the man to "Fuck off, I got my own rockets bro, and I know my rights, motherfuckers. Where does it say in the Constitution that I can't set these off?" But also perhaps the launches near the base were a way to get close to the kind of life he could never have—one of respectability and acknowledgment by his equals—or possibly even a way to commune with his father, an Air Force pilot who had died some time after Don had left home. For many years, Don had told friends he missed him.

But it was through rockets that he tried reaching not just for the past, but for the future, his own son. The movie *October Sky* tells a true and similar story about a father and son who connect this way, although it is the boy who initiates the journey. In the case of Don and Jello, the trajectory was the reverse, with the father introducing the son to rockets, hoping to show him a way out. The act of guidance was witnessed one day when a sister of Don's paid him a visit, elated to see her brother and her nephew toiling away on a new projectile, putting the final touches on quite an impressive-looking missile, loading it into a launcher that Don had fashioned from his cache of desert junk. "Okay, hold that pose," she said, raising her camera, and then father and son did so, holding the pose as if they belonged that way, next to each other and leaning against the rocket and grinning away. At this moment they were boys forever, igniting fires, watching things fly, attaching the past to a thing of their own making, and sending it into the endless sky of the Antelope Valley. But in a few years, their relationship would crash and burn, and then some time later, so would Jello. Soon after that Edwards would join the hunt for Donald Charles Kueck.

Some of Jello's friends blame his demise on "a chick named Samantha." A young woman who worked at a record company in Los Angeles, she had connections with hot new bands such as the Red Hot Chili Peppers and Nirvana and was passing out demo tapes in clubs around So Cal, including Spanky's, which is where she met Jello. The pair struck up a friendship, and the three amigos remember that it was heroin-based. She was beautiful, bisexual, and a junkie—and she got Jello back into shooting it. In fact, Jello spent the night with Samantha before he moved out to the desert, getting high on smack—and he was floating on the high when he embraced his father after stepping out of his friend's truck. From then on, he was never able to shake the habit. But of course the problem was much more complicated. There wasn't a drug he hadn't tried or wouldn't. When he wasn't down in the well getting blasted, he was above ground getting into trouble. For instance, there was the time he either ate or smoked some jimson weed—his friends don't remember the manner of ingestion, but it happened, and there were serious consequences. Jimson weed—or datura—is a deadly plant with beautiful white flowers native to the desert. When Don would guide Jello through the terrain, he had pointed out the various plants and their functions—you could make a healing poultice out of creosote or sage, just as the Indians did—and he made a point of showing Jello jimson weed, telling him not to eat it and even giving him a pamphlet about its dangers. But every son rebels, even the son of a rebel, and so he consumed the plant and went blind—a strange echo of Don's own story about having gone blind in San Francisco after an acid trip. Afraid to go outside, he stayed in the van for two days, in his leather jacket, Total Chaos T-shirt, and combat boots, playing his tapes and listening to the radio while Don brought him food and water. When his sight returned, he emerged from the van.

But from then on, Don's early concern about sharing his kingdom was confirmed, even though his roommate was his son. Yes, they had hooked up over a couple of things—being boys together, running around in the desert, setting off rockets—but the arrangement just wasn't working. Jello was one pissed-off kid; although he was sometimes too high to act out, the very act of getting fucked up and hanging out in a well for hours on end was not a good sign, and when he was not high, he was raging, lost in rants about cops, society, the world. Later, one of the amigos suggested that the two had been feeding off of each other's anger. During his time in the desert, Jello had told Don about what happened to him in jail—how the cops had thrown him into a tank filled with skinheads, doing so, in his view, so he would get a beating. It was around the same time, oddly, that Kueck and Sorensen had their encounter on the road. Together father and son were a team united against rules and regulations, pissed off at the man, never talking about their own choices in life—or if they did, not telling anyone about it—and for sure, they did not make the big moves necessary to correct them. There in the sands of Llano, they festered and mulled things over, convinced that the deck was stacked against them. Their paranoia was nurtured by the relentless sun and an endless cocktail of drugs, sprouting new shoots all the time. Together they had reached a wall.

For refuge and advice, Don turned to fellow parent Virginia Smallwood. He would get in his old Lincoln or one of his Dodges and head into Riverside, stopping en route at his daughter's, spending a day or two with her and her children before heading to the Smallwoods'. There, in modern civilization, he'd have a home-cooked meal, again joining the others who had come in for a moment of grace, and he'd speak of his son's problems as well as philosophical matters and religious practices and he iterated the names of ancient warriors. The kids who gathered round Mrs. Smallwood's table regarded him as an old soul who wandered in from some mysterious place, an elder whose mind was operating on some other level. When the night wound down, he'd watch television sometimes, amazed at the number of channels that were available as he flipped through them, accustomed to receiving only the Home Shopping Network out in the desert. On many occasions he slept over, on the couch or on the floor, which he preferred, because of the pain from his old back injury. By all accounts, he liked having the contact with what was becoming a kind of extended family, even though the situation with his own son was a mess. On several occasions, Don had resorted to locking Jello in the van, to get him to sober up. "I don't know what to do," he'd say. "He's out of control." Chris and his sister, Amanda, commiserated and agreed, and so did their mother. She was okay with the fact that Jello had decided not to hang around her house or kids any more, hoping this new relationship with his father would work out. But Jello's friends had watched his descent into harder and harder drugs over the years, and once he had gone down the heroin road, they figured the game was over. Mrs. Smallwood was never one to give up on the lost kids of the Inland Empire, but even she had reached the end of her rope. "You need to man up," she would tell Don. "It's time for some tough love."

There came the day that he gave it—not in the way she meant, like organizing an intervention or getting him into rehab—but give it, he did. After all, when you got down to it, he just liked being alone. He was not cut out to be a hands-on parent, whatever that meant. He wanted to dream and think and putter whenever he felt like it. Yes, it was one thing to hang out with your son and watch the stars or launch rockets, but having to deal with all of the fucking problems was just not part of the program. "You can't live here," he said to his son one day. Where and in what manner he said it we do not know. Maybe he had joined his son in the well, waiting for a break in the music, smoking a joint with him, and then as the high kicked in and calmed them, he told his son that things weren't working out. At that point, maybe Jello passed out in a drug haze, or maybe Don climbed back out of the well and cranked up the music as a fuck you. Or maybe they were having an argument, and that's when Don said it. At some point toward the end of their time in the desert, Don had once again locked Jello in the anarchy van, trying to keep him from running around the desert and scoring drugs. Jello was stranded there, detoxing presumably, with only the well as a refuge. After a few days, Don let him out. There was a fight, and the reunion was over. Jello had been out there for a year. He left the desert and headed for Seattle, where he could have all the heroin he wanted. And Don retreated back into his own private world, with one less fetter keeping him there.

A Break in the Case

Sleep with one eye open
Grippin' your pillow tight.
    —Metallica, "Enter Sandman"

BY THE MORNING OF TUESDAY, AUGUST 5, THE LOS ANGELES County Sheriff's Department issued a special bulletin, and Kueck's face began appearing everywhere. WANTED FOR MURDER OF DEPUTY SHERIFF it said in red lettering, and it showed two booking photos of the fugitive taken at a bust two years earlier. Some cops wondered why the flyer hadn't been issued earlier, but in any case here it was, up on the "Most Wanted" boards in bus stations and post offices, and broadcast throughout the day on reports of breaking news. For friends of Kueck's who had never seen the photograph, it was shocking: the handsome hermit with the craggy face and the Fu Manchu now looked like the man law enforcement said he was—a killer. "Suspect Kueck should be considered ARMED AND

DANGEROUS," warned the flyer, and then listed his personal stats and the names and phone numbers of Sergeant Joe Purcell and Detective Phil Guzman, the lead investigators.

Tips continued to pour in, and it was around that time that Purcell and Guzman got a call from C.T. Confirming their belief that Kueck was in the area and that it was only a matter of time before someone dropped a dime on him, he told them that he was a buddy of Don's and that he had seen him twice that week. The cops immediately left LASD headquarters in Commerce and headed for Palmdale in an unmarked car, meeting C.T. at a secret location in the desert. The ex-con looked frazzled and scared. He did not appear to be high, although one of his busts had been for narcotics. He told them about Kueck carrying two guns when he had dropped by on the day of Steve's murder, and also that Kueck had asked for food and water. C.T. was concerned that Kueck would return; since C.T. was wanted on a parole violation, Kueck figured that he would not tell law enforcement he had been there, lest C.T. be busted as an accomplice or for aiding and abetting a fugitive. That would have been a third strike; in the California penal code, it meant game over. But Kueck was desperate now, with his face plastered everywhere; "he might kill me," C.T. told cops, and take off again. There was also another angle; a $25,000 reward had been posted, and C.T. wouldn't say no to a piece of it. For law enforcement, things were falling into place, and with C.T.'s help, they started planning how to take down Kueck if and when he returned to the remote desert compound.

Meanwhile, investigators were working a different aspect of the case. Many of the tips that were pouring in involved tunnels. We do not know if these tips were coming from people who knew about the burrows around Kueck's property, but we do know that some of them were coming from those who knew the Mojave. The tipsters were convinced that the fugitive hermit had gone to ground, because that's the only way to survive extreme desert heat during the daytime. Given the fact that Kueck had been surfacing at night and vanished during the day, investigators came to embrace this view as well. The problem was what to do about it. Where were the tunnels? How would they flush him out? On the other hand, the tips about tunnels were coming in so fast that they became a joke among law enforcement. They knew Kueck could have been hiding out in a mine shaft, but come on—a whole system?

By Day Four of the manhunt, it was becoming clear that Donald Charles Kueck was no match for law enforcement teams trained for street battles. Locals knew that the longtime student of desert survival, buddy to four-legged and winged creatures of the Mojave, could easily have made adaptations that would help him remain underground for a long period of time. Clearly, they reasoned, he had entered the Mojave tunnel system, resting in coolness and shade by day, possibly finding water that was trapped in underground seeps, regaining his diminishing strength, and then emerging at dusk and traveling through darkness like all desert creatures in temperatures that will not destroy them. Where he entered we do not know, but sometime on the fourth day, it appears that he—or someone else wanting to leave a message—ended up back at his trailer. Perhaps he had traversed a labyrinth that ran for miles or, more likely, made his way close to home above ground, in the dark, and then had gone to ground in the tunnels that coursed near his home. Hunkered in a cavern, he might have used his homemade periscope for the very thing he had long expected—that he would be hunted down—extending it carefully and methodically, lest anyone spot movement, surveying the area, deciding that no one was there and proceeding with his plan. In the morning hours of the fourth day, investigators returned to his trailer for another search. There a message awaited them—a rattlesnake nailed to the front door. Once again, the man who was now starring on "America's Most Wanted" had slipped through a massive dragnet, and on the fourth day of the manhunt, he was telling cops to come and get him.

At sundown on Day Four, some residents of Lake Los Angeles were gathering in a local park. They remembered all of the times Deputy Sorensen had helped them, on good calls and bad. The American and California state flags were at half-staff, and town officials were standing behind a bank of microphones. In the crowd were about twenty or thirty people of all ages, races, and manner of desert persuasions. They held candles and sang "Amazing Grace" and told stories about their local protector. This was the first of several memorials in Steve's honor, and in some ways, because it was the first and therefore the most spontaneous, it held a certain kind of raw energy and some of it was about kids. There at the front of the crowd stood Miss Lake Los Angeles and her court, a pretty teenage girl with hair in a flip, solemnly facing . . . what exactly? For sure, it was her first such experience; a cop had not been killed in the line of duty in this area since 1992, despite its reputation as a rough place. Now here she was, representing the town in the aftermath of carnage that surprised even veteran cops. Perhaps it was an obligated public appearance, maybe her first, but in any case, it was a tribute to Steve, who had sunk roots in Lake Los Angeles for its beauty and chance to start over.

As dusk rolled across the big sky of the Antelope Valley, and prayers were murmured at his memorial, the hunt for Kueck became ever more fevered. Police vehicles from other jurisdictions were still racing to the scene. Hearing reports of sightings on their scanners, some would quickly turn around and try to head in the opposite direction, gunning their engines when their cars became mired in washes or roadside shoulders and running out of gas. In online chat rooms, locals were reporting that some cops were simply abandoning their cars and heading into the desert on foot, trying to help out in any way they could, carrying no water or supplies and not dressed for a desert pursuit. Others spoke of a police Suburban being hauled out of the area by truck, apparently after its driver burnt out the engine in the desert heat. There was

chatter about the chaos of the operation, and people wondered
how so many vehicles could keep showing up with no one telling
them exactly where to go. But no matter what they were saying,
the posse had taken on a life of its own, expanding and spreading
out along every vector of the sixteen-square-mile search area.
Adding to the traffic were news vans, racing across the valley and
responding to scanners like anyone else who was listening, and in-
terviewing residents along the way.

There were a lot of kids who wanted to talk about Steve, not
only beauty queens, and not Boy Scouts or Girl Scouts, but kids
who were on a different path and outside the mainstream. For example, a thirteen-year-old who had a ring through her lower lip,
looking like a lot of kids everywhere. "Steve set you straight if he
saw that you were hanging with the wrong crowd," she said. "A lot
of people don't like cops," another kid added. "But Steve was one of
the good ones." A couple of parents nodded and their kids teared
up, and then someone spoke of Steve's own son, a two-year-old
toddler, and they mentioned that he too would be feeling the loss.
Three days later the little boy would be standing next to his
mother at Steve's funeral.

Earlier that day some news had broken, and a few in the crowd
spoke of it after the event. When investigators had searched
Kueck's trailer in the aftermath of Steve's death, one of the things
they found was the letter Don had written to the heads of law enforcement agencies in which he had recounted what happened on
that August day, almost ten years earlier, when he and Steve had
their first encounter. That's how they learned that the two had
more in common than just living in close proximity. Within hours,
news of the prior run-in began appearing in media coverage of the
manhunt, and it raised questions among cops and friends and family members of both men. Was it possible that neither Steve nor
Don knew that they lived in each other's backyard? The answer
was yes, but not likely. Steve had made a point of getting to know

everyone on his beat, not that such a thing was always possible given how many residents didn't want anyone, especially cops, to know them.

As for Don, everyone knew who the local cop was, not because they had necessarily met him, but because sooner or later, if you went anywhere in Lake Los Angeles or surrounding areas, you'd run into him. Don in fact had probably run into Steve several times at the local Frontier Mart on Highway 138, where he went every week in his Dodge Dart to pick up a new supply of propane. When he returned, he would tell friends that there was a cop in town who was always giving him dirty looks, and they got the impression that if the eye contact had a musical score, it would be written by Sergio Leone. Now, to be sure, many a cop might have given Don a dirty look. They had been doing it since the 1970s, when his long hair translated as outlaw, and the situation was especially aggravated in the South, where he grew up. In more recent years, he looked and sometimes acted tweaked, meaning paranoid and agitated and hostile from use of meth and other drugs, and sometimes was. Plus, when he stepped beyond the moat of his desert kingdom, he was a trouble magnet. While it's one thing to hate the man when you're a kid and into your twenties and thirties, the edge never softened, and in fact was only amped by jail time, drugs, and personal failures and loss. For Don, especially toward the end, it was a point of pride to stand against those who enforced rules and regulations, a thing that fueled him and qualified him for residence in the remote Mojave. So whenever he saw a member of law enforcement, especially, as he once told his daughter, white ones, his hack went up and he may have said some things, and even if he said nothing, he was a guy whose looks and demeanor said, "Oh yeah, buddy? I don't think so."

Yet in all the times he complained about "this cop who's hassling me," he never mentioned the cop's name, and he never said anything about this particular cop being the guy who had once busted him on the road. Quite simply, time had passed, and in his final months, he was undergoing a loss of mental acuity, perhaps forgetting the name of the sheriff against whom he had nurtured a serious grudge, or never getting close enough to read the name on Steve's badge when he saw him in the store, or not remembering what he looked like. Also we must consider that sometimes bad memories fade all on their own, perhaps still troubling when they send the last angry tentacles before receding forever. And sometimes they are just gone—or smoldering, waiting for a match.

As for Steve, he had once told a few friends that there was some tweaker who lived down the road, and he was keeping his eye on him. He never associated this person with a name. Of course, he could have been referring to any number of people, but from the direction Steve was pointing when he would make that remark, friends later theorized that the reference could have been to Kueck, even though he was not a known tweaker, meaning he hadn't been busted for meth use or cooking it. What's interesting about this comment is what he didn't say: "I can't believe I bought this house. There's this lawsuit nut living down the road, the same guy who tried to get me fired." In fact, Steve never spoke of their earlier run-in, as far as anyone remembers, and when it was reported on the news, it was the first time that those in his immediate circle had heard of it.

Yet an encounter such as the one Kueck and Sorensen had is not likely forgotten. Years before Steve was killed, one of his partners was Sgt. Paul Dino. The pair became close friends, and months after the manhunt for Kueck had wrapped up, I spoke with him on the phone. He remembered the time Steve had saved his life. It was a domestic violence call—other than traffic stops, the most deadly of police tasks. Someone is usually armed when you get there, and they are willing to take you and anyone else down. At the time, 1997, they were working in Altadena, on the south side of the San Gabriel Mountains. When they arrived at the scene, a woman was standing on the front porch. She said that she and the man in her house—whether he was her husband or a boyfriend the cops didn't know—had been arguing over tacos. Her eyes were swollen shut. "Did he do this to you?" Dino asked, and the woman nodded yes. Steve moved to cuff the guy, but he spun away and punched Dino in the face, breaking his nose. The cops tackled him and fell into the living room. "He's got my gun," Steve called out. Dino grabbed the guy's head and pulled it up, jamming his weapon against it. The man dropped Steve's gun. "The second we put the cuffs on," Dino said, "the fight was on. Lesson learned," he added. "Keep going no matter what, and don't underestimate a call." And then we talked about whether or not cops remember all of the busts they have made, who was in what house or car, and what happened to each of those cases. "No," he said. "You don't always remember. But you never forget a bad call."

The backstory of what happened between Steve and Don was ultimately of little consequence to Steve's brothers and sisters in the sheriff's department, and they steered clear of reporters' questions on the subject. Quite simply, members of law enforcement do not do gray. Which is not to say they weren't interested in the things that led to the downfall of their colleague, or of anyone for that matter. It is to say that bad things have consequences, and they are there to make sure that the law is brought to bear.

In the middle of the memorial, the red light on top of a Crown Vic in the parking lot started to flash and the siren screamed and the screech of pedal to metal was heard. The police vehicle turned hard on the Pearblossom Highway and headed west. Kueck had been sighted in Saddleback Butte, and black-and-whites from San Bernardino County were on the way. The last major preserve of Joshua trees in Los Angeles, Saddleback Butte was as good a hiding place as any in the Mojave, rumored to be riddled with mining shafts and the ghosts of frontier hermits. Meanwhile, investigators were trying to track down other associates of Kueck. One of them, believed to be a "close acquaintance," had not been seen since the murder. Perhaps he was harboring Kueck at his shack on Avenue R. SWAT deployed and surrounded the place. "DONALD CHARLES KUECK, THIS IS THE LOS ANGELES COUNTY SHERIFF'S DEPARTMENT. COME OUT WITH YOUR HANDS UP" came the announcement over SWAT's speaker system. They repeated it several times and made the same announcement for Kueck's associate. No one emerged. Finally, the search warrant they had been waiting for arrived. It was a high-risk service, which meant that there was a probability of encountering armed individuals on the premises. With five men remaining in position around the house, two approached the front door on either side, and that night's team scout, Mark Schlegel, knocked it down and entered, followed by his men. The house was empty and the team left, heading back to the Mount Carmel convent. They took off their gear, laid down on the floor in the main wing, and, with the nuns finishing up their prayers in the chapel, called it a day. For Bruce Chase, hitting the cold cement felt good, a relief from the outdoor furnace. He found himself thinking about the manhunt he was on and, well, his whole life. Yes, he was a fan of Louis L'Amour, but there was more to it. He had a degree in economics from William and Mary and he could have followed the trail to Wall Street. That of course was brutal in its own way, with brokers engaged in blood sport that was far removed from a hands-on engagement with the law and those who broke it. But how did he end up out here in the desert, in temperatures of over 110 degrees, running through the sand lugging sixty pounds of tactical gear toward a deputy's lifeless body? Would they find the man who killed him? So far, he felt like he was chasing a ghost, and it was hard not to believe he was in the Twilight Zone.

DAY
FIVE

Jello's Last Hurrah

Every junkie's like the setting sun.
>—Neil Young, "The Needle and the Damage Done"

KURT COBAIN DIED IN 1994, ON APRIL 5 ACCORDING TO THE coroner's report, although his body wasn't found until April 8. He had shot himself in the head. The rock idol and longtime junkie was twenty-seven years old and joined a list of other rock stars who had checked out at the same age, including Jim Morrison, Janis Joplin, and Jimi Hendrix. For a lot of kids, and especially musicians, the age had become diabolically magic. According to Cobain's sister, Kurt had wanted to die at that age, and as he wrote in an anguished suicide note, "It's better to burn out than fade away." The rise and fall had happened in Seattle, where all things rad had coalesced in the mid-1980s and early '90s, a response to the canned chart-topping hair bands that reeked of marketing

ploys and the music industry at its corporate worst. Lost boys and girls from across the land were heading to Seattle, and one of them was Jello Kueck.

No one knows exactly when he arrived, but it seems to have been a year or two after the death of Cobain. There he began his final descent, even as he was becoming a hero to other wastrels and flowering among strangers. The pounding waves and big cumulonimbus clouds of the Pacific Northwest must have been a reprieve from the desert. There was no need to wait for rain, for a drink, a break from the crashing white light of the Mojave; Seattle was gray and any way you cut it, it was wet—there were people on the streets, in bars, on the pier, on the floor, coffee'd and junk'd up, making music, making art, saying no, saying yes— it all smelled like teen spirit. Through his friend Samantha, Jello had met kids who were on the grunge scene, which was still thriving although not as intensely since the loss of its biggest star and ensuing breakup of his band. Jello began hanging out at local clubs, and one thing led to another, and soon he found himself playing in a band called Fuckhole. He had also become friends with drug dealers, as well as bouncers such as Dave Oberweber, who worked security at a place called the Color Box. Dave was in his forties, and Jello was about twenty-one or twenty-two. As the nights unfolded, Jello laid out the bits and pieces of his life story—leaving home at thirteen because of abuse by his stepfather, getting beaten up by skinheads, and things that even some close friends in Riverside didn't know about, such as a number of suicide attempts, like jumping off a truck with a noose around his neck or driving a car off a cliff only to end up in a tree. The stories were extreme, and possibly not true, but Dave realized early on that the kid was a handful and incredibly depressed. But he also noticed what everyone in his old crew well knew—that he was charming, brilliant, and, if his talents could be harnessed, someone who had a lot to offer the world.

Dave offered him a place to stay, and Jello took him up on it, staying with him for the next eight or nine months in his two-bedroom house in White Center, a neighborhood that was a mix of artists, musicians, and working-class people who had gigs at the docks or bars. "His room was a masterpiece," a girlfriend named Ford remembers after I reach her on the phone one day, years after she had been with Jello. The walls were decorated with his poetry and art, as well as lyrics from favorite songs, including one that he had penned called "I Don't Fit In." On the ceiling was a poster of his idol, Cobain, and he often told Ford that he'd die by twenty-seven. What can you say when someone makes such pronouncements? Of course she tried to point out reasons to outlive the tormented rock star, and she wasn't sure that he was serious. After all, he wasn't the only one who wanted to follow in Cobain's footsteps; many a bedroom was plastered with Nirvana posters, and especially those of its front man. In Seattle, and across the country, who didn't want to go out like Kurt Cobain? Yet it was no secret that Jello was a junkie, and Dave knew he had been shooting dope off and on since about sixth or seventh grade. It wouldn't surprise him if he turned up dead at some heroin hovel at some point. Still, Dave hoped that Jello would clean up, and became a kind of foster father to the kid who by then was calling him Dad. Along with a woman named Elaine Simons, the founder of Peace for the Streets by Kids from the Streets, he helped the lost boy from the Inland Empire start to make a change.

Elaine's organization is a Seattle drop-in center for local homeless and at-risk kids and young adults founded in 1995, at a time when the city had become a mecca for the young and disenchanted, thousands of whom had converged on Seattle to join up with the kindred spirits of the grunge scene. Jello had been hanging out on Capitol Hill, an area favored by street kids who were mainly into heroin (as opposed to the university district, which was known for its meth freaks, or downtown, where older, hardcore derelicts gathered). There they would stake out their turf and ask for spare change from passing tourists. Elaine was a regular among the pedestrians, talking to the drifters and locals who worked the streets, hoping to throw them a towline. One day Jello stopped her and spun out a story about needing some new guitar strings. She gave him a couple of bucks and invited him to check out her center, just a few blocks away on Summit Avenue. "He seemed really decent," she recalls years later. "I was hoping he'd come by." He did, and by all accounts, he had doubled down on his fabled charisma. Within months, local kids viewed him as a hero.

Yet there was something genuine under the sparkle. For sure it came through when Jello was high, but when he detoxed through a methadone program that Dave got him into, even more so. He began helping Elaine with her group's needle exchange program, at one point accompanying her to the state capitol in Olympia to testify at hearings about rampant teenage drug use in Seattle and what to do about it. His testimony was so impressive that he won an award. As he began moving away from heroin, he threw himself more passionately than ever into writing music and lyrics. And he became ardently involved in protests against the government, putting the words he had been writing and reading and tattooing on his skin into action. In 1998, a close friend of his named Megan died of an overdose. Jello was distraught, and helped her grandmother get through the grieving process. After that, he immersed himself head-on in the battle to rescue America's flailing children, heading back out to the streets, planting himself at the bus station or abandoned warehouses where kids were living, counseling them in whatever way the situation demanded. In a way, he had become a parent, doing for all the young denizens of the street what his mother and father had not done for him, finding kindred spirits among America's legion of castaways.

One of them was a street kid named Zoey. They met through some mutual friends in 1996 but fell out of touch, and then in October of that year, Zoey spotted Jello while she was panhandling, his hoodie up over his green Mohawk. It was her fourteenth birthday, although she told him she was turning sixteen. He gave her all the change in his pockets. They didn't see each other again until the following summer, although Zoey had been writing to him and calling from a road trip. When she returned, she phoned him, went to his house, and moved in. "I didn't have anywhere to go," she recalls. "And he didn't want me to leave." During the time they were together, Jello was trying to clean up, drinking mostly, and going every day to a methadone clinic. He didn't tell Zoey much about his life, but she told him all about hers. She had run away from home because her father was a strict disciplinarian. She cried and cried and cried over the punishments he had meted out, and Jello would hold her and listen. In the way of young lovers everywhere, they promised each other they would never stray, and Zoey was convinced that she had met her Prince Charming. One day, they had a spat; Zoey went back to her parents' house and was planning to bake a cake for Jello for his birthday, the following day. But her parents had arranged for her to be taken to a controversial "therapeutic boarding school" run by the Worldwide Association of Specialty Programs and Schools, and that night several people whisked her out of her bedroom to Utah, then Florida, and finally Jamaica for seven or eight months. While away, she and the other teenagers were repeatedly told that their parents were always right and whatever their parents told them to do, they should do. Throughout her time at boot camp, she pined for Jello but told administrators her tears were for her mother and father, lest she say the wrong thing. Sometime after she returned to Seattle, she went to visit her old friend. He had a new girlfriend, and she herself had a new beau. Confused and broken by her experience, she was preaching the mantra she had learned at camp because she didn't know what else to say: "Go back to California and visit your family," she told Jello. "That's what you need to do." It was the last time she saw Jello, in

1998; to this day, she regrets not having been there on his birthday, with the cake she was not allowed to bake, figuring that Jello took it as one more blow from a cruel world. She was right; she didn't know that on his eighteenth birthday, for instance, he had shown up in tears at the Smallwoods' house, explaining that his mother had kicked him out of her house yet again. Today, Zoey is a self-made and successful career woman, far away from the streets of Seattle. But she still thinks of the guy with the green Mohawk as the best boyfriend she ever had.

Later that year, an anti-globalization action was planned for Washington, DC. There was a growing worldwide fury against multinational corporations, and in America nowhere was it more intense than in the Northwest. Jello joined a group of people in Seattle who rode an old school bus across country, heading for the nation's capital, stopping en route at an anarchy camp in Pennsylvania for a baseball game pitting anarchists against socialists. Once in DC, they hooked up with others from around the country who had gathered to express their anger. Jello eagerly participated in the political mosh pit that was raging on the streets of the nation's capital, and later chained himself to a rail at the Pentagon subway station, sending the crowd into a frenzy. Back in Seattle the skinny guy in the big Mohawk and Sid Vicious spikes commanded a lot of attention. Not a day went by that he wasn't asked to speak at a rally for homeless kids or show up in defense of someone who was about to get kicked out of a shelter. As always, a lot of the attention came from girls. For all of his newfound stardom, he had not improved his personal hygiene; he was still slovenly and still gave off a rank odor. Yet it didn't matter, and nowhere was this more apparent than on the streets, where there was always an audience—and money. While Jello sometimes worked at the Color Box to earn it, he couldn't refrain from spare-changing tourists. They were easy marks, and many of them were attractive and well-heeled women. One of them, from Romania, took him back home for a month-long affair. When he got back, he was a junkie. Actually, he had never really cleaned up. What had happened in Seattle was a repeat of his old pattern—he'd detox and then relapse, and then it would all start over again.

Throughout his four years in Seattle, Jello had maintained an on-again, off-again relationship with Ford, who played guitar with him in Fuckhole. To her, he spoke of his hopes and dreams; some day, he said, he wanted to teach history. Some day, he said, he wanted to tour in a band. Some day, he said, he wanted to be a writer. Yet, as he told his friend Dave, he felt obligated to take care of his ailing father. In spite of the early abandonment and the later eviction, a tight bond remained. He never went into details in his conversations with Dave, but it was clear that he knew his father's hold on things was tenuous, and that he may have been the last thing between the old man and oblivion. Maybe he should go back to the desert, he said. His father was incapacitated by chronic fatigue syndrome, he explained to friends. He was out there, all alone. . . . It was really a goddamn shame. But at the same time, as he well knew from counseling addicts or people in other sorts of trouble, you can't save someone who doesn't want to save themselves. Moreover, he was gripped by a fear that he was turning into his father and appeared to be fighting off a curse. "No way am I going back there," he'd say sometimes. Not gonna happen. "Guess I'm stuck in Seattle," he'd tell Dave. "It's a punishment or a joke." Whatever was going on, the general trend wasn't good. He was writing suicide notes about once a month, and had been since his arrival. "Whoever finds me," the notes usually said, "I want my belongings to go to—" and the name always changed but the words were the same and at some point, after all the times in and out of rehab, there was nothing anyone else could do, other than be there for Jello should he reach out.

In 2000, Jello returned to Southern California, possibly drawn by the blood tie. Back in Riverside, he immersed himself in the burgeoning arts and music scene, moving into the Life Arts Building at the corner of University and Lemon Street. The structure was once Scientology headquarters for the Inland Empire but had since gone through several occupants until it was finally abandoned—except for the homeless kids who were partying and hanging out there, giving their own meaning to the Scientology credo of "getting clear" and echoing Manhattan's Chelsea Hotel, where Bukowski and many pioneering punks who followed his path had found sanctuary, and where Sid Vicious allegedly killed his girlfriend Nancy Spungeon during a heroin blowout and then later overdosed himself. "Please bury me next to my baby in my leather jacket, jeans, and motorcycle jacket," Sid had written in a suicide note. "Goodbye." In the old arts building, Jello was shacking up in one of the rooms with a girlfriend, and both were shooting heroin.

One of the girls on the scene was Angela Asbell. Like the other kids in her community, she had a rough upbringing. When Angela was a young girl, her mother, reluctant to remain with her father in Texas where they were living, was hospitalized with a nervous breakdown. Angela went to Riverside to live with her grandmother, a school-crossing guard who worked a second job cleaning downtown office buildings. Always creative, Angela was writing poetry as a kid and liked to hang out with the local artists and musicians. One night when she was fifteen, she went to a party at an old house on the banks of the Santa Ana River near the Riverside airport. There were bands playing in different parts of the house, plenty of booze flowing, and drugs being consumed every which way. At some point Angela began winding her way through swarms of people lining a hallway, trying to find a bathroom. A guy in a massive Mohawk stopped her and said, "Hey, do you have a pipe?"

"My friend has one," she said. "I'll go get it." The pair wandered off to retrieve the pipe, and the kid handed Angela a beer. "I'm Jello," he said, and from then on Jello and Angela kept running into each other at shows around town, soon exchanging phone numbers and becoming good friends, even more so when they learned that their birthdays were both in January, just a few days apart. As it happened, she was into making music too. Every now and then Jello would be back at his mother's apartment, along with his friend Ian, a homeless kid who stayed with them until Jello would push the limits and get kicked out again. Asbell, a close friend of Ian's, would visit the boys often, and Jello taught her to play bass.

Throughout this time, the desert was calling, and Jello had been traveling out to Llano, spending a few days here and there, trying to reconnect with his father. As the end of the year 2000 approached, he, along with countless citizens across the land, had an idea for a party. He wanted to ring in Y2K out in the desert, the land of new beginnings, and he wanted his father to join him. So he organized a shindig in a dry riverbed in Lake Los Angeles and invited about a hundred people. One of them was Don. It was a cold and beautiful night as midnight approached. All over America and around the world, something truly profound was unfolding. Contrary to the many predictions about the new millennium ushering in an apocalypse, resulting in an amped-up police presence in places of significant religious import such as the Holy Land—another desert, a million miles away—traditional enemies held their fire, and citizens of the planet appeared to celebrate as one community, as if a new and shining path had suddenly appeared and we could all live happily ever after. Under a twinkling Mojave sky in an ancient wash in Lake Los Angeles, Jello and his crew joined the world's tribes and played their guitars and pounded their drums and drank and smoked intoxicating substances, beating out that rhythm that we all know, the one that mimics the heartbeat—the sound of life. Among the revelers was Jello's devoted and younger half-sister, Sharon Booth. Although she was not feeling well, down with strep throat and two ear infections, the ever-charismatic punk wanted her to be there, and she followed. "After all," she said many years later, "he was my older brother."

And just as Jello had planned, his father was there too—manic and social, to the surprise of Sharon, who had never seen him "like that," and at a party, no less. It crossed her mind that maybe he was on speed—as others well knew, he did have his manic episodes—but she also thought that maybe he was actually happy, or maybe it was the spillover effect of a mood that seemed to be sweeping across planet Earth, affecting even people who just wanted to be left alone. In any case, everyone was having a good time; it was one of those events that found its groove, and it was all because of the neutrons in that particular cell at that particular moment, all working and dancing and sparking in harmony, and maybe even fathers and sons could have some kind of life together along with all of the nations of the world. But what good is a party, especially on Y2K, if the cops don't show up? Arrive they did as the music and shouting had reached a crescendo, and then they told everyone that they were partying in a protected area and had to leave. To everyone's surprise, Don stepped forward and presented himself as a chaperone. "I've lived here all these years and can guarantee that we'll clean up," he said to a woman in uniform, handing her his driver's license and asking her to hold it as a personal guarantee. "We know you've been here for a long time," she said, obviously a person who was familiar with Don. "Are you sure you want to take the responsibility for all these kids?" He reiterated that as a local, he cared about the place, and insisted that he would make sure it was not damaged or harmed. As dawn broke on the New Year, Jello and his buddies began the task of cleaning up the wash, retrieving their cartons and plastic bags and bottles and whatever other paraphernalia and trash they had dropped. The sentiment was that Don had put himself on the line for them—"Your old man is cool," someone said to Jello—and they wanted to help him make good on his promise. Also he needed his driver's license back. Soon enough the party dispersed, and everyone headed back to the outside world, which no one was able to contact all night long because there was no cell phone service in that part of Lake Los Angeles. "Maybe the world ended," Sharon and Jello and some of his friends had joked throughout the evening after they tried to make a few calls. "What if we get back and it's gone?"

About a year and a half later there came another party. It was in January, and it was a joint birthday celebration for Angela Asbell and Jello, her twenty-fourth and his twenty-seventh, the magical year of death foretold. The party was at Angela's house, the same one where she had been living with her grandmother. At the time Jello's address was a place called "the cave" on Van Buren, a dive on a forlorn stretch of pavement near the Riverside airport. The ragged cave folk were fed up with Jello and his heroin habit, and tried to evict him by shutting him out of conversations. He didn't leave, and finally they kicked him out. That night at their party, Angela sensed that he was at the far end of his long downward slide. Always a bag of bones, he looked worse than ever. She made falafel for him as people wandered in and out of her kitchen. He was leaving for Seattle the next day, he told her; he had to get away from Southern California, a place that was destroying him. At some point that night he slept with Angela's roommate, shot up in the bathroom, erased everything from a board on its wall, and wrote a note that puzzled Angela when she discovered it the next day. "Dear Angela," it said, and as she began reading, she smelled the smell that junkies leave behind, the acrid evidence of the thing that was coursing through their veins. She recognized it from a sense memory of a bathroom at another party, one where Jello had holed up in for hours. "I want you to know that no matter what happens, we'll always be friends, in this world or next. I'll always respect you no matter what happens . . . " Of course Jello had left a trail of such notes, and in a way, his life had been a series of sprints between these postings. At least one more would appear a few months later.

The day after the party, or possibly the next week—the exact time frame is not clear—Jello called his friend Dave in Seattle and asked him to wire money for a bus ticket. Dave did so, not realizing how strung out Jello was and hoping to bail him out one more time. Jello took the money and partied, never getting to the depot in LA and missing the bus. Instead he called his old amigo Chris Smallwood and asked for a ride to the station. Chris agreed, and during the two-hour drive, Jello tried to talk him into shooting dope. "You're going off the reservation," Chris said, as he had on many other occasions, declining his friend's offer. At the station, Chris helped Jello get a new ticket. Then they embraced, and Chris kissed him on the forehead. "Bro," he said, "I love you."

Chris Smallwood heard from Jello one more time after their farewell at the bus station. "Dude," he said, in a phone call the next day. "Come pick me up." He had missed another bus and was calling from somewhere in downtown Los Angeles. Chris was pissed off and said no. Jello called his sister Sharon and she said no, she was studying for a final exam. A few other calls were made and everyone said the same thing. Finally, he reached his old friend Aaron Blair, another musician who was then living with his parents in Riverside. "Dude, I just got out of jail," Jello said. "Get your ass back here," Aaron replied. His home was one of the various sanctuaries for Jello upon occasion, and once again he was extending an invitation. But Jello was pissed off about everything and went on a long rant. "Call me later on the cell," Aaron told his friend after explaining how to jump the Metro and get back to Riverside. "I gotta leave for work." Later, Jello called and left a message—on the family's house phone instead of the cell. Aaron's mother picked it up, but it was too late, and when Aaron called back the next day, there was no answer.

No one knows exactly what happened after Jello's last phone call to his friend. "You're not supposed to get off the boat," Chris Smallwood says years later, referring to the scene in *Apocalypse Now*, in which the soldiers leave their boat, go ashore, and are attacked by a tiger. "He was supposed to get on the bus and go to Seattle."

There were no more calls, not even to his father, whom he had been calling with some regularity in his last few weeks. His father was worried, and in fact long before Jello's first trip to Seattle, he had confided to Virginia Smallwood that sooner or later, Jello was going to kill himself. He called a few of Jello's friends, including Angela Asbell, who was also concerned that Jello might have been missing, especially after finding that strange note in her bathroom. "Do you know where he is?" Don asked Angela. She didn't, and neither did anyone else.

The answer came on July 4, when Jello's mother received word from the police that her son had been found dead of an overdose in a warehouse on Skid Row in downtown Los Angeles. Rebecca, Jello's older stepsister, decided that his friends and father ought to make a pilgrimage to the site and contacted Don and the others to arrange it. A few days later, Mike Cazares, Fritz Aragon, and Fritz's girlfriend drove to the place where Jello's body was discovered. Don drove in from the desert and accompanied them on the trip. It was true that Jello had died in a seedy part of town. But it was characteristic of him that in terms of the exact location, he went out with a flourish, in the old Palace Theatre at Broadway and Sixth Street, a once-grand establishment where Fred Astaire and Harry Houdini played to high-ticket audiences in plush red velvet seats. One of Houdini's famous presentations was the Needle Trick. He'd begin by swallowing several of them, followed by a length of thread. Then, to the audience's delight, he'd regurgitate a series of threaded needles. Over time, the theatre fell into disrepair and decay, mirroring the story of downtown Los Angeles. A few years ago, a renovation restored its former glory, polishing up the marble entranceway and the gold leaf surrounding the murals flanking the theatre's stage. But regardless of its condition, drama had always found a home at the Palace. During its lean years, homeless people had burrowed through its crumbling walls and roof, wandering through, some making a home in the warrens that ran above, below, and around the theatre in adjacent buildings. Each of these drifters had a story and a name, and one of them was Jello Kueck. As it turned out, on his way to meeting Kurt Cobain, he had spent his last days with the ghosts of Al Jolson, the Marx Brothers, Will Rogers, and strangely, Harry Houdini, who had survived his own kind of needle trick on the stage of the grand old theatre.

On a bright summer day, Fritz parked his car in a downtown lot, paid the hefty parking fee, and headed with Don and his friends toward the address they had been given. Not realizing that it was a theatre, he was a bit surprised, and then noticing that it was undergoing renovation, he wondered if they had been given the correct information. His girlfriend carried a bouquet of flowers. As they approached the building, a security guard stopped them, took note of the flowers, and asked where they were going. As they explained their mission—to pay homage to a friend who had recently died and been found at this location—the guard became excited and related a disturbing story. "I'm the person who found his body," the man said, in broken English laced with a lot of Spanish phrases and words, and physical mannerisms to break the language barrier. For a few days, he continued, he had been hearing a strange sound coming from one of the doors in the back of the theatre. "I thought someone was banging on it," he said. Superstitious, he was reluctant to find out what or who was there. Maybe the place was haunted, he said. Demons could have been living there. Maybe he should call a priest. But something kept telling him to open the door. Cautiously, he approached and tried to open it. But there was something in the way, on the other side, and he pushed harder. When he peered in, his fear was confirmed—there was a man's body leaning against the door. He was dead. There was a needle in one of his arms. Later, a guy from forensics told the guard that the noise had been caused by the man's boot kicking the door as rigor mortis settled in. Strangely, around the same time, someone made a drive-by past Jello's mother's place in Riverside, tossing his backpack into the front yard. Inside was a suicide note. It seems to have vanished at some point, but as far as anyone remembers, it echoed the long symphony of farewells.

As the guard wrapped up his story, Don "went crazy," Fritz says, and ran to the metal door. It was locked with a bar, which he wrenched off with his bare hands. Then he tore it down and rushed into the abandoned building. The others followed, and the first thing they saw was a large blood stain on the floor. Jello had been found there. "Maybe it's Jello's aura," Mike Cazares thought, and they placed a candle there and lit it. With Don leading the way, they stepped away and began picking their way through the dark surroundings. He had brought a flashlight, and its scant light helped them stake out a path around mounds of trash and wrecked mattresses and deep into an urban wasteland—a strange echo of the scene in the desert, a way station for squatters that was all walls and no sky and had no way out.

At some point Don found a miner's hat with a light on it, put it on, and led the way up an old staircase and into the theatre balcony. There were no railings, and with nothing to hold on to, the four mourners walked carefully across the upper reaches of the Palace, unsure the rafters would hold them and trying to maintain their balance on the narrow walkway between the seats and the orchestra section below. Sunrays filtered through the stained-glass windows like dim stage lighting, and all around were odors of decay. The group kept walking, into the nether reaches of the theatre and behind the balcony and up near the roof of the building. The shaft of light from Don's helmet swept across a hovel where someone had been living. He stopped and so did the others and they surveyed the squat and understood right away that this was the place: there was a comb, a book, a necklace, and bracelets with spikes that everyone recognized. And there amid a pile of junk was the gun Don had given to his son. He picked it up, checked it out—it wasn't working. He teared up and then held back and then was pissed off, blaming others for the disaster and then retreating and blaming himself. Cazares wondered what Don was going to do next, and they stood in silence for a moment or two, waiting for him to take the lead.

At some point, he sat down and so did the others and they placed the bouquet of flowers on the floor. Looking around the area, someone spotted some writings on the wall. It sounded like stuff Jello would say and then sure enough, there it was—the name Jello scrawled in charcoal. It was time to toast their departed friend. Fritz had some weed and he and Mike were looking for rolling papers; Don saw their dilemma and pitched in, scrounging up cigarette paper from some butts that were lying around. Then, to Fritz's surprise, he picked up a rat trap and used it as a poker to stuff the joint with pot. "Jeez that's hard-core," Fritz thought as Don handed him the joint. He lit it up and took a hit, but he hadn't met Don prior to that day, and he didn't know if he smoked and wasn't sure if he should hand it back, but offered it anyway. Don took a hit and then passed it to the others and they smoked it down and stayed for hours, pondering Jello and his fate and not saying much as the sunlight began to fade. Fritz noticed that Don had checked out once he had smoked the weed. With the sun now setting, he said it was time to go; Fritz had only paid for so many hours of parking and he didn't want to spend the night amid the squalor. The four of them headed out, and as they turned a corner, they noticed more flowers and candles. Back in the lot, the security guard told them he had placed them there. There was half an hour of parking time left and Don made the most of it, talking to some kids who were hanging around, asking if any of them knew or had seen Jello in the days prior to his death. The answer was no. A month or two later, he went back to Skid Row, staying there for weeks and trying to find out what happened to his son. The answer wouldn't have mattered. From the moment Don stood at the place where his son's body was found, Jello's sisters and friends knew that it was only a matter of time before the old man lost it.

Back in Seattle, when Dave learned that the money he had sent Jello for the return bus trip had gone up his veins, he berated himself. But as everyone knew in their heart of hearts, Jello would have gotten his hands on the money to score one way or another, and there wasn't much else they could do for someone who had vowed to check out at twenty-seven. When Elaine and the kids at the community center learned that he had joined the Twenty-Seven Club, they organized a memorial. Several among the seventy-five people who had gathered gave testimony about his friendship and impact on their lives. In the middle of the service, two girls faced off over the lanky ladies' man from Riverside, nearly taking each other down in a shoving match. Later, Peace for the Streets by Kids from the Streets added a plaque for Jello on its memory wall.

He left his belongings at his girlfriend Ford's place. After he left, she opened his suitcase. Inside it was a tape, some clothes, a Greyhound ticket, and a big book on space.

Cloud of Dust

Happy trails to you, until we meet again.
—Dale Evans and Roy Rogers, "Happy Trails"

DEPUTY STEVE SORENSEN'S FUNERAL WAS SCHEDULED FOR THE following day, August 8, at 10 in the morning. It was hoped that Kueck would be captured before Steve was laid to rest. But that outcome was not guaranteed, and among the local cops who were Steve's friends and colleagues, frustration was mounting, compounded by feelings of anger and humiliation. Thousands of representatives from law enforcement agencies all over the country were on their way to Lancaster for the service. The governor of California, Gray Davis, would be there. Sheriff Baca and all high-ranking members of the LASD would be in attendance, along with countless rank-and-file deputies. Of course family members would be at the memorial. What would it be like to honor and bury a beloved and embattled town sheriff while his killer might be hiding in the

brush nearby? Or worse—on his way out of the area, the state, or even the country, permanently slipping through the tentacles of the law?

As is customary, local cops had been out of the loop since Day One, with LASD Homicide and Major Crimes running the investigation. But they had been asked to help and were proceeding with their own groundwork. One of the units in particular, the Safe Streets Bureau—a team of experienced gang investigators—pitched in. A member of the unit had been keeping a running blog throughout the manhunt called *A Fallen Hero*. "In the days following Steve's murder," he wrote, "gangs had not been one of our priorities. Local gang members were probably quite surprised that we weren't 'visiting' them as much as usual. It was a good time to be a gang member," the blogger said in bold face, "and a bad time to be a 52 year old white male bearing a passing resemblance to Queck! [sic]." On Wednesday, the fifth day of the pursuit, various members of this unit headed to Lake Los Angeles and met up with deputies who patrolled the area with Steve, and then tried to locate an unnamed associate of Donald Kueck's whom law enforcement had been seeking for several days. In a caravan of police vehicles, they headed out across the desert, visiting a number of remote locations in temperatures soaring to over 100 degrees, each man weighted down with body armor and some thirty pounds of additional gear.

When they reached Avenue S, they spotted a run-down farm complex that was boarded up and had a "For Sale" sign posted outside. It appeared to be abandoned, but something was strange: a trailer was parked next to the main building, and it had not been there when one of the deputies had driven by on an earlier reconnaissance mission. The team of cops staked out positions and surrounded the building, approaching slowly and cautiously as they moved in across the open and flat terrain. The structure was empty, they found, but someone was asleep in the trailer. "He turned out

to be an unknown acquaintance of Queck," the blogger wrote. "He
had information that we realized Homicide might need to know."
As cops continued speaking with the man in the trailer, a truck
slowed and began turning into the driveway that led to the front
entrance of the farm. Spotting the black-and-whites, the driver
peeled off and sped away, heading west on Avenue S and crossing
170th Street East where it becomes a dirt road. Two units were on
its tail, clocking in at over eighty miles per hour, flying across the
desert gravel and into clouds of dust kicked up by the accelerating
truck. Suddenly the cops were intercepted by another police vehicle. They had stumbled into the Major Crimes Bureau—the people
who were running the investigation—and told to break off. They
headed back to the farm building, where the other members of the
gang team had detained the man in the trailer for trespassing. Soon
he was taken in for an interview with Homicide. Several miles
away at the Lancaster station, Captain Carl Deeley was preparing
remarks for Steve's funeral.

That same night SWAT was sweeping a quadrant of the desert
near C.T.'s place. Once again, dogs were deployed, bloodhounds
now instead of the Malinois. On the side of a dirt road, the men
spotted something strange—a fresh bowl of peaches. Perhaps
someone had set it out for Kueck. Or maybe it was for them. Or
maybe it was just there. You never know in the desert. That was
why they didn't live there—too much strange stuff going on. They
kept going, in the dark and under the stars. Under the sage the
desert gave up something else. There were several Hefty bags and
some other items, all part of a portable meth lab. "It was like it
dropped out of the sky," says Deputy Rick Rector, the scout on
SWAT's Blue Team during the manhunt. On the men trekked,
deeper into the nether reaches of the Mojave, and it began to feel
that they were getting close to Kueck, and in a moment, the feeling was confirmed. There was a compound with trailers, behind an
old western-style gate, like the entrance to a cattle spread. It was

illuminated with one floodlight and the place looked spooky and Rector thought about places like Area 51 and how you weren't sup- posed to be there. No one else was—or so it seemed. SWAT sent the dogs in and the animals alerted on human scent, drawing the team's attention to another strange sight inside one of the trailers: a mattress with fresh bed linen and a glass of water that had just been poured. Had cops stumbled on one of Kueck's hideaways, where he kept clean sheets in case of an emergency? Had someone laid out the linens, knowing that it would have been a comfort to a man on the run? Did they lay them out specifically for Don, knowing that he had a thing about cleanliness? Or was it just another desert mys- tery? "I knew he was there," Rector recalls, as we talk about the manhunt a few years later at a chain restaurant in Orange County. Chances are, he was.

LOCKED UP WITHOUT A VIEW: A DESCENT INTO THE CALIFORNIA PRISON SYSTEM

Sometimes I give myself the creeps.
    —Green Day, "Basket Case"

THE SUMMER OF 2001 IS KNOWN FOR A COUPLE OF THINGS, mainly because it is now seen in light of the attack on 9/11, which forced an examination of the months preceding it. Let us recall that it was a period of intense celebrity coverage in the media, some of the most intense that we have experienced, with the topic of Britney Spears dominating the news ethers. There was also the subject of shark attacks, which had reportedly reached an all-time high that summer, forcing swimmers up and down the coasts to stay out of the water at some of the country's preferred beaches. Among the

many things that did not make the news that summer was the death and ensuing memorials for Jello Kueck. It is noteworthy that during that period there was not just the one service in Seattle for Jello Kueck, but several, a testament to the impact that this lost child of the Inland Empire had on the lives of those in his various circles. They did not all know each other, but in addition to knowing Jello, they had one thing in common; they were trying to carve out a new world, with the personal and cultural deck stacked against them. Now one of their own was down, and they honored him that summer on at least three different occasions. One of them was a memorial party at his friend Aaron Blair's house in Long Beach, this one for close friends and family members. Other than trying to retrace Jello's path in downtown Los Angeles, Don had once again sequestered himself in Llano and was reluctant to attend this tribute. But his daughter, the surviving amigos, and various other friends and relatives of Jello sent him a series of letters about why they wanted him to be there, and he consented. Chris Smallwood drove out from Riverside to pick him up. "Hey, man, check this out," Don said when Chris walked into Don's trailer. Chris was struck by how bad Don looked; always lanky, he had lost a lot of weight, and it really showed in his face, with a look that was kind of grizzled and more intense than before. Now from a compartment in the trailer, Don retrieved an assault rifle. Chris knew that Don had guns but was surprised to see this one. "Wow, dude," he said, "that's like the A-team." Don stashed the gun away and then they headed out of the desert and down the 14 to the 405 to the 710, arriving in Long Beach for the afternoon celebration. All the while, Don was carrying a container of Jello's ashes.

As they sat in Aaron's crowded living room, each person spoke somberly or humorously about their recently departed friend. At the conclusion of the ceremony, Don, visibly upset, stood up and thanked everyone for attending the event and having been a friend to his son. Virginia Smallwood took Don aside, having noted how drawn and strange he looked. She asked him if he were sick, and he said yes he was—he had desert fever. She wasn't sure if that was a joke, and Don assured her that it wasn't. But don't worry, he said; sooner or later, everyone picks it up out there and now it was his turn. Well, Virginia wondered, who wouldn't be sick after finding out that their son had OD'd, but she didn't say it out loud, because she figured that Don didn't need to hear it. Then someone suggested making a time capsule of Jello's life; a canister was retrieved and people wrote remembrances and deposited them, along with wallet photos and some tapes and CDs that were his favorites. The capsule was sealed and handed off for future burial—no one remembers exactly who received it—and Jello's uncle passed out urns of his ashes. Don made special entreaties to certain people, those who knew Jello best, inviting them out to the desert and asking if it was okay if he stayed in touch. It was a way, they realized, for him to connect with his son. They were happy that Don had reached out; they liked him, even though they knew that a big part of what destroyed Jello was that his father had vanished into the desert and the kid had been fending for himself for years. But they promised to maintain contact and come out and visit; for them as well, it was a way to keep Jello's spirit alive. Yet, in the words of Chris Smallwood, Don was now "leaner and meaner" than they had ever seen him and he and his sister were convinced that "it was only a matter of time" before Kueck went off the rails.

After the tribute in Long Beach, the crew headed back to Riverside and continued to party at the Smallwoods' house. A few of Jello's friends were huddling in a corner. Someone was playing Alice in Chains or maybe it was Soundgarden; Chris can't remember, but whoever it was, it made them realize that the punk scene that Jello had so much been a part of was over. "Dude," someone said, "I'm gonna smoke him," reminding everybody that one of the many requests Jello had made about his impending death was "when I die, put my ashes in a cigarette box." Someone else had a pipe and they packed it up with weed and ashes of Jello, alternating layers, and then someone fired it up and inhaled and then they passed around their departed amigo, with each taking a hit, a long one. "This is to you, you son of a bitch," someone said, and soon the party broke up. The next morning, Chris had a sore throat. Jello had returned.

Within twenty-four hours, Don erupted. After the service, Don had headed to his daughter Rebecca's place in Riverside to spend the night with her family. The following day, he drove her to the county Department of Public Social Services, where she had some business with a social worker. Everything seemed to catch up with Don in the building's parking lot, where a heated exchange of words led to a violent altercation with a wanted man. Several weeks later, he was sentenced to hard time, joining California's ever-burgeoning felon population and later returning to the desert, like many other parolees, as an unstable figure whose grudge against law enforcement was now a living thing.

What happened was this: a Riverside local named Gilbert Arias—a parolee at large, wanted on a felony warrant for burglary—drove into the lot and parked his red 1990 Plymouth Voyager minivan in a No Parking area. Like Kueck, he was on a family errand, dropping his wife and kids off so they could enter the building to attend to a social service matter. After they went inside, he got out and closed the passenger door, taking a few minutes as he rearranged some items in the van. Someone began yelling at him through the open driver's window of an adjacent car. "What did you say?" he called out, over the loud music in his own van. "You're in a No Parking zone" came the reply. Arias explained that he was dropping off his family. By then the man, Donald Kueck, was out of his car and approaching Arias. A security guard outside the entrance yelled at the men to stop, but the incident was rapidly escalating. "You son of a bitch," Kueck said, swinging his right arm and making a wide, arcing, and slashing motion at the stranger's abdomen. Arias staggered slightly, looked down and saw that he was bleeding. "Man, he cut me," he called out to the guard. A cop arrived and trained his weapon on Kueck, who put the box cutter into a back pocket, refused to get on the ground, pushed the cop away, and began to flee. The cop subdued him with pepper spray as two other members of law enforcement arrived. "I told him to move his van, man," Kueck said by way of an explanation. "He got mad and walked towards me." Afraid, Kueck pulled the blade from his pocket and swung it when Arias was "close enough." Then he ran.

Anyway you looked at the incident, the theme was Don't Tread on Me: don't park in my space and don't enter my personal space. For a man on the edge it was serious fuel. Both men were arrested on the spot; Arias was taken to the hospital, where he received ten stitches for the laceration across his stomach, and then locked up on the outstanding warrant. Kueck was taken downtown. He was charged with a felony knife attack and two misdemeanors involving the use of force against a peace officer and interfering with a peace officer and an EMT in the discharge of their duties. A deal was made, and Kueck pled guilty to the felony, receiving a three-year sentence, reduced to one year and credited with time served. He then entered the Robert Presley Detention Center in Riverside County, becoming a member of the prisoner nation of California—one of the biggest and most notorious in the world, frequently mentioned with countries such as China, Singapore, and Malaysia in studies of penitentiary conditions and what happens to the incarcerated.

By the end of the year 2000, 1 in every 143 US residents was behind bars in a state, federal, or local jail, with California—always blazing the trail—along with Texas and the federal penitentiary system holding 1 in every 3 of the incarcerated. At the time of Donald Kueck's entry, disturbing news about life in the padlocked shadows of the Golden State had been coming to the surface for months. In 1999 there had been riots at Norco state prison, an otherwise scenic and bucolic location in Orange County where locals can still ride their horses into town and hitch them up at a local bar. Later that year at Corcoran, the state prison that was then housing Robert Kennedy's assassin Sirhan Sirhan and some of the Manson women, guards were busted for staging gladiator fights in which inmates were pitted against each other in death matches. In Riverside, where Kueck was doing time, there were rumors of such fights being staged in the old wing of the detention center; at one time in the center's history, one of these fights involved two old men, according to Jello's friend Rande Linville, who witnessed it when he was held there during the era of the three amigos in River-side. In the newer and more modern section, where the cells surrounded a pod where guards were stationed, as opposed to a row of cells with hallways that the guards walked up and down every fifteen minutes to half an hour, such activities did not happen. With his chronic fatigue syndrome and other ailments, Kueck may have been housed in the medical wing. It may also be that he was not provided with the pain-killers he depended on—a typical jail-house situation—and he certainly had no official access to drugs that would amp him up or had the ingredients for speed, such as certain nasal sprays. But he could have acquired them through the jailhouse underground, or prison doctors may have provided him with drugs that took him in the opposite direction, quieting his mind—a not unknown jailhouse practice. Still, with nothing to do but think, and in a place that was the antithesis of the desert, Kueck was probably going mad.

But the decline had begun long ago. In the years before Jello had died, and even in the years before Don had reentered the lives of his children, his sisters noticed the downward slide. While stationed in San Diego, the navy nurse Lynne would visit Don in the desert every month during a period stretching from 1996 to 1999, driving up the freeway in her pickup truck with her dog Nimitz, named after the carrier she had served on. Sometimes Don seemed fine, carrying on with his rockets and discourses as always, clearly meant to be living in the wide-open space, off the grid, and free like the ravens and bobcats and rattlesnakes all around him. His brother, Bill, occasionally visited as well, and he and Don would go hiking and deepen their connection under the big welcoming sky of the Antelope Valley. But other times there were signs of illness; for instance during a couple of winter visits, Lynne noticed buckets of frozen vomit outside Don's trailer. He complained of headaches, and some of his behavior seemed obsessive and focused on a grim albeit touching plan—amassing gems from the Home Shopping Network as a legacy for his daughter. Lynne began to suspect that maybe Don had a frontal lobe tumor; as a nurse, she knew that it caused certain symptoms and headaches and obsession, and planning for the end fit the general pattern. Sometimes, when she approached his trailer, she made sure to listen for sounds; she feared that he might have killed himself, so any sound at all would have assured her that he was still alive. On a less dire note, she was also concerned about all of the empty peanut butter jars around the premises; there was a chemical in peanut butter, she learned from a relative who was a chemist, that could cause dementia, and if that was all you were eating, a serious problem could ensue. Don's sister Peggy, sometimes visiting from Florida, noticed that Don seemed paranoid at times, not just gripped by the usual round of fears and phobias, but convinced that the universe was sending him signs that the end was near. These signs, to others, were minor—lost or missing mail, things that didn't work. During various visits, Peggy would drive him to doctor appointments or appointments with social workers to make sure he'd continue to receive disability checks. But there was often lost paperwork or some other snafu— more proof that forces were conspiring against him and there really was no reason to be here. Once, when Don went on a vacation for a few days, he returned to find that scavengers had broken into his trailer and stolen some things, confirming a fear that he shouldn't have left. By then so many things had gone wrong in Don's life that Peggy was beginning to think that he was indeed stranded in a cycle of bad luck, bad choices, and more. Whatever was going on, it all served to amp up his edge, and others too had noticed a problem. For all of his mellow, seemingly Buddha-like nature, Don could snap easily—and sometimes did, frightening people as he veered close to something they did not want to experience. And so they steered clear of him, for a while at least, until he simmered down and became the guy they revered as a wise old hippie with strange thoughts and stories and a serious way with animals.

When Don got out of jail, one of the first things he did after returning to the desert was make contact with his daughter Rebecca and Jello's friends. He held tightly to Rebecca especially, bringing her kids odds and ends from the desert and trying hard to have a relationship with them. He started to make good use of the cell phone his sister Peggy had gotten for him in earlier years, calling Jello's friend Angela Asbell every day. Often he spoke of his time in jail, sharing with Angela a passion for radical politics, refined during the period of his incarceration. She looked forward to the calls because she too had concerned herself with the political situation in America; as a lesbian activist and writer, she had penned many pointed and funny essays for a way-out zine she edited called *Bitch Kingdom*, under the pseudonym of Angela Chaos. Like Jello, both she and Don had taken note of the "injustice, racism, and classism" in the country, and Don was especially concerned with racism, a thing that was most apparent to him while he was in jail, where there is no pretense among inmates of trying to get along in a diverse society and the population divides itself into race-based tribes. Their conversations sometimes went on for hours, with Don citing chapter and verse from various historical tracts on a wide range of subjects, but sooner or later it all dovetailed back into a general obsession. What is government for and what is the role of the individual? These were rich questions but there was something underlying them, a thing that Don seemed to be dancing around. Like all of Jello's friends, Angela knew that Don loved rockets but now his passion had gone beyond the dream of possibility and flight. "People need rockets for protection," he told Angela one day. "Government can't be the only people with weapons." For the first time during their many conversations, Angela felt kind of nervous as Don spoke about such matters, and there were some others who did as well. He was reading books about how to disarm a policeman, he told a couple of friends, and he was giving himself a refresher course on search-and-seizure law.

It was around this time that Chris Smallwood happened to pay Don a visit in the desert, and once again, there he stood with the assault rifle. At the very least, it was a parole violation; once released, felons were not allowed to possess firearms, and if found to have possession, they could be returned to prison for a long time. In Don's case, it would be a second strike (with three felony counts meaning a mandatory life sentence), but there was no sign that such a thing concerned him. As Chris approached, Don was out behind his trailer, taking aim at a large Porky the Pig cutout planted in the sand. It was wearing an ATF hat and badge, and when Don finished off some rounds, he handed the weapon to Chris. While Don watched quietly, Chris shot off a clip. He left later that day. The next time he saw Don he was on television, wanted by every cop in the country.

DAY SIX

Requiem for a Cop

*These old people I talk to, if you could of told em that there would
be people on the streets of our Texas towns with green hair and
bones in their noses speakin a language they couldn't even understand, well, they just flat out wouldn't of believed you. . . . All of that is
signs and wonders but it don't tell you how it got that way. And it
don't tell you nothing about how it's fixin to get, neither.*

—Cormac McCarthy, *No Country for Old Men*

ON AUGUST 8, 2003, DEPUTY STEVEN SORENSEN WAS LAID TO
rest. In addition to the vigil in his honor held in the middle of the
manhunt, there had already been a funeral at the Twin Lakes
Community Church in Lake Los Angeles, where his friend John
Wodetzki was the pastor. Wodetzki and Connie Mavrolas—the
two surviving members of the trio that had come together with
Steve to take on what they saw as a corrupt local government—
were still concerned that townspeople who had been making

threats against Steve might have been responsible for his death. They also pondered their own fate. Law enforcement—aware of the ongoing battle in Lake Los Angeles as well as the civil suit in which Steve had announced that he feared for his life—placed Pastor John, Connie Mavrolas, and Steve's family under twenty-four-hour protection for several days after Steve was killed. Although Kueck was wanted for his murder, at that point there was still a lot of speculation. Was Kueck acting alone? Maybe some bikers were involved; after all, you can't be a cop in the Mojave and not piss off certain constituents. Better to play it safe than to risk more violence.

But behind it all, given what Connie and Pastor John knew about the area and the fact that there was a continuing endeavor on the part of many concerned citizens to keep the desert from becoming one big parking lot for transients, they were convinced that Steve's mission on behalf of people who had lived in the region for generations was righteous. If he had a previous run-in with Kueck, so be it; by then it was common knowledge that he had gone out to Llano to deal with a long-time squatter, and perhaps, some theorized, he had even made that turn down Kueck's driveway to warn him about a problem drifter in the area, letting bygones be bygones, knowing exactly who was living at the end of the gravel path with the "No Trespassing" sign but fearing not. Or maybe it was just plain simple: "He let his guard down," some cops told me many months later. "It just happens sometimes." After all, they said, cops are human, and sometimes that's just the way it goes. At the church in Lake Los Angeles, friends of Steve's, including many of those he had helped over the years, gathered to pay their respects. In front of a banner that depicted the Lion of Judah, a band played a song, and Pastor Wodetzki eulogized the man who had become such a close ally in a short period of time. He praised Steve's short-lived mission and talked about his devotion to community and family. "His best friend Christine was always with Steve when he was not at work," he said. "They shared and told each other everything. Together they worked tirelessly on a list of projects to complete: trees to plant, walls to paint, animals to care for. . . . St. Jerome said, 'A friend is long sought, hardly found, and with difficulty kept.' . . . Had I known this day was coming, I would have done it all again." Then Pastor Wodetzki asked for prayer that he and the congregation be used by Jesus to turn the tragedy into a victory for the kingdom of the Lord.

There is nothing like the pomp and circumstance of funerals for members of law enforcement or the military who have gone down in the line of duty. Sometimes, to those who reside in the civilian world and know little or nothing of how it is among the men and women who walk that thin blue line so others can be protected, such ceremonies seem overblown or in some way excessive. They make people feel uneasy and wary of the warrior way. But this is how it must be, with flags and dirges and uniforms; can you picture it otherwise, lesser tribute, for citizens who spill their blood in service to town and country?

On the sixth day of the manhunt, at Lancaster Baptist Church, one of the largest Baptist churches in the West, several thousand people gathered to say farewell to the resident deputy whose mission was short-lived and profound: the boy who had wanted to help people for as long as anyone could remember had grown up and continued doing exactly that, for five decades, until the end. It wasn't a glamorous calling, and the acts of kindness had been carried out in silent ways, but few among us follow their first path, and now the impact was loud and clear. Getting groceries for the housebound or cleaning up an elderly person's squalor or speaking up on behalf of cleaning ladies or old vaqueros who ran feed stores—the list went on and up and down the pews as friends and acquaintances remembered, privately and to each other.

In the moments before the service, video screens on the church walls showed photographs of Deputy Sorensen as a baby, with his parents (no longer living at the time of his death), with other deputies, and at his wedding. Most photographs showed Steve with his son, Matthew, his greatest joy, holding him on his shoulders or inside a judge's office for a visit, or happily astride his horse, his arms around the toddler as they went for a ride. It was a testament to the bond between father and son—a counterpoint, or in a strange way, a parallel to the other father and son story that, unbeknownst to authorities, played out in the awful thing that had gone down six days earlier and brought everyone to this church.

Among the mourners there were some who wondered how their old friend made his way to the desert, not even knowing he had been there for so many years until they saw what happened on the news. There sat Julie Franks for instance, Steve's neighbor in Manhattan Beach, one of the girls who had a crush on the cute surfer who did odd jobs for the folks on his street whenever there was a need. She hadn't seen him since he left for the army long ago, with his polished boots on the front lawn announcing his departure, as if—it seemed in retrospect—the very shoes had made the man, just like the old saying goes. Nor had Kimberly Brandon-Watson seen her former beau since many years earlier, when they had broken up in Manhattan Beach and gone their separate ways. She felt compelled to attend the funeral for her old boyfriend, stunned by what had happened to the young man who forsook the waves and endless promise of surf for what she had long regarded as a darker place—with some vague fear she had long held now confirmed.

Yet all of the hows and whys were quelled, if only for a few moments, as pallbearers entered the church carrying Deputy Sorensen in a flag-draped casket, with sheriff's deputies and members of the California Highway Patrol standing at attention in double lines leading up to the pulpit, saluting their fallen brother. Then two deputies lifted the flag and folded it, handing it to Sheriff Baca and Captain Carl Deeley, Sorensen's commander at the Lancaster station. Baca and Deeley knelt and handed the flag to Christine

Sorensen, Steve's widow, who was sitting in the front row with family members and friends. "Greater love has no one than this, that one lay down his life for his friends," said Captain Deeley, as he eulogized Deputy Sorensen before his family, Governor Gray Davis, and thousands of spit-shined deputes and cops from all over the country who filled the pews and spilled out onto the somber streets. The utterance from John 15:13 is oft-quoted at such funerals, but that does not render it less true; it is the ancient mandate regarding duty, a word that is generally spoken on patriotic holidays and in military and law enforcement circles, but not much elsewhere, sadly bereft of meaning in a country without any form of required national service or sacrifice.

Next to make a tribute was Sheriff Baca. "I think I have a right to be mad as hell," he said. "I think everyone here has the same right, but I don't want all that to get in the way of what this means to all of us. I want to focus on Steve Sorensen." Then he turned his attention to Steve's widow. "Chris," he said, "I'm so sorry. It is manly to weep. We'll continue in Steve's way." Several years after the killing of Deputy Sorensen, I sat in Sheriff Baca's office in east Los Angeles, talking with him about the incident. An intense man admired and scorned for his spirituality and sensitive manner and, as this book goes to press, in trouble as his department faces a raft of scandals, he seemed to pulse with a calm kind of outrage when we got to the heart of the conversation: What happened to Steve? I could tell that he was still angry about the loss of his man and the way in which it happened, and we spent a long time talking about the nuts and bolts of the manhunt, and the task that had sent Deputy Sorensen down the rutted driveway into what Sheriff Baca referred to as Kueck Nation. As we spoke, I could feel the full force and history of the Los Angeles County Sheriff's Department coming right through him, 160 years of standing on the thin blue line.

"If you're here to ask about the fire," he said, "I'd do it again." He was referring to the final conflagration, a thing that became the subject of controversy and an investigation. That wasn't why I was there, I explained; others had looked into it, written about it, and I was telling another part of the tale, the one that kept leading me right back to the same big question.

"Where is God in this story?" I asked the head of one of the most powerful law enforcement agencies in the world, hoping he might have a clue. "You know the answer," he said, and then was silent for a moment, maintaining his gaze, making the most penetrating eye contact I have ever experienced and working the fingers on both of his hands as if reliving Steve's final moments and the entire manhunt as well. "This is an old story and it never ends."

At Lancaster Baptist, the story went on, and the grief-stricken cops who knew it were uneasy. The thing that bothered them from the moment the pursuit began was still on their minds. What if Kueck were hiding somewhere, now looking through a rifle scope at the congregation as they laid their fallen deputy to rest? They prayed for their fellow officers who were still out searching for Kueck, wondering why nothing could flush him out, not the bloodhounds, not the two-bit snitches, not the cell-phone signals, not the thermal-imaging helicopters, not even bad luck. They knew that every outlaw in the desert was suddenly living with a proud defiance—one of their own had outsmarted the system. The world was watching, and if Kueck got away, the cops would be nothing.

Then, shortly after the bagpipes sounded and an honor guard placed Deputy Sorensen's coffin into the hearse for the last ride, they got a call. A phalanx of black-and-whites screamed out of the church parking lot and into the desert sands. Kueck, they were told, was cornered.

THE ALLIES ARE SUMMONED

Everyone comes to a meeting with a point of view.
  —Simon Baker, "The Art of Decision Making,"
  www.myCEOlife.com

IT WAS ANOTHER FALSE LEAD; KUECK WAS NOT CORNERED AT
all—at least in the sense that the cops were hoping for. Although
no one knows for sure, it seems most likely—and this is the conclusion that many searchers came to themselves—that by day six of
the manhunt, Kueck was hiding in the tunnels that tips kept pouring in about, emerging at night, like all desert creatures, to hunt.
Unlike those who were chasing him—equipped with all sorts of
elaborate gear and optics—he had no need for such trappings,
knowing well how to take advantage of such things as the excellent
nocturnal visibility of the Mojave Desert. "Its light-colored soil,"
wrote the naturalist Raymond B. Cowles, "varies from pale buff to
soft pink, and the plant life is so scanty it throws few shadows. All

the natural light from moon, sky, and star, vivid in the clear air, remains to aid one's vision." In just a few minutes, with automatic ocular adjustment, Don was able to move easily through the night, foraging, drinking, and returning to his subterranean safe house before sunrise.

Is it possible to know which tunnel our hermit would have hidden in, on this, his last day of freedom? Perhaps it was the one near his trailer, with the periscope that he had shown Jello's friends. Or perhaps it was an outlying tunnel, which he had shown no one. Or perhaps it was a tunnel that even he had not seen before, had only read about as he wandered the pages and visions of the old shamans. A portal might have appeared out of nowhere, drawn open by some unseen power or force, or there might have come an opening to a pack rat's nest, and it might have enlarged, or possibly it was already large enough for a man to crawl through and into, entering a world that could have held him for who knows how long. There's a strong chance that the tunnel in which Kueck was hiding in these final hours was not really a tunnel, but a kiva, a holy room, possibly the very one in which the shaman that had been unearthed by the bulldozer at the Anaverde development nearby may have once danced and prayed, in what manner we do not know, for so little is known or understood about the Indians of the western Mojave, the place that seems to have removed so much of its past and even recent history, as if in defiance of being remembered.

Given that Don may have been inside a kiva, of which tribe might this room of worship have been affiliated? Among the first peoples of the Antelope Valley were the Shoshone, and then there were their descendants, the Kitanemuk, the Vanyume, the Serrano, the Southern Paiutes, the Northern Mojave, and the Kawaiisu. All of these tribes invoked animal totems, some carving depictions of these creatures on rocks and on basalt walls, in tribute and perhaps as a route of spirit access, after certain plants were ingested or appropriate ritual was carried out.

Inside the kiva, on this, his sixth day as a fugitive, Don may have been undergoing withdrawal from powerful pain medication; he may have lost considerable weight, the result of not being able to acquire enough food or water in spite of having quenched himself at his friend's house and at various caches and quite possibly faucets in the yards of the unsuspecting. He may have been hallucinating, seeing all manner of ghosts and demons, and was it not in a moment such as this that the Devil had come to him some time ago and shown him the way out?

With the walls literally closing in, he may have called on certain powers he had read about in his beloved collection of books, some of which or whom he may have communed with at one time or another. Like many of his generation, he had read the works of Carlos Castaneda, the celebrated and mysterious author who had journeyed to Mexico and encountered the Yaqui shaman Don Juan, who guided him on the inward journeys that transpired after ingesting magic plants, instructing Castaneda about the parade of power animals that crossed his path and loaned the pilgrim special powers. In a book found in Kueck's belongings when it was all over, *The Second Ring of Power*, Castaneda encounters a powerful female figure called la Gorda, and finds himself confessing all sorts of personal torment while sitting in a desert gully. For example, he tells her that he once had a son whom he dearly loved and then one day forces conspired to take the boy away. To understand this dilemma, he had gone to consult Don Juan, asking the sorcerer to help him regain his son. Don Juan explained that a true warrior should not seek comfort after the fact. Instead, he could achieve results simply by the force of his own awareness and intentions. But it's too late even for that. "If I would have had the unbending intent to keep and help that child," Castaneda laments, "I would have taken measures to assure his stay with me. But as it was, my love was merely a word, a useless outburst of an empty man."

Alone in the ground, Kueck may have replayed these words over and over, flaying himself with rebuke, simmering down in a self-obsessed stew of regret and shame, crying out what little water he had left, calling out to his son, and trying again to make contact, just like Dr. Moody had said you could do, his mind now a big mishmash of pathways and crackling neurons, fear and disbelief. Yet all of the good doctor's suggestions for how to contact the dead were not working. In fact, they never had—who was this guy kidding, no wonder his relatives locked him up; there was only one way to talk to the dead and everyone knew what that was, and Jello, my son, do not fear, I am on my way, even though I am many days late and dollars short, but here I come you fucked-up son of a fucked-up father, here I come.

But first there were a few more things to take care of, farewells to be made, or hey, who knows, maybe I can still get away, it's still a free country, right, and I'm still a free man, I got my rights. . . . It was time to call in his friends the animals. Oh, you could always count on them when the going got tough. They didn't judge the way people did; they didn't care if you ate your meals out of a can or snarfed drugs from the dirt if you ran out. And so here came Scorpion, who said, 'Stay stealthy,' and here came Bobcat, who advised that perhaps the time had come, but not without a fight, and then raven came—and Don thought, Raven? Underground? You are indeed some bird, one helluva bird if I may say so, and I thank you for finding me in my hour of need—and the black creature with the chevron wings hopped on Don's arm, as always, and then the hermit looked him in the eye and saw his own reflection and he looked so bad and gnarly that it scared him. "Fear not," Raven said. "I will help you fly away." And then Don gave that some thought, and as he pondered, there came Ground Squirrel, and then several, and they hopped on his lap and on his shoulders, and they were running up and down his shattered body and chattering and just as the Indians used to say, they had come with news of the forest—or in this case, the desert, ha ha, the joke was on Don, for what they said was "You cannot win, my friend, give yourself up, there's thousands of men out there and believe you us, they are heavily armed," and the hermit knew that what they stated carried great weight and that he should probably heed their words.

Yet there was one tribe not yet heard from and this was Snake. Their absence disturbed him, as this was their domain, and he knew that some of the ancients, the Hopi in particular, that most unknowable of tribes, would go underground, taking snakes with them, and there they would dance, imbuing the rattlers with prayers for rain and then later sending them out to the four cardinal directions when they emerged, understanding that the snakes would carry the desires of their people with them and answer with the seasons and cloudbursts and life. Where were the Mojave greens who stood sentinel at his doorstep and who permitted him to handle them with no interference just because he lived with no fetters like they did out in the middle of nowhere? He couldn't bear that the very creature who embodied the thing that he lived for— Don't tread on me—had now forsaken him. And as he thought and thought and mulled it over, finally one of his beloved snakes may have appeared, though in a way that was not friendly, making it clear that he was no longer an ally. "Everything is out of whack," Snake said. "Things are not right with you. We can no longer be of service." It was all over then; there was clearly only one way for Don to get where he needed to go.

Or maybe it did not happen like that at all.

Darkness swept the sky on the night of August 6, 2003, and our hermit made ready for his last stand, figuring out how he would get from where he was at this moment to the place where he wanted to stand his ground. Sometime before daybreak, deep under the Mojave sands, Donald Charles Kueck understood that there was no refuge except what was supposed to happen, so he emerged from below to play the last scene out, promising himself that he would go out like a motherfucker. "Bring it on, old man," came a voice, maybe his son's. "Let's see what you got."

It was August, after all, the time when the end of things is on the wind; leaves are beginning to turn and fall, and even in the desert, the light is shifting, recalling, signaling, for those who have known it, the coming coolness and snap of impending freeze, the time of hibernation, sleep, and death.

DAY
SEVEN

Last Stand

Let's do it.

　　—Gary Gilmore at his execution before a Utah firing
　　squad, January 17, 1977

*I will meet them as a bear that is bereaved of her whelps, and will rend
the caul of their heart, and there will I devour them like a lion: the wild
beast shall tear them.*

　　—Hosea 13:8 (King James version)

"MRS. WELCH, GET OFF THE PHONE." HOMICIDE DETECTIVE
Mark Lillienfeld was calling Kueck's daughter on the special cell
phone that another investigator had given her the day after Kueck
killed Sorensen. The trap and trace operation that was running
since Day Two of the manhunt had picked up a signal from Don's
cell and traced it to Rebecca's phone. Kueck, it told them, was back

at C.T.'s place, but this time, his buddy was gone; fearing for his life, he had moved to a local motel. Inside his unmarked Crown Vic, Lillienfeld was tearing through a mountain pass across the 60 to Riverside and then placing the urgent call. "Your father is trying to call you," he said. Becky knew from the tone of Lillienfeld's voice that things were reaching a finale. But one of her kids had knocked the receiver on her land line off the hook, and the phone was busy. She immediately replaced it and awaited her father's call.

Throughout the week, Kueck had been phoning, strung out and crying and apologizing for never being able to see her again, saying how much he loved her and recounting a bizarre although possible version of the murder in which he had shot the deputy with Sorensen's own gun, suggesting that there was hand-to-hand combat before he opened up on him. "He kept coming," Kueck had said, "and I said, 'Stop, man, stop.'" Cops later attributed the story to Kueck's attempt to lay the groundwork for a defense, should he be taken alive, but some of his friends and relatives and a few on-line regulars who had been tailgating police scans believed that that's how it had gone down, affirming their unfettered belief in the right—and beyond that, the necessity—to bear arms.

Now, in Kueck's last hours, Rebecca Welch was walking an emotional tightrope, trying to help the sheriff's department and at the same time calm her father down as he threatened to go out like Scarface. Meanwhile SWAT was closing in, setting up a perimeter with snipers after moving into place early that morning. In fact, they had figured that Kueck would return one more time to C.T.'s compound. To make sure he didn't elude them again, they had em-barked on a sensitive operation two days earlier in which they switched places with the family who lived in the adjacent house, under cover of darkness. Detectives had been in contact with the woman who lived there—Steve's friend, who worked in a church thrift shop—since her sightings of Kueck earlier in the week. To take Kueck down, they knew there had to be an element of surprise.

The surprise was being at C.T.'s place when Kueck arrived. So a Spanish-speaking detective contacted the family and explained that they had to get out of the house—that night. Within minutes members of the SWAT team arrived to help them vacate. They had two dogs and several cats, and they wanted to take them. This was not allowed, to the sorrow of the children. The family piled into their white Toyota minivan, and six SWAT guys in full gear climbed in with them for protection, lest Kueck—or anyone else— had them in their sights. Then they drove to the convent, trying to be as inconspicuous as possible. But the fifteen-minute ride was frightening—for the family and for deputies. "We were crammed into the van and couldn't move," Bruce Chase recalls. "We talked about what could happen if Kueck opened up on us. We knew we were Swiss cheese."

Arriving safely, SWAT dropped off the family with the sisters at Mount Carmel. The kids were crying and asked again if they could go back and get their animals. The answer was no. Now SWAT had the cover of the family's van, and they headed back to C.T.'s place and parked in their usual place. They had told the family to leave the house unlocked, and entered the house through the front door. Kueck, they feared, may have returned when he saw the family and could have been lurking. Avoiding the use of lights in case that had happened, they staked out positions at each room in the house, then cleared them one by one in the darkness. Kueck did not come back that night, and the following morning, the red team returned, ramming down doors to all of the structures on the property and clearing them. Again there was no sign of Kueck.

Now, one week after Steve Sorensen had been killed, SWAT was ready. Snipers had returned to C.T.'s place in the white minivan, then staked out their positions. It was time for the heavy artillery. A SWAT commander placed a call to the LAPD, requesting the BEAR, the Ballistic Engineered Armored Response, a tactical vehicle that weighs 28,000 pounds and can rapidly deploy up to fifteen cops against urban combatants armed with assault weapons. In the open terrain of the desert, law enforcement had been at a disadvantage all week, even though in terms of manpower the odds had been overwhelmingly in their favor, with hundreds of cops trying to hunt down one man. But they were unprotected, not trained in wilderness tracking, and easy targets as they walked skirmish lines across the valley flats. The BEAR had been rolled out during the Gulf War, and at the time of this incident, few police departments had one. LAPD—the law enforcement agency that first deployed tanks in the city—was one of them, and they had just gotten the vehicle a week before this call. Within minutes, the massive tank was being driven up the freeways to the Antelope Valley and into the desert, tested in a foreign land and now deployed for another desert war on the home front.

Bear power cannot be underestimated in this, the final act. For just as our hermit had his team of animal allies—creatures whose ways he knew so well as to have been helped along his wilderness path—so too did his hunters invoke animal spirit. Regardless of the acronym, it was not for nothing that the tank used in modern street and desert warfare is called the BEAR. In California, where the grizzly was exterminated long ago, the bear had become an official symbol, like many a bygone creature, forever depicted on the state flag. Gone as a physical presence, its energy is drawn on in mysterious ways. Like the ancient warriors who donned eagle feathers and skin of wolf and head of elk and painted their horses with lightning bolts and arrows, the six-man SWAT team—tan, on this, the last day of the manhunt, with experienced deputies from other teams added to the crew—climbed inside the BEAR, heading to the final siege. The tank gave them an edge, named for a fearless apex predator, covering them with metal skin that can repel fast-traveling bullets—or so they were hoping as the fierce gun battle soon broke out.

But it wasn't only bear medicine that was being invoked in this assault; other animals were being called on from inside the tank and in other ways. There was dragon, an elaborate version of which lay coiled in ink around the arm of Deputy Mark Schlegel, eyes glowing and presence conjuring breath of fire, deployed later that day. And there was dog, in the physical form of Rik, the Malinois, returning with Joe Williams after searching on the first day of the manhunt and finding Sorensen's belongings.

Other team members that day called on other powers in their own way, each seeking an edge and protection for an event involving mortal danger. Years earlier, Bruce Chase had served with team scout Rick Rector when they were partners at the Century station in South Central LA, a violent beat. Several times they had been involved in shootings where people tried to kill them. They had a bond, and although he had Saturdays off, he readily agreed when Rector called him early that morning and asked him to step in on this, the final siege. As he climbed into the BEAR, he thought of Psalm 23, which helped him calm the adrenaline rush that arrives with fear, just as he had when he and his team entered the compound two nights ago in the dark, now delving deeper into the channels of the Old Testament watchwords. "You prepare a table before me," went the familiar words, "in the presence of my enemies. You anoint my head with oil . . . "

Deputy Fred Keelin found comfort in the BEAR itself. Two days earlier, his pager went off moments after taking his son to get his driver's license on his sixteenth birthday. He was asked to report in for a SWAT operation, and he tossed his son the car keys and headed out to the command post on Palmdale Boulevard. At the age of fifty-five, he was the oldest member of the SWAT team, having been on the force for twenty-one years and involved in all manner of deadly situations. For Keelin, the tank was a thing of religious ferocity. "The BEAR was like God to us," he recalls several years later. "Kueck was in his element, and we were not."

As the vehicle headed across the sands to the compound where Kueck had staked out his position, police radios were going berserk with news that the fugitive was cornered. Deputies from three counties burned down the highway, racing toward the site, where they joined other law enforcement personnel and stood arm to arm at the outer perimeter, a human barrier through which no one could escape. Across the way at a nearby house, an arrest team was in place, ready in case the day concluded with Kueck's surrender. With everybody positioned, an announcement was made—"DONALD KUECK, THIS IS THE LOS ANGELES COUNTY SHERIFF'S DEPARTMENT. WE KNOW YOU ARE IN THERE. COME OUT WITH YOUR HANDS UP." There was no response, no movement. Was Kueck really in there? Many of the frazzled deputies wondered. Or had he escaped the noose once again?

At 1:20 PM, Rebecca Welch got another call. It was her father. He had been trying to contact police on Sorensen's radio. After exchanging greetings, Don launched into a disjointed stream of thought about what happened, his fears about returning to jail, and regrets, stating that he was calling from the house of an old acquaintance where he had gone to get some food. "The SOB came at me with his gun pointed at my head," he said. "So I dug up the gun and put it together. . . . I was gonna kill a rattlesnake. . . . What was I gonna do—let him starve to death? . . . They found me yesterday morning when I was asleep. I put cardboard over me. . . . They can't read the thermal thing. . . . The cardboard blocked me. . . ."

"I heard from Bill," Becky replied, referring to Don's brother, and trying to stop the train. "He said to tell you he loves you. Lynne told me to tell you don't hurt anyone else."

"They froze me to death in jail," Don said. "Gave me food I couldn't eat. . . . For the past few years I've been getting signals that my life is over. I didn't think I'd live this long. . . . There is an afterlife—I know that. . . . a scientific fact . . . You suffer for the pain you caused and then . . . Tell Ann I love her," he continued, referring to another sister, a prison guard in Arizona. "They gave her hell for going by the book. . . . I made it to the grocery store once, and it wiped me out. . . . I was backing up. . . . I didn't have nothing in my hands. . . . When I got close enough to the car, I grabbed his gun, and I shot him. . . . He wouldn't quit. . . . If only cops would follow the law . . . Only low-income people know . . . The ex-con who attacked me in the parking lot . . . I opened the bolt cutter just to scare him. . . . I'll shoot myself in the head first before going to jail. . . . I had the snake for three weeks. . . . I considered dumping him, but he might have bitten a hiker. . . . Don't worry about me—they're gonna kill me. . . . I'm not scared. . . . I'm not even nervous. . . . "

"Your granddaughter Lolly was crying all night," Becky said. "Someone told her you killed a cop."

"I wish my family had never found me," Don said, then continued his downward spiral, conflating various experiences from different periods of his life in a continuous timeline. "I love it in the desert. . . . It's warm. . . . I'm too exhausted, honey, to talk. . . . I love you, baby. . . . Lynne tried to help. . . . I left money in the trailer. . . . I could hear their voices. . . . They circled me for about an hour . . . wider and wider. . . . It was two days ago, or it might have been this morning or yesterday. . . . There were two choppers less than a hundred feet right over me, and I was lying on my side. . . . I have to sleep with my legs curled up because of the cot in jail. . . . When the black-and-white got there, the guy said, 'I'm gonna pepper spray you.' . . . "

"Can we get through this without you dying?" Becky said.

"I won't live for long," Don replied. "I tried to stop him— knock him down—I said stop stop stop. . . . We're losing the signal. . . . I went to my neighbor. . . . Everyone out here is stupid. . . . They have no morals. . . . Don't ever move out here. . . . I was walking. . . . I got as far as one-quarter mile, a hundred or two hundred yards, at some guy's house because I knew the hose was on in the backyard. . . . The TV was on, and I was on it. . . . It was a struggle to get water. . . . I had a one-gallon water container. . . . I'm laying down. . . . I feel great. . . . It's 80 or 90 degrees, ideal, with less than 20 percent humidity. . . . I'm ready to die. . . . I wish I had died sooner. . . . If I'm still alive, I'll call you back. . . . I'm close to C.T.'s house . . . can't go no further. . . . He's not involved. . . . He gave me some water and tea and a potato. . . . He doesn't have much. . . . They'll find my fingerprints at his house. . . . I can't sleep in the daytime, not with this noise. . . . I'm in my right mind. . . . I'm in the shade and sage brush . . . laying down. . . . I don't want a cop to kill me. . . . I'd rather have anyone else kill me but a cop. . . . "

"Dad," Becky said, "don't kill someone else."

"Would killing Mengele or Hitler be bad?" Don said. "Sometimes I get better for a week or two. . . . Sudafed helps a little."

"I love you, Dad," Becky said. "Your granddaughters love you."

"I never wished anyone any harm," Don said, now crying. "I have a hard time killing a rattlesnake. . . . I'm glad I'm with God now. . . . Bye, baby, I love you."

There was another brief exchange in which Don again talked about the conditions in jail. He added that his phone was giving out and that he was trying to contact law enforcement, noting that he had Sorensen's walkie-talkie. "I'm sure they'll respond," Becky said. "They don't want to kill you. . . . Wait, someone's at the door. . . . " Detective Lillienfeld had just arrived. "Dad, the sheriff's right here," Becky continued. "You talk to him." By now, every satellite van in Southern California was racing toward the scene.

Who among us thinks about the last conversation you might have before checking out? What topics would be covered, beyond the usual round of farewells? And, perhaps more importantly, with whom would you be speaking? Of all the last conversations Donald Charles Kueck found himself having, it was with a cop—the figure with whom he had been shadow wrestling for years. Now a member of law enforcement was his final buddy, deathbed confessor, and possible savior.

Kueck was fortunate in that the person he ended up talking with was Detective Mark Lillienfeld. They were of the same generation—Mark was fifty-two to Kueck's fifty-three (in fact the negotiation occurred on Lillienfeld's birthday)—and in other circumstances, they might have learned that they shared a similar trajectory, at least in terms of geography. Like Kueck, Lillienfeld had come west as soon as he could. He spent his childhood in Illinois, with many a fondly remembered summer watching baseball at Wrigley Field. As a teenager, he moved with his family to Waco. At seventeen, he headed for California, longing for the coast. He didn't know anybody there and had no place to stay, except his car, a Pontiac station wagon, which he parked in Elysian Park. He spent six months on the streets, using the showers and restrooms at USC and UCLA when necessary, and working at various construction jobs around town. "It was great," he recalls in one of many conversations we had at a cop hangout near the Firestone station where he was working a case. "I was in LA!" Some time later, a friend suggested he join the LASD; always a person who wanted to stand up to the bad guys, he took the test and entered immediately.

In talking with Kueck, he brought something beyond their love of California. A cop with a different manner, more brash, for instance, would not have been able to stay on the phone with the fugitive for more than five minutes. Lillienfeld was a self-effacing guy whose unobtrusive nature gave no hint of his accomplishments as a homicide detective with twenty-five years of experience in the LA County Sheriff's Department. For instance, in 1998, he was called to the scene where racing legend Mickey Thompson and his wife had been murdered in the foothills of the San Gabriel Mountains. For the next thirteen years, he followed the killer's trail, until their business partner was finally charged. While on the prison gang strike force during the 1980s, Lillienfeld investigated the Aryan Brotherhood—one of the Big Four gangs in the country, all of which had coalesced in California. At the time, there had been forty murders over a ten-year period, all of them in prison. The victims were "unappealing," he told a reporter at the time. "Bad men." Most people couldn't care less that they had been whacked. "But I worked on the case for three years," he said. "You develop compassion for the victims. They weren't that different from you or me. They had families, hopes, dreams—they just happened to turn left where you or I turned right." In the final hours of the manhunt for Donald Kueck, it was more than his identification with the other guy that permitted a conversation, strange though it was, to unfold. It was his very voice itself. Quiet and soothing, it may have provided Kueck with a few moments of grace before he went up in flames. Beyond that, after listening to the tapes of the conversation many times and hearing Kueck's voice waver and then come back strong, I can say that it may have even caused him to think twice about his decision to make a last stand.

The situation was equally unexpected for Lillienfeld, not that homicide cops are surprised by much. But here it was, his birthday weekend, and he gets a call because the regular hostage negotiator is not available. He figured something might come up on the weekend, because not a Saturday night goes by without someone getting whacked in Los Angeles County. But still, getting called to a crime scene was a lot different from having to get on the phone and negotiate with a fugitive. Plus, there wasn't really a hostage, other than the man himself. Quite simply, Mark Lillienfeld was tasked with convincing a man who had vowed never to return to jail into surrendering and possibly facing the rest of his life in prison—without taking a few more cops out before he gave up or killed himself. Then there was the possibility that Kueck wanted to kill himself—commit suicide by cop—and that the entire episode had been one prolonged version of this increasingly common way to go out. According to the *Annals of Emergency Medicine*, at least 10 percent of the shootings involving the Los Angeles County Sheriff's Department are such incidents. Of course, if that was the goal, Kueck was about to get his wish.

But the end was hours away.

For over five hours, as Kueck tried to recharge his faltering cell-phone battery with the one in Sorensen's radio, there were dozens of calls made back and forth from Lillienfeld to the staging area at Mount Carmel in the field. All the while, the detective was sitting on the couch in Welch's small living room, with Rebecca right next to him, taking care of her children and toddler while at the same time watching the siege unfold on television and wondering what her father was going to do—and receiving periodic calls from him on her land line. It was hot in Riverside that day, over 90, and there was no air conditioning in the apartment. "I drank a lot of water," Lillienfeld recalls months later. "I got very hungry." At one point during the siege, a local cop stopped by, and Mark gave him some cash for a pizza run. When he returned with replenishments, Rebecca's kids devoured the food, leaving a slice for the detective. Throughout the negotiation, he was holding a phone in each ear— one for talking to Kueck, and the other an open line to SWAT command HQ in the field, through which he was relaying what Kueck was saying, and then they in turn would relay the information to LASD headquarters in Commerce. At times, there were problems with connections, with lines cutting out and a ten-minute delay between SWAT, staging from the convent, and HQ. Whenever contact was lost, Lillienfeld had to wait for Kueck to call back. It was not possible to call the fugitive; wanting to avoid a situation where the GPS tracking could pinpoint his exact location inside the general vicinity of the compound, Kueck initiated all of the calls, and maintained contact for brief spurts only, which eliminated the ability to zero in on his whereabouts. Although everyone knew he was on the grounds of a complex of sheds at a certain address, they did not know if he was calling from a tunnel, a bedroom, or behind a creosote bush.

Well into the negotiation, Lillienfeld's cell phone was fading as well, and a black-and-white was sent to Riverside to deliver new batteries. With Kueck's cell phone dying by the minute, he kept trying to talk on Steve's radio. But he couldn't read the small channels because sometime during the past week, he had lost his reading glasses, which he may have been carrying in a backpack he took with him on the day he fled the crime scene. Toward the end of the lengthy negotiation, Lillienfeld's arms were tired from holding phones up all day in the heat. Kueck himself was spent—"dehydrated, scared, mentally ill, and surrounded by thousands of cops," as Lillienfeld said. The detective kept prompting him to surrender before dark. "I wanted a good legal admission," he tells me months later at LASD HQ in Commerce. "I've just spent six hours in a hot room with a cop killer."

Pieced together, the abbreviated exchanges between the two adversaries, recorded on tape, comprise a kind of two-man drama, a play within our play, involving a character who was throwing out lifelines and a man who was wavering between coming in and not, and degenerating as the hours ticked by.

MARK: Hi, sir, how are you? My name is Mark, and I'm a detective with the LA Sheriff's Department.

DON: My cell phone battery is on its last legs.

MARK: Talk to me as long as you can.

DON: No, sir, please, can you turn the walkie-talkie on? It has many channels.

MARK: To talk on the radio, you push the red button on the side. Is there something we can do for you?

DON: I don't want to be rude, but you can't because once I get in there, those two Asian doctors are worse than Mengele. . . .

MARK: We got all kinds of doctors in there. Why don't we let you see some non-Asian doctors?

DON (making an allergy reference): I can't use a wool blanket. I need cotton.

MARK: Are you allergic to Top Ramen?

DON: I can't eat beans, tomatoes, MSG.

MARK: The sheriff is telling me he agrees to all that.

DON: Put me in solitary, not with four Crips. I'm really weak. . . . I have chronic fatigue syndrome. . . . I take Ritalin. . . . Some of those cops are gonna shoot me on sight.

MARK: No, they won't.

DON (crying): Don't tell my mother. . . . My father was in the Air Force. . . . I gotta go. . . . You're breaking up.

MARK: Look at L-TAC1 on the radio. . . . I can have the sheriff phone back in ten minutes. Keep the phone on for five minutes. Donald, do you still have the deputy's gun—the Beretta and the other gun? We don't want a little kid to find it.

DON: I don't either. . . . I'm gonna get my glasses so I can see. . . . I'm in the desert. . . .

MARK: Talk around L-TAC1. Hang on, Donald. Stay with me. . . . You're gonna hear someone talk on the radio. . . .

DON: I have a question about mode 7 star.

MARK: You gotta quit moving channels around. We'll find the one you're on.

DON: It says "mode 7 emergency."

MARK: Don't touch any other knob. . . . We're a bunch of dumb cops—you gotta bear with us here. . . .

DON: I gotta take a leak. It might be a minute before I answer. [back on the line] The radio's getting hot.

MARK: That's typical of our equipment. . . . We'd like to kind of resolve this thing before it gets dark out. It's 3:20 now. . . . You sound like you're smarter than I am when it comes to police radios.

DON: I don't wanna get arrested or killed before sundown.

MARK: Nobody wants to kill you. . . . There's probably a million cops out there. . . . Why not come out now? It's light out.

DON: I'm too damn weak to walk. . . . I'm peaceful, but if you're lying to me about this radio, I might have to defend myself with the little thing I have.

MARK: I'm an old detective, and I haven't carried one of those radios before. . . . When I was in patrol, I walked a foot beat, and I'm just not that familiar with it, or else I'd be smart enough to tell you how to work it right. Honest to God, I'm just not that bright as everyone knows. That's why I'm here at Rebecca's house and not out there with you and all the other cops. . . . All we want to do is see you stand up and walk with your hands up. . . .

DON: They're gonna shoot me.

MARK : They're not gonna shoot you. . . . Can you hit the button so it says not to scan? Push the menu button and see what it says. . . . Turn on the channel one click at a time. . . . What happened on Saturday?

DON: I was in bed. He says come out. I said, 'What's up, buddy?' He wouldn't say. . . . I alternate my meds. . . .

MARK: Talk around Seatac 2. . . . Hey Donald, is there an orange button at the top of the radio? . . . Is there any way I can convince you . . . I understand you know how to defeat the infrared.

DON: Well, I barely did. . . . The helicopter was going exactly over my position at a low altitude that woke me up, and that's when I put cardboard over my head.

MARK: I'd really like to end this silliness in about five minutes . . . get you some water and take care of you. . . .

DON: Five minutes won't do it.

MARK: Nobody's out to do bad stuff to you. . . . I drive a desk. I'm not good at being out there in the field. . . . This getting old is not for sissies. . . .

DON: Yeah . . .

MARK: How old are you?

DON: I'm almost fifty-three. . . . My health is so bad. . . . [crying] My son passed two years ago. . . . I'm fucked up.

MARK: Tell me what you want, and I'll do it. I give you my personal guarantee that I'll make it happen.

DON: (possibly not hearing Mark): This is Donald. Can anybody hear me? If I had an hour or two, I could wire this battery to my cell phone.

MARK: I'm sure you could. Donald, push the red button and say, "This is Donald. Can anybody hear me? Emergency." . . . If you push the button and you key the microphone, they'll hear you. . . .

DON: It's an emergency. Please respond. This is Donald. Can anyone hear me? . . . I wanna say something. . . . The first day I came by C.T.'s . . . he had cleared out. He had nothing to do with this. He ain't no saint, but he wasn't in on this. . . . The Antelope Valley is a fucked-up place to grow up.

[Connection lost; Kueck recharges cell phone, calls again.]

MARK: Hey, Donald, tell me what I can do to get your butt out of there and get you to the hospital. What would it take? No one's gonna put you in a cell with a buncha Crips. . . . I don't want you out there after dark. It's dangerous for you; it's dangerous for cops out there. . . . It's 4:36 right now, Donald. . . . We got till about 8. . . .

DON: Let me tell you something, buddy. . . . The last few years [choking up]—excuse me . . . Since I got out of jail . . . all the tools and everything I needed to live was gone. . . . I knew it was my time to go, or it was getting close, so I've made my peace with God. . . . All they have to do is believe me and not look at my long hair and think I want dope. I promised a friend who went to Nam that I'd cut it when he came back. He never did. Twenty-five years later I thought about cutting it, but I couldn't do it.

MARK: Twenty-five years is a long time to go without a haircut. . . . Where are you? Near C.T.'s or out in the desert?

DON: I can't tell you. Some of those cops are gonna shoot me on sight. . . . I love the desert. The first time I went out there I was with my buddy and his older brother. He was racing a dirt bike. . . .

I loved the desert so much and wanted to move here. . . . I even started racing and got a good bike. . . . We had two bikes so you'd have parts. . . . I was at the Vegas 400 race. . . . Too many rats are coming down from the mountains now. . . .

MARK: Those dirt bike promoters made a ton of money. Did you race with guys from LAPD?

DON: They were probably out in some of the races.

MARK: I guess the heat is good for your back pain.

DON: I have chronic fatigue syndrome. . . . The desert makes me feel good, like a piece of toast. . . . The disease affected my body temperature. . . . I can barely get a charge, and these guys are moving in . . .

MARK: Can you see deputy sheriffs moving in?

Earlier that afternoon, Sheriff Baca had flown to the staging area on Palmdale Boulevard and 180th Street. At 3:30 PM he stepped out of the Air 5 chopper and was escorted to a bank of microphones to address the news media. He gave an assessment of the situation and the suspect, and ended the press conference with a terse summation: "We're down to what's known in this business as dead or alive."

At 5:05 PM, SWAT commanders positioned the BEAR and set up a tactical plan. Ground intel was telling them that Kueck was making spider holes and burying himself, and that comported with what Lillienfeld was hearing from Don on the phone—that he was moving from location to location and maybe the signal was cutting out because he was underground. SWAT was ready to deploy gas. But there had been a delay—the battering ram wasn't rigged to send in the fuel. To arm a delivery system, team members scoured a safe zone beyond the perimeter and found baling wire. Then they loaded the burnsafe—a large metal canister—with gas and attached a 550 parachute cord to the pin. With the burnsafe ready to go, they would punch through each of the four sheds on the property, deploy gas, let it cook, and wait for a response. Back in Riverside, Mark Lillienfeld tried one last time to get Kueck to surrender. The connection was lost. At 5:26 PM, the loudspeaker began blaring—"DONALD KUECK, COME OUT WITH YOUR HANDS UP." As the announcements continued, SEB and patrol sounded a roll call, and a gun shot rang out. By 5:43, over fifty announcements had been made. Three minutes after the shot was heard, Don activated his phone and called Mark Lillienfeld. "Hey, tell those guys—" he said, and then the call cut out again as the loudspeaker kept telling Kueck to surrender. He called back one more time. "I can't get much charge," he said, and then the connection cut out, and the penultimate line of the final conversation of Donald Kueck's life was Mark Lillienfeld asking, "Don, can you hear me?"

Now the BEAR was on the move, lumbering across the sands and heading toward the sheds where Kueck was making his last stand. The first round of tear gas was deployed, quickly followed by a second. As the gas billowed through the main compound, Kueck called Lillienfeld at 6:14 PM claiming to be in the bushes and daring him to "send in the dogs."

SWAT launched another volley of tear gas and then backed away from the location to discuss the next action. At 7:23 PM, Captain Spencer okayed a request to knock down the walls of the sheds and the BEAR moved in for the kill. At 7:27, two more shots were heard, and roll calls for SEB and patrol were immediately taken. Three minutes later, another shot was heard by containment positions, and deputies tried to locate the shooter. By then the BEAR was rolling toward the main compound. Kueck opened up with his automatic, spraying the giant assault vehicle with gunfire. "How many rounds can these windows take?" someone asked inside the BEAR. LAPD sergeant Rick Massa, piloting the vehicle, didn't know, and tried calling his command post for the stats. Meanwhile the situation in the BEAR was growing more tense. At the sound of

the first gunshot, the team had figured Kueck wanted to make
them think he had killed himself so they'd get out of the vehicle.
Through a porthole, Bruce Chase returned the fire. When Kueck
responded, they saw the heat signature—not a bright orange flame,
since it was daytime, but a small circle rippling from the weapon—
and they knew his location. They blasted off a volley of .308 rounds
from their long rifles, the firepower pouring out of the tank and
through the compound. As the shots screamed over the sand, Chase
couldn't shake the feeling that all along, he had been chasing a
ghost; now, for the first time in his career, he wasn't able to see the
man who was trying to kill him. Hot shell casings poured down his
back as the weapons ate up the rounds, and the team kept reloading
and firing, trying to bring their lone adversary down. At some point
SWAT started to run out of ammo. A call went out on the police
band, and Sorensen's academy classmate Bernard Shockley heard
the news. As the heated firefight continued, he headed west across
the 15 from his home in Victorville to deliver more ammunition.
Shockley got a flat in Hesperia and pulled over, followed by an old
couple in an old car, offering help. "Turns out the man had a huge
floorjack from Pep Boys," Shockley says years later, recalling the bit
of good fortune. He changed tires and raced to the scene, thinking
that the episode was a mirror image of what Steve had done in his
life—Samaritans on the road, and elderly ones at that, stopping to
help a stranger in need.

By the time he got there, the place was on fire.

Inside the BEAR, Rik the Malinois had his hack up, way
more than usual. Like Joe Williams and the others on the team,
he had never been in tight quarters like this, in extreme heat,
with hundreds of hot rounds going off around him, heading toward an enemy as gunfire screamed off the surrounding metal
skin. Joe tried to calm him as shells from the firestorm fell down
the collar of his uniform and onto his back, a painful occurrence

that precluded a normal response lest Rik sense danger and react in the enclosed space.

Meanwhile Rick Rector was undergoing another first. Because LASD did not have their own BEAR, he and the others hadn't been inside one until today. Now he was up in the turret and felt vulnerable. As a deputy in LASD during the Rodney King riots in 1992, he had walked the streets of Compton, exposed and a target. But this was different; he was confined to the BEAR and could not escape. From his vantage point he was throwing flashbangs into the compound—a diversionary device—to try to flush Kueck out. But the tactic wasn't working, and in fact after lobbing a flare into one of the sheds, he watched in amazement as Kueck appeared, grabbed it, and tossed it aside. He continued to launch tear gas canisters by hand, but that wasn't working either; the high winds were blowing the gas away from the sheds along with the fuel from the burnsafe. But the BEAR kept moving until the walls on all four sheds were knocked down. Inside it, although protected, Bruce Chase wondered if the vehicle would suddenly plunge into a sinkhole or tunnel, to be consumed by that mysterious system that Kueck had been in and out of all week long and that some of the men had seen firsthand.

By 7:42 PM, Air 5 and 6 were hovering over the sheds as fires broke out in one shed, then two, then a third, as Kueck—perhaps shot himself—darted in and out of the flames, continuing to blast off rounds. "He has a shitload of ammo," Fred Keelin was thinking, and by then SWAT had gone through so much of their own that they had been leaving to reload at a supply line and then returning to engage. By 8:45, the entire compound was on fire, and the fire grew, and as the moon appeared above the Mojave, almost full, it became a conflagration with giant freak-show flames that scorched the heavens, and some wondered if it was the Twilight of the Gods, and the news choppers came to the fire like mechanical moths, relaying the image to millions who watched the flames dance on television, the phony hearth that interrupted regular programming with coverage of The End. Around the perimeter of Kueck's last stand, hundreds of deputies and law enforcement personnel watched the grisly bonfire burn and wondered if they had finally got him. A few miles away at Mount Carmel, the nuns watched the flames in the distance and prayed, and out in Riverside, a few hours later, Mark Lillienfeld delivered the news to Rebecca Welch, who had stopped watching television when the gunfire erupted and left the room. "It's over," he said and then after a while, he and Rebecca said their good-byes and he hit the road. Like Steve Sorensen, Mark Lillienfeld rescued dogs. There was one he had recently adopted from the pound, and as he headed west on the 60 out of Riverside, he was looking forward to seeing her when he got home.

AFTERBURN

Eddie would go.
   —Tribute to fallen lifeguard and big-wave surfer
Eddie Aikau

AT MIDNIGHT—MORE THAN THREE HOURS AFTER THE FIRE BEGAN
raging—SWAT was ordered to search the area. Now, two teams
were sweeping the field. They still didn't know if Kueck was alive
or had escaped yet again. They formed skirmish lines and began
walking through the rubble. Once again, they felt vulnerable. Yet
odd things can go through your head at any given time. At least
half of the men on site were planning to leave for a golf trip in
Nevada later that day. They had put down their deposits months
ago. "We gotta hurry up," Bruce Chase was thinking. "If we don't,
we'll miss our plane." But of course what they were doing had no
timetable, and on they walked, as if into a literal representation of

the twenty-third psalm, the one that Chase often though of when in danger.

Strangely, although all four sheds had burnt to the ground, the main house where the Hispanic family lived was completely intact. In fact, as the compound had gone up in flames that night, Bruce remembers watching the blaze get bigger and bigger, moving toward the main house, while noting that a tree next to the house was on fire but the house was not, even as more of the tree's branches began crackling with heat and flame. Except for a propane tank next to it, the tree was the only thing between the house and the rest of the bonfire. Oddly, the tank did not erupt either. Now, as Chase walked across the fallen timbers and ashes, the tree was still smoldering—and only half of it at that. There weren't many trees in that part of the desert, in fact hardly any at all. This one was a mesquite, a tree with a root system than can run deep and run wide in order to tap into water. Far away in another desert there is a mesquite known as "the tree of life." It's the only tree for miles, and residents of the town of Bahrain where it lives have long regarded it as the marker of the Garden of Eden. Here in the Mojave, it was as if the tree had been protecting the house where Carmen lived, Steve's friend, the devout woman who toiled in a church thrift shop that helped provide the destitute people of the valley with clothing and other provisions. It was some kind of miracle, Bruce figured. Yet that was not the only one. Inside the house were the family's animals, left behind when they evacuated, safe and alive and well, waiting for everyone to come home and start over.

Other strange sights awaited SWAT as they continued to walk through the dregs of the compound. The power had been turned off several hours ago, and they were searching in the dark, with powerful handheld lights. It had been a long siege, and they were spent. Even Rik the Malinois stopped in his tracks. Joe Williams knew it was time for the dog to go home. He was replaced with another K9 who had been standing by, and the men continued their weary march. Ten minutes after the search began, Bruce Chase spotted two femurs jutting through the ashes. The men moved in for a closer look. Donald Kueck was on his back, nearly cremated, clutching his rifle. When they went to move the body, it crumbled. A few days later, his family scattered his ashes off the Three Sisters Buttes, the formation he looked to at dawn.

* * *

On August 11 at 8:06 PM, the dispatcher announced the traditional end-of-watch roll call for a deputy killed in the line of duty. "Lancaster 110 Charlie," she called, and from his patrol car he responded, "114Boy, it was an honor to know you and a privilege to work with you, God speed," and then from all over the desert the messages poured in—from 110 Lincoln and 110 Lincoln Adam and 110 George and 113 Sam—"Steve, you will never be forgotten, my brother. . . . Your family's in good hands here, and we know you're in good hands up there. . . . Rest in peace, my brother."

* * *

Months after it all went down, the crime-scene tape at Kueck's trailer still fluttered in the wind. There were some old jars of peanut butter and a pair of Nikes (size 11)—just waiting for the next hermit with a dream. The land remained a scavenger's paradise of busted bicycles and generators, engines and furniture, lawn mowers and tables and chairs. There was a broken-down La-Z-Boy facing the buttes—Kueck's chair, the one he sat in when he watched the sun rise over the Mojave. From here he could survey his strange desert kingdom. He had come out here to escape civilization, but he knew he could be evicted at any point. The desert was shrinking, and civilization didn't like people who violated its codes.

"Lynne," he said in one of his last letters to his sister, "I'm writing this down because I get choked up when trying to talk about personal issues. . . . I know the next life is waiting for me. . . . I don't want you to blame yourself if the inevitable comes to pass. This feeling has been growing for the last one to two years." Then, in a burst of optimism, he added, "Of course the future *can* be changed, and it would be fun trying. Since I was twenty years old, I've had the dream of building a little place in the desert."

To the right of the La-Z Boy sits a pallet stacked with eighty-pound sacks of lime—construction material for the house that Kueck never built. One of these days, he was going to make a course correction. But as always happens with men such as this, he never got there—and never would. Instead, he had picked up a spade and dug his own grave at the edge of his property. It's the first thing you see on the way in and the last on the way out, a project he made sure to finish, now filled in by wind and erosion. Months after he had gone out in the blaze, Jello's friends drove out to the old man's trailer, retrieved some mementoes, and scattered the boy's ashes on top of Don's grave.

EPILOGUE

For Whom the Bell Tolls

AFTER IT ALL WENT DOWN, DON'S FRIEND C.T. SMITH MOVED into an RV and parked it near Littlerock Dam, his pad now burnt to smithereens. A few days later, detectives arrived with his share of the reward money—one-quarter of $10,000—but he didn't know how to cash the check. They took him to a check-cashing place and walked him through the process. Around that time, he was listed in the paper as one of the people sharing the reward. Now known as a snitch, he retreated more deeply into the desert. At some point, he moved into a house in Lake Los Angeles. On October 10, 2005, after failing to report to his parole officer and register with the Los Angeles County Sheriff's Department as a sex offender, he retrieved a gun from under his roommate's pillow, stood near a bathroom doorway, and shot himself in the head. He had told friends he was never going back to jail, which he knew would happen because of the aforesaid violations and the fact that he had been doing speed and would therefore fail the mandatory drug test. As soon as she heard the shot, his roommate called 911. Paramedics quickly arrived, and within minutes C.T. was pronounced dead.

On the thirteenth of every month, a devout woman named Maria Paula Acuna leads followers into the desert near California City, where others go to wait for desert tortoises to emerge from their burrows in spring time, a sign of magic and rebirth. Paula and her constituents were awaiting a vision of the Virgin Mary. They make the pilgrimage to the spot in the Mojave on the same date and same time because that's when the Holy Mother had first appeared as a cloud of white fog years ago, at 10:30 in the morning, and said, "I am the Lady of the Rock, Queen of Peace of Southern California. I come to bring you the peace and love that is so needed." One week after the manhunt for Donald Kueck had reached its conclusion, thousands sat under the clear blue sky in lawn chairs, on the ground, on rocks, and waited. Someone saw a beam of light and inside it an apparition. "Mary," called a child, and others rushed toward the beam, crossing themselves and falling to their knees and someone cast off their crutches. "Madre de Dios," others said, and later, depending on how you looked at it, a Polaroid showed an image of a woman in a cloud. . . .

Shortly after Steve was killed, the town council of Lake Los Angeles was rearranged, replacing those who had opposed him and his allies Pastor John Wodetzki and reporter Connie Mavrolas with those who supported their work, ushering in a more inclusive policy, and transforming how things were done in the town where Steve had been resident deputy. On October 18, 2006, a portion of State Route 138 was named Deputy Sheriff Stephen Sorensen Memorial Highway. The six-mile stretch that runs through Llano is marked by signs at 135th Street East and 195th Street East, the east-west borders of the sheriff's beat. Just to the north of the pavement are the ruins of the old commune, faltering every hour and every minute, yet still somehow standing. . . .

The way of the future, they say, is logistics, a curious endeavor once associated primarily with the military and now a college major at various institutions of higher learning around the country. Logistics, according to *Wikipedia*, is the management of the flow of goods between the point of origin and the point of destination in order to meet the requirements of customers or corporations. Logistics involves the integration of information, transportation, inventory, warehousing, material handling, packaging, and security. To accommodate logistics, there are plans for a High Desert Corridor in the Mojave, a sixty-three-mile freeway consisting of four, six, or eight lanes, depending on what parts of the desert it traverses, running from Highway 14 in the Antelope Valley eastward to Highway 15 in the Victor Valley, facilitating connection between the ports of Los Angeles and Long Beach with rail lines and airports in the Inland Empire. "The corridor uniquely positions the High Desert to distribute goods on a global scale," as the plans say. "A talented labor force and low land costs make the High Desert a great place to locate your business." The corridor will be completed by 2020 if all goes according to plan.

The proposal is not without merit. It will certainly bring jobs to a region where jobs are scarce. It may alleviate problems on the 138, aka Tweaker Highway aka Blood Alley, site of so many fatal accidents, siphoning off fast-moving truck traffic from a roadway that can't handle it and loosening up bottlenecks that form on the freeways of Southern California when travelers must drive around the western Mojave instead of across it. But the corridor would also pass through the last remaining wide-open space in Los Angeles County—the land that Donald Kueck and Steve Sorensen called home. This would change the nature of the place, alter the quality of living for those who have spent fortunes and time and blood erecting kingdoms great and small, and it would drive the region's remaining castaways deeper into the desert, rigging their tents, planting their no trespassing signs, scavenging on the far reaches of civilization, desperados displaced one more time. Already, like their brothers and sisters in the animal nations who detect the approach of a tsunami or earthquake and flee in advance of a cataclysm, they have picked up signals, organized meetings (perhaps a first in the annals), "contacted the media" . . . Yes, the man has come a-knocking, in pursuit of code violations, expired smog checks, other misdeeds, and they suspect that their days in the far reaches of Los Angeles County are numbered. John Wayne once lived in these here parts. One of the things he said about the Antelope Valley is that it taught him how to be a cowboy.

On a final note, let us recall the mysterious character known in this story as Mr. X. You remember him? The squatter who triggered the chain of deadly events? The last I heard, he was living at El Mirage, the dry lake bed near Barstow where Don and Jello sometimes went to launch rockets. The High Desert Corridor will pass right by the northern edge of this ancient sink, carrying goods consumed elsewhere and destined, sooner or later, for a hermit's house in the Mojave.

NOTES ON THE
WRITING OF THIS BOOK

IT'S NOT OFTEN THAT A MAP LEADS TO THE HEART OF A STORY, but in this case it did, and I had it. "Go down V Avenue," it said. "Just before the pavement ends there is a small fenced-in area with some gas lines in it. Take a right-hand turn. Then go 0.9 miles and take a left where a house used to be. Go 2.3 miles, take a right-hand turn, then go 0.45 miles and turn left—you might notice some Christmas tinsel in the sage brush. In another 3.5 miles take a right at the intersection. At this point, if you look into the mountains, you should be lined up with a road going towards them . . . "

The map came to me by way of Donald Kueck's sister Lynne Kueck, whom I began speaking with shortly after his death and continued to do so throughout the time I was working on my *Rolling Stone* article "The Great Mojave Manhunt," the one on which this book is based. The directions led me right to the scene of the crime and other things; it was as if I had dropped through some freeway sinkhole in Los Angeles and ended up in its sad and lonely heart—an hour away from the Warner lot, just beyond the San Gabriel Mountains, where Donald Kueck had watched the stars, studied search-and-seizure laws, and talked to animals. And nearby, as I would later learn, Deputy Steve Sorensen watched those self-same constellations, communed with desert creatures, and was deployed for the laws that so many a desert hermit deliberated over in their solitude and ruminations.

As the months unfolded, I made several trips to the site where Don had lived, sometimes with his son, Jello—the same site where Steve and Don had faced off for the final time. On these trips, I was accompanied by the photographer Mark Lamonica, an early guide through the Antelope Valley and the person who encouraged me to write this story; a long-time wanderer of the Mojave to the east of Los Angeles, I had not spent much time in the desert to the north of LA until Mark invited me out for a visit after we communed over a mutual affinity for Joshua trees. In addition to having a map and an escort through the nether reaches of the Antelope Valley, I also had a pit bull named Buddha—a loving, loyal, and good-to-go protector whom Mark and I had raised together. Buddha accompanied us on various explorations into these lands where many had animal guardians (and did not always treat them with kindness); his watchfulness was a grace and his presence a comfort—he seemed to have become his name. And his sixth sense was an alert to who knows exactly what, telling us when it was time to leave.

Months and even years later, artifacts of a hermit's life remained at the scene, and these objects became vectors for the story. Sometimes I would sit in the lounge chair that was Don's, read through books that were still there, and ponder the Three Sisters Buttes directly to the east—the formation that rendered solace and protection to him, as well as to Steve Sorensen, the nuns at the convent nearby, and so many others who lived in this region. Many things became apparent in those buttes and in the sands that stretched out in their shadows; it's easy to walk through time in the desert—in fact, it *is* a walk through time. The playing field of history is literally level, and after a while the parade is right there: the ancients, the moderns, the attempts of all who tread the path.

Look, up there in the rocks, an Indian is making ceremony! And see that conquistador across the plain, on his horse, harquebus at the ready! How soon he vanishes—and now come the tractors and backhoes and the men who man them and then the desert grows silent again and as I sit in the old chair a late afternoon wind blows in and I hear the rattling of the creosote and the banging of a door left unclosed somewhere and then come other signs of civilization—the sound of plastic bags flapping through the air until they are impaled on brush, now windsocks forever. After a while, as the sun sinks westward ho, the skies of the Antelope Valley fade to red—crimson, then deeper, an outpouring of blood, and then ribbons of indigo. It's time to go, but one more sound draws my attention: the rustle of—what? I'm not sure, but I follow the sound to its source, and there is the pear tree Don had planted when he first moved in—scrawny, its few leaves dry but still there, sending out a call, yes, another silent wail from this patch of earth, ready to revive if enough rain comes along, struggling for a hold, waiting—as is the way of things in the drylands.

Across the way at Steve's house there were other messages, and I heard them as its new owner guided me through it. So many times in recent years it was the horse that led me to things I needed to know, and now, once again, they were leading the way. My previous book *Mustang: The Saga of the Wild Horse in the American West* was an account of the wild horse on this continent, from prehistory through the present, and to learn its story I had followed its tracks across the centuries. One of the places they led to was the Antelope Valley, specifically a sanctuary called Lifesavers, where mustangs that have fallen through the cracks of modern management systems live out their lives amid Joshua trees and the wide open space that is their birthright. One day as I was nearing completion of my book, I attended an event at Lifesavers, a "bomb-proofing" exercise in which untrained horses are taught to become accustomed to loud and unexpected noises, thus becoming prepared for service in the outside world, such as with law enforcement agencies or on the trail carrying boisterous dudes at a ranch. At this event, I began talking with Palmdale resident Kate LaCroix and her son Austin; they had adopted several mustangs, Kate told me, and as we conversed, one thing led to another, and I was soon telling her about this book. "Have you been to Steve Sorensen's house?" she asked. As it happened, I had been trying to do that for several years; not being the kind of reporter who simply shows up and knocks on doors (except as a last resort—and even then, I think twice), I told her that I had driven past it several times but that was all, and also how important it would be to be able to walk the grounds he had called home. It turned out that she knew its current owner, the woman who had bought it from Christine Sorensen after Steve had been killed. "Steve's animals are still there," Kate said. "Maybe you could go for a visit."

I was stunned by this turn of events—and then not; sooner or later in the course of things, usually later, people come forth, information emerges, doors open, and I'm on my way down the trail. Soon after meeting Kate, I contacted Kristie Holladay, the current owner, and was touring the house where Steve had lived, meeting the dogs he had rescued, and looking at the world from his vantage point—the very center of his beat. The house itself was saying something, and so were the grounds, the view, and of course the animals Steve had rescued. It's not often that animals remain with a house once their owner has left, but it seemed fitting—the place was theirs after all, and perhaps they too were waiting, in their case for the man who had taken them in from a hard life in the Mojave. But of course Steve's spirit was there, because he had poured it into his house and the act of making it better, and then there was that powerful artifact in his office: his coffeemaker. Yes, a cop and his coffee! I thought. What else should remain? And of course it wasn't just any coffee; here he once was, making it himself, just the way he used to when he lived at the beach and surfed the nice hollow sets of the South Bay, and here too were the mugs he drank from as he looked out across the desert, watching it and trying to keep it the way it was—ever the lifeguard, answering calls of distress.

But it was after a trip to the Los Angeles County Sheriff's Department Museum in Whittier, California, that I gained a deeper insight into Deputy Sorensen. The museum is a little-known destination—that is, outside of members of law enforcement—an unprepossessing structure far away from the city's museum row, on an old high school campus that is also home to the Major Crimes, Family, and Narcotics bureaus. Among the exhibits are a 1938 Studebaker patrol car, saddles from early posses, booking ledgers from the 1800s, frontier wanted posters, various weapons, drug paraphernalia, Vegas slot machines, illegal carnival games, a piece of an old hanging tree and the rope that went with it, a Hughes 300 helicopter that was part of the department's first Sky Knight squadron—a complete mishmash of memorabilia, in that sometimes strange LA way of things whereby the past becomes mixed up with the present in spite of attempts to impose a timeline. But there's often something unexpected in these museum driftnets, and as I made my second pass through the halls, I found it: up on a wall, not easy to spot—kind of hidden away, since cops play few of their cards—there was a letter, a law enforcement decoder, I realized as I began to read it, another key to the secret universe of those who stand on the thin blue line.

"Dear Mr./Ms./Mrs. Citizen," it began.

Well, I guess you have figured me out. I seem to fit neatly into the category you placed me in. I'm stereotyped, characterized, standardized, classified, grouped, and always typical. I am the lousy cop. . . . Unfortunately, the reverse isn't true. I can never figure you out. . . . You pride yourself on your polished manners, but think nothing of interrupting my meals at noon with your troubles. . . . You talk to me in a manner and use language that would assure a bloody nose from anyone else. . . . You have no use for me whatsoever, but of course it's OK for me to change a tire for your wife, or deliver a baby in the back seat of my patrol car en route to the hospital or even forsake time with MY family working long hours overtime trying to find your lost daughter. . . . So, dear citizen, you stand there and rant and rave about the way I do my job, calling me every name in the book, but never stop for a minute to think that your property, your family, and maybe your life might someday depend on one thing . . . ME.

Respectfully,
A Lousy Cop

After reading the letter several times and thinking about it for a while, I came to a realization that should have been obvious but wasn't, I guess because all tribes have their secrets: behind the weapon and the badge, cops are just like everyone else— misunderstood and not appreciated, or so they feel, and therein lies the tale or part of it. In the end, their secret is ours.

When I left the museum, I was traveling along Telegraph Road and saw a bus marked "Sorensen Avenue," as if the day belonged to Steve. It was heading through the adjacent town of Santa Fe Springs, and I found myself following the bus for a while until it turned off and headed for its destination. At that moment, I looked to my right, and there at the intersection of Norwalk Boulevard was one more lit- tle-known Los Angeles monument. "Heritage Park" said a wrought iron sign, and past the sign was a beautifully landscaped spring gar- den in bloom, as well as a Victorian greenhouse and a well-preserved carriage barn—something that harked back to a time of elegance and planning to please the senses. The sight on this industrial side of town was startling, and I decided to stop in and take a look. As soon as I entered the park, the calling was clear: markers pointed past the barn, past the excavated adobe from an earlier settlement, down a trail to what was here first—the prehistoric Tongva/Gabrieleno village, made by the Indians who flourished at the local springs, constructing domes of willow and reed, leaving their myths and their stories. Here their village has been reconstructed in tribute, and just over there, coiled around it, was a giant totem—Snake Fountain, it's called—a multicolored representation of a rattler commissioned in tribute to the original citizens of Los Angeles.

And so the story had come full circle. The rattlesnake of the desert had wound its way back into the story, or perhaps it was here all along, connecting the two sides of Los Angeles, the Antelope Valley with its more famous and glamorous twin, the city of LA "down below," as if it had uncoiled from the Don't Tread on Me flags that flutter in the Mojave winds and traversed the mythic tunnel system that runs beneath the region, emerging at an ancient site—in stone. I sat in the old Indian village for a while and thought about what message the old serpent might have been carrying. Brother rattler is a sign of transformation and change, old skin for new, an end and a renewal, and when I left the park, I realized that the time had come to finish the story; following the trail for many years had led me right back to the beginning.

But the experience was a change-up pitch. A few days later I received some additional information about this story, and I began to examine it by way of a new prism. The information came from a friend of Steve's, someone I had spoken with before. This person did not want to be identified in connection with this piece of information, but the secret could be kept no longer. "Steve called me the day before he was killed," the friend said. "He was very upset. He had just been diagnosed with a brain tumor, and the doctor told him he didn't have much time." The friend was stunned and expressed sadness to Steve and then asked, "Is there anything I can do?" Steve asked for the friend's confidence, and the secret remained untold—until the day I was contacted, seven years later. There was no way I could verify the information; Stephen's wife,

Christine, was not available for interviews regarding my original magazine piece or this book. And out of deference to her, his close friends would not have corroborated the information, if they knew it, and I had no idea what doctors Steve might have consulted (those records would not be released anyway). Still, after I heard from Steve's friend, I began to wonder. Over the years I had heard many theories about "what really happened to Steve." Some people think he was ambushed. Others think he was set up. A few say he was a gung-ho cop and when they heard about what happened, they were not surprised. And then there was the Antelope Valley psychic who told a reporter that two people whacked Steve and one, Donald Kueck, was caught. But the new information went under the surface—in a physical sense and every other way. Don's sister Lynne, the navy nurse, had suspected that her brother might have had a brain tumor. Was I now telling a story about two men who were afflicted by a terrible invader? Did Steve tell anyone apart from his friend? Or did he not want to burden his family with this sad news? Again, I thought about what had made him turn down that road on his last day and head toward Don's. Here was a man with everything to live for—his wife, a son, a future—and then there was Don, a man with a tenuous hold on things until his own son died, and then telling those around him that the end was near. But what if the man with a future found out that he didn't have one? What effect would that have had on his actions on his last day? The question has no answer, only raising more questions, but for sure adding one more strange cast to the deadly encounter at Don's trailer.

As Ellen Gilchrist once wrote, "the truth has a biological urge to come out," and it was around the time I had heard from Steve's friend that I began receiving other calls, as if other elements of the story now wanted to come forward. These were from Jello's friends, some of whom I had been trying to reach for years. They were ready to talk about Jello, Don, the last days of both of these men;

even as I was I wrapping up the story it seemed to be wrapping up itself—stopping me and telling me more.

Yet I must also say that there was one more map into this story. This one was an audio map, and it consisted of the tapes of Donald Kueck's final conversations, the exchanges he had with Mark Lillienfeld, the LA County detective who had spent hours with him on the phone, trying to convince him to surrender before cops closed in. What does a voice carry? Yes, of course, there were the words, so important at a critical moment such as this, when two men are engaging in a life-and-death negotiation. But here was the palpable sound of the song that Donald Kueck had been broadcasting from his trailer for so many months, the timbre of loss, anguish, defiance—amped up because it was the end. Perhaps the most telling moment was when Detective Lillienfeld told Don to talk on a certain channel and say, "Emergency. This is Donald Kueck." Kueck goes ahead and says it—the exact words—and after I listened to them while sitting in a room at LASD homicide headquarters, I stopped the tape to recover. The statement could sum up Don's last couple of years, I thought, perhaps his entire life, but beyond that it was the call we are all making at any given time, and who's listening?

After the story had completed itself once again, I was walking with SWAT veteran Bruce Chase on Speedway in Venice, parallel to the beach where we had just met at a restaurant, talking about some elements of this tale. As we walked and talked, I thought about the manhunt and what it must have been like to be on it. I wondered what it was like to have gone right from the weeklong manhunt for Donald Kueck and the last siege inside the tank and then having to walk the smoldering ruins of the sheds after the inferno and uncovering bones and ashes to, of all things, a golf tournament in Mesquite, Nevada. Here was a man who had undergone the terror and the beauty of the desert, within days, not as an observer but from deep inside the experience. Cops are not especially talkative about their lives and the contours of the circumstances they cannot escape; these are things they coexist with, in their own ways, and it's hard. But Bruce was well aware of the extremes that marked this particular episode; he had in a very physical sense walked through the fires of hell and emerged on a heavenly patch of well-tended desert, and one that was in a town named for the tree that survived the inferno and protected the house and animals that belonged to Steve's friends. Did God have a hand in any of this? Throughout this story we had talked of right versus wrong and the nature of good and evil; various players in this saga saw the ancient conflict afoot here, and I too felt that angels and demons were upon the land, taking up residence in the desert because, hey, there's a lot of space out there and why not? Strangely, just as we were discussing whether or not the guy with the pitchfork and cloven hooves had a part in this matter, Bruce noticed something shiny, a silver chain dangling from a pipe on the side of the pavement, just behind an old beach pad. It had caught the sunlight, and he walked over to take a look. I followed. It was a necklace with a pentagram—of all things to find, speaking of the Devil! It was creepy, and Bruce knew it, although certainly it could have been placed there by Wiccans, not Satanists, or anyone, really, for any reason at all, and in any case, it was the kind of thing sold all over the beach at Venice, along with talismans of other persuasions and prophets, from Jesus Christ to Bob Marley. Or so I told myself as our discussion of good and evil finished itself up and we called it a day.

* * *

What are the flashes of the human mind and the storms of the human heart? They are all prayers—the outpouring of boundless longing for God.

—Micah Joseph Berdichevski

ACKNOWLEDGMENTS

THIS BOOK IS BASED ON MY *ROLLING STONE* ARTICLE, "The Great Mojave Manhunt," which was published on September 22, 2005. I would like to thank my editors there, Will Dana and Eric Bates, for giving me this assignment when the incident happened in 2003, and Eric, for his thoughtful editing and patience as I worked on the story for two years. I would also like to thank Kathleen Anderson, my agent at the time. The article was reprinted in *The Best American Crime Writing* 2006, and I am grateful to Otto Penzler and Mark Bowden, editors of that anthology, for including it.

To write the article, I consulted police and coroner's reports; a project such as this can't be written without them, and although they must be prepared when it comes to any crime or murder, I'd like to thank the people who take the time to put together these lengthy and complicated statements. I also turned to the following people for help (job titles for members of law enforcement are generally the ones used at the time of interviews): Lynne Kueck, Peggy Gilmore, and Ann Ghent—Donald Kueck's sisters; his daughter Rebecca Welch; his neighbor Wayne Wirt; Deputy Stephen Sorensen's sister Dixie Bear; friends and colleagues from different phases of his life, including Kimberly Brandon-Watson, Julie Franks, Connie Mavrolas,

Pastor John Wodetzki, Richard Hedges (founder of the Outlaw Pigs law enforcement motorcycle club), Los Angeles County Sheriff's Department members Sgt. Christopher Keeling, Deputy Vince Burton, Deputy Paul Dino, Deputy Randy Heberle, Deputy Melissa Sullivan, and Captain Carl Deeley; Sgt. Larry Johnston and Officer Victor Ruiz of the California Highway Patrol; Sister Mary Michael of Mount Carmel in the Desert; LA County District Attorney David Berger; LA County Deputy District Attorney David Evans; Norm Hickling, aide to LA County Supervisor Mike Antonovich; Los Angeles County Sheriff's Department Detectives Philip Guzman, Joe Purcell, and especially Mark Lillienfeld; LASD Sgt. Paul Delhauer; former Antelope Valley Press reporters Kim Rawley and Nicole Jacobs; former Fox news reporter Lorena Mendez-Quiroga, and LAPD SWAT officer Rick Massa (now retired).

To write this book, I turned once again to police and coroner's reports. Thanks also to my former writing students Mark Takano and Carol Park for help in navigating Riverside and various agencies there. And thank you to Celeste Fremon, reporter and founder of WitnessLA, for background on sheriff and police department enforcement of immigration codes. I owe a debt of gratitude to reporter Connie Mavrolas and Pastor John Wodetzki, who continued to provide important context and facts, and spoke from the heart about their own experiences inside this story. I am grateful to Steve's friends Steve Kirchner and Dan White, as well as the following members of the Los Angeles County Sheriff's Department (some of whom now have different titles or are retired): Sheriff Lee Baca; Detective Joe Purcell; Detective Steve Katz, Deputy Steve Propster; Sgt. Richard Valdemar, and SWAT team members Deputy Mark Schlegel, Deputy Rick Rector, Deputy Fred Keelin, Sgt. Joe Williams, Deputy Bernard Schockley, and Deputy George Creamer. In addition, I am most thankful to two veteran cops, LASD Detective Mark Lillienfeld and now-Lieutenant Bruce Chase, without whose help I could not have written this book. Over the eight years I worked on this project, Det. Lillien-feld spent many hours talking with me about his life in law enforce-ment and his role in the final hours of the manhunt. I met Bruce Chase after my article was published, and throughout the years I worked on this book, he also spent a great deal of time filling me in on his experiences in the sheriff's department, and guiding me through the manhunt and SWAT's role in it.

Along the trail of this project, Antelope Valley residents Kristie Holaday and Kate LaCroix were also helpful, and I'd like to thank Jill Starr of Lifesavers, the wild horse rescue organization in Lancaster, for the introduction to Kate.

Over the eight years I worked on this book, various friends and relatives of Jello Kueck began to come forward and were gen-erous with their time, providing much insight into their departed friend. They also provided important recollections of both Jello and his father and the nature of their lives—and their own at the time of this story and beyond. Their participation in this project was crucial. They include Fritz Aragon, Angela Asbell, Aaron Blair, Sharon Booth, Mike Cazares, James Finch, Ford, Rande Linville, Dave Oberweber, Elaine Simons, Chris Smallwood, Amanda Small-wood, Virginia Smallwood, and Zoey.

I would also like to say thanks to John Carver for the fine book trailer, and to pay serious acknowledgement to the fine crew at Nation Books—my wonderful editor Ruth Baldwin, for being simpatico with my work and supplying all manner of help with this project, editor Carl Bromley for his support, Marissa Colón-Margolies for emergency aid and reminders, and publicist Dori Gelb for guiding this book along its public path; my publisher John Sherer at Basic Books; and their colleagues who have done such fine work on production, copyediting, and design, including Collin Tracy, Linda Mark, and Jed DeOrsay at Perseus, and Beth Wright at Trio Bookworks.

Finally, I am grateful to Mark Lamonica for not only encouraging me to write this story, but also for insight and moral support along the way. I would also like to thank my agent, Liz Darhansoff, and her associate Michele Mortimer for their critical role in this project. And as ever and always, I am so grateful to my mother, Eleanor Stillman, for being in my corner throughout it all—and telling me not to barrel through intersections, advice that has served me well.

BIBLIOGRAPHY

BOOKS, PAMPHLETS, AND ARCHIVES

Antelope Valley: Early Future Envisioned in Early Days. Van Nuys, CA: Valley Federal Savings and Loan Association, 1965–1966.

Bach, Richard. *Illusions: The Adventures of a Reluctant Messiah*. New York: Dell, 1977.

Banks, L. A. "Buzz." *Policing the Old Mojave Desert*. Victorville, CA: the author, 1994.

Baumgardner, Randy, editor. *Los Angeles County Sheriff's Department Annual*. Paducah, KY: Turner, 2000.

Bergon, Frank. *Wild Game*. Reno: University of Nevada Press, 1995.

Bloom, Howard. *The Genius of the Beast: A Radical Re-Vision of Capitalism*. New York: Prometheus Books, 2009.

Castaneda, Carlos. *The Eagle's Gift*. New York: Pocket Books, 1981.

———. *The Second Ring of Power*. New York: Simon & Schuster, 1977.

Chimbole, Larry. *Palmdale: First City of Antelope Valley*. Anaheim, CA: Creative Continuum, 2006.

Comstock, Phyllis. *Indian Uses of Plant Sources Found in the Antelope Valley*. Lancaster, CA: Friends of the Antelope Valley Museum, 1991.

Conley, Cort. *Idaho Loners: Hermits, Solitaires, and Individualists*. Cambridge, ID: Backeddy Books, 1994.

County of Los Angeles Department of Regional Planning. "Antelope Valley Areawide General Plan." A component of the *Los Angeles County General Plan*. Adopted by the Los Angeles Board of Supervisors, December 4, 1986.

Darlington, David. *The Mojave: Portrait of the Definitive American Desert*. New York: Henry Holt, 1996.

Davis, Mike. *City of Quartz: Excavating the Future in Los Angeles*. New York: Verso, 1990.

Dunaway, David King. *Huxley in Hollywood*. New York: Harper & Row, 1989.

Eargle, Dolan H., Jr. *The Earth Is Our Mother: A Guide to the Indians of California, Their Locals and Historic Sites*. San Francisco: Trees Company, 1986.

Fages, Pedro. *A Historical, Political, and Natural Description of California*. Ramona, CA: Ballena, 1972.

Gifford, Edward Winslow, and Gwendoline Harris Block. *California Indian Nights*. Lincoln: University of Nebraska Press, 1990.

Gordon, J. Shelton. *Incredible Tales of Some of the Antelope Valley Pioneers, Compiled with Love and Affection for All of the Antelope Valley Pioneers*. Palmdale, CA: West Antelope Valley Historical Society, 1973.

Gossard, Gloria Gine. *Antelope Trails and Pioneer Tales*. Tehachapi, CA: Yellow Rose Publications, 1993.

Greenstein, Paul, Nigey Lennon, and Lionel Rolfe. *Bread & Hyacinths: The Rise and Fall of Utopian Los Angeles*. Los Angeles: California Classics Books, 1992.

Gurba, Norma H. *Images of America: Lancaster*. Charleston, SC: Arcadia, 2005.

Hassler, Lynn. *The Raven: Soaring Through History, Legend & Lore*. Tucson: Rio Nuevo, 2008.

Hauth, Katherine B. *Night Life of the Yucca: The Story of a Flower and a Moth*. Boulder: Harbinger House, 1996.

Hayden, Dolores. *Seven American Utopias: The Architecture of Communitarian Socialism, 1790–1975*. Boston: MIT Press, 1976.

Hinterland. Culver City, CA: Center for Land Use Interpretation, 1997. Exhibition catalog.

Hough, Susan Elizabeth. *Finding Fault in California: An Earthquake Tourist's Guide*. Missoula, MT: Mountain, 2004.

Hunt, John J. *The Waters of Comfort: The Story of Desert Hot Springs, California*. Desert Hot Springs, CA: Little Morongo, 1997.

Huxley, Aldous. *Tomorrow and Tomorrow and Tomorrow, and Other Essays*. New York: Harper & Brothers, 1952.

Jalbert, Matt. *Up Above: The Geography of Suburban Sprawl in Southern California's Antelope Valley*. Written to fulfill the senior thesis requirement, Department of Geography, University of California, Berkeley, 1995–2007. www.radicalurbantheory.com /AntelopeValley/index.html.

Johnston, Francis J. *The Serrano Indians of Southern California*. Banning, CA: Malki Museum Press, 1965.

Kroeber, A. L. *Seven Mohave Myths*. Anthropological Records, vol. 11, no. 1. Berkeley: University of California Press, 1948.

L'Amour, Louis. *The Lonesome Gods*. New York: Bantam, 1984.

Leadabrand, Russ. *A Guidebook to the Mojave Desert of California, Including Death Valley, Joshua Tree National Park, and the Antelope Valley*. Los Angeles: Ward Ritchie, 1966.

Llano del Rio Colony. Papers, 1896–1967. Manuscripts Department, The Huntington Library, San Marino, CA.

Los Angeles County Sheriff's Department. *Code 6 in Region 1*. Field Operations in Region 1 Headquarters. Los Angeles, 2007.

McWilliams, Carey. *Southern California: An Island on the Land*. Santa Barbara, CA: Peregrine Smith, 1973.

Moody, Raymond. *Visionary Encounters with Departed Loved Ones*. New York: Ballantine, 1994.

Moore, Edra. *American Indian Peoples of the Antelope Valley, Western Mojave Desert, 12,000 Years of Culture and History*. California State Parks, 2003.

Olsen, Jack. *Give a Boy a Gun: A True Story of Law and Disorder in the American West*. New York: Dell, 1985.

Peretti, Frank E. *This Present Darkness*. Westchester, IL: Crossway Books, 1986.

Pruett, Catherine. *Aboriginal Occupation in Sand Canyon*. Master's thesis, California State College, Bakersfield, 1987.

Read, Nat B. *Don Benito Wilson: From Mountain Man to Mayor, Los Angeles, 1841–1878*. Santa Monica, CA: Angel City, 2008.

Reisner, Marc. *A Dangerous Place: California's Unsettling Fate*. New York: Penguin Books, 2003.

Robinson, Roger W. *Prehistory of the Antelope Valley, California: An Overview*. Lancaster, CA: Antelope Valley Archaeological Society, 1987.

Rolle, Andres. *Los Angeles: From Pueblo to City of the Future*. San Francisco: Boyd & Fraser, 1981.

Rosamond, California: Hub of Antelope Valley. Rosamond, CA: Rosamond Chamber of Commerce, date unknown.

Schuler, Stanley, editor. *Cacti and Succulents*. New York: Simon & Schuster, 1985.

Settle, Glen A. *Bears: Borax and Gold*. Rosamond, CA: Kern-Antelope Historical Society, 1965.

———. *Here Roamed the Antelope*. Rosamond, CA: Kern-Antelope Historical Society, 1963.

———, editor. *Lancaster Celebrates a Century, 1884–1984*. Lancaster, CA: City of Lancaster, 1983.

———. *Tropico: Red Hill with a Glamorous History of Gold*. Rosamond, CA: Kern-Antelope Historical Society, 1959.

Shah, Diane K., and Daryl F. Gates. *Chief: My Life in the LAPD*. New York: Bantam, 1992.

Stark, Milt. *A Flower Watcher's Guide to Wildflowers of the Western Mojave Desert*. Lancaster, CA: the author, 2000.

Stone, Bonnie D. *San Andreas Ain't No Fault of Mine*. Lancaster, CA: Fawlty, 2005.

Storm, Rory. *Desert Survivor's Guide*. New York: Scholastic, 2001.

Sutton, Mark Q. "Comments on the Symposium: Prehistoric Archaeology of the Western Mojave Desert." Paper presented at the annual meeting of the Society for California Archaeology, Pasadena, 1992.

Tomo-Kahni State Historic Park (brochure). Kawaiisu Native American Village Site, Mojave Desert State Parks, Lancaster, CA.

Waldie, D. J. *Where We Are Now: Notes from Los Angeles*. Los Angeles: Angel City, 2004.

Waters, Frank. *Book of the Hopi*. New York: Penguin, 1977.

Williams, Rod, editor. *Aldous Huxley Slept Here*. Lancaster, CA: MousePrints, 2006.

ARTICLES FROM NEWSPAPERS AND JOURNALS

Arellano, Gustavo. "The Assassination of Sheriff James Barton by the Mexican Juan Flores." *OC Weekly*, January 8, 2009.

Blankstein, Andrew. "Sheriff's Department Faces Scrutiny in Fatal Standoff." *Los Angeles Times*, October 28, 2003.

Bosquet, Jean. "Lizard People's Catacomb City Hunted." *Los Angeles Times*, January 29, 1934.

Bostwick, Charles F. "Coroner Releases Report on Kueck." *Daily News*, November 21, 2003.

———. "Sheriff Admits Lit Flares Used in Kueck Battle." *Daily News*, January 31, 2004.

Botonis, Greg. "Deputy's Killer Filed Complaints Against Him in '94." *Daily News*, September 7, 2003.

Burdick, Dan. " . . . Like No Other Cop I've Known." *Lake Los Angeles News Shopper*, August 22, 2003.

Cardenas, Jose, and Eric Malnic. "Standoff Ends in Flames." *Los Angeles Times*, August 9, 2003.

Duersten, Matthew. "Who'll Stop the Reign?" *LA Weekly*, February 3, 2005.

Fausset, Richard, and Richard Winton. "Man Sought for Clues on Slain Deputy." *Los Angeles Times*, August 4, 2003.

Fleischer, Matthew. "Policing Revolution." *Los Angeles Times Magazine*, April 2011.

Hickling, Norm. "In One Word, Steve Sorensen Was a Man Who Gave." *Lake Los Angeles News Shopper*, August 22, 2003.

Liu, Caitlin. "Thousands Mourn Slain Lawman." *Los Angeles Times*, August 8, 2003.

Mavrolas, Connie. "LA County Threatens Closure of Lake LA Business." *Lake Los Angeles News*, January 3, 2003.

Morin, Monte. "Action in Death of Armed Man Found Lawful." *Los Angeles Times*, March 25, 2004.

Sutton, Mark Q. "On the Late Prehistory of the Western Mojave Desert." *Pacific Coast Archaeological Society Quarterly* 24, no. 1 (1988).

Thermos, Wendy. "Deputy Felt Threatened, Suit Says." *Los Angeles Times*, August 8, 2003.

Wormser, Marci. "Zoning Laws Threaten Local Businesses." *Daily News*, January 9, 2003.

INDEX